BEYOND THE ACADEMIC GATEWAY

BEYOND THE ACADEMIC GATEWAY

Looking Back on the Tenure-Track Journey

Edited by

Timothy M. Sibbald
Victoria Handford

University of Ottawa Press
2020

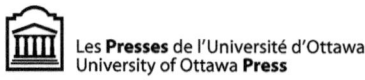
Les **Presses** de l'Université d'Ottawa
University of Ottawa **Press**

The University of Ottawa Press (UOP) is proud to be the oldest of the francophone university presses in Canada as well as the oldest bilingual university publisher in North America. Since 1936, UOP has been enriching intellectual and cultural discourse by producing peer-reviewed and award-winning books in the humanities and social sciences, in French and in English.
www.press.uOttawa.ca

Library and Archives Canada Cataloguing in Publication

Title: Beyond the academic gateway : looking back on the tenure-track journey / edited by Timothy M. Sibbald, Victoria Handford.
Names: Sibbald, Timothy, 1966- editor. | Handford, Victoria, 1957- editor.
Series: Politics and public policy (University of Ottawa Press)
Description: Series statement: Education |
  Includes bibliographical references and index.
Identifiers: Canadiana (print) 20200207954 | Canadiana (ebook) 20200207989 |
  ISBN 9780776628905 (softcover) | ISBN 9780776628943 (hardcover) |
  ISBN 9780776628912 (PDF) |ISBN 9780776628929 (EPUB) |
  ISBN 9780776628936 (Kindle)
Subjects: LCSH: College teachers—Tenure—Canada—Case studies.
Classification: LCC LB2335.7 .B49 2020 | DDC 378.1/2140971—dc23

Legal Deposit: Third Quarter 2020
Library and Archives Canada

© University of Ottawa Press 2020
All rights reserved.

No part of this publication may be reproduced or transmitted in any form or by any means, or stored in a database and retrieval system, without the prior permission.

Production Team
Copy editing   Robert Ferguson
Proofreading   Michael Waldin
Typesetting   Transforma
Cover design   Steve Kress

In the case of photocopying or any other reprographic copying, please secure licenses from:

Cover image
The Blackstone River where it crosses the Dempster Highway about 125 km South of the Arctic Circle. Courtesy of Dick Smith.

Access Copyright www.accesscopyright.ca
1-800-893-5777

For foreign rights and permissions:
www.iprlicense.com

The University of Ottawa Press gratefully acknowledges the support extended to its publishing list by the Government of Canada, the Canada Council for the Arts, the Ontario Arts Council, the Social Sciences and Humanities Research Council and the Canadian Federation for the Humanities and Social Sciences through the Awards to Scholarly Publications Program, and by the University of Ottawa.

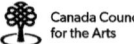

The Cover Photo

In searching for a cover photo to serve as a metaphor for destination of tenure-track tripartite faculty in universities, we decided on one depicting the individualistic setting of the Blackstone River in Yukon Territory, Canada. Those few people who visit the Blackstone River must journey to a remote watershed in a territory with few people. They can experience magnificent views and water that can challenge experienced paddlers. Yukoners love its difference, and while they may struggle with how different and poorly understood living conditions are in the north, they treasure its beauty and uniqueness as well as its camaraderie.

    The Yukon, with its population of 37,000—slightly less than 1 percent of the total Canadian population—can seem lonely. University faculty members in Canada with earned PhDs also make up less than 1 percent of the population (Statistics Canada, 2011); few outside academia understand their work. Just as some of us may not recognize the ecological importance of the Blackstone River, visitors to higher education frequently misunderstand what is essential to the ecology of the university. The research, teaching, and service environment of higher education is distinctly different than other workplaces. It is important to identify, and deeply understand, what is valuable and why.

The landscape in the picture is an environment with many different paths and possibilities. Such is a faculty role in higher education—there are many paths, many obstacles, and many possibilities. The photo used on the cover of *Beyond the Academic Gateway* contrasts with the blue and white mountains on the cover of our related book *The Academic Gateway: Understanding the Journey to Tenure*. Whereas *The Academic Gateway* presented lived experiences while the same group of authors were in the tenure-track, this latest volume comprises chapters written after, or very close to, the tenure decision. Reflecting this difference, the photo shows a move from a tough survival landscape of the mountains to an environment that, on its surface, is brighter and less hostile. Although the peaceful solitude of wilderness is inviting, one knows that a trip along Blackstone River would not be a leisurely walk. This book reveals this similarity between nature and higher education.

Table of Contents

Acknowledgements ix
Introduction 1

Section 1: The Review of Literature

1   Are We There Yet? Understanding the Meanings of Tenure
Manu Sharma 11

Section 2: Reflecting on the Tenure Journey: The Individual and the Institutional

2   Of Joys and Sorrows: Lessons Learned in Applying for Tenure and Promotion
Carmen Rodriguez de France 33

3   Starting From Scratch After Tenure to Run a New Lab in France
Margarida Romero 45

4   Transitioning to the Academic Tenure-Track at Mid-Career: Exploring Adaptive Responses Through the Lenses of Resilience, Grieving, and Institutional Logics
Peter Milley 57

5   Tenured Life: Rhythms, Time, and Energy
Cecile Badenhorst 87

6   Women Reflect on Remaining an Academic: Challenges and Supports
S. Penney, G. Young, C. Badenhorst, H. McLeod, S. Moore, and S. Pickett 101

Section 3: Reflecting on the Tenure Journey: The Systemic and Institutional

7   For Academy's Sake: A Former Practitioner Settles in Academe
Lloyd Kornelsen 125

8   Indigenous Scholarship: What Really Matters and to Whom?
Onowa McIvor and Trish Rosborough 137

9   Establishing Balance to Define a New Normal
Timothy M. Sibbald 155

10 The Mid-Career Indigenous Scholar: Navigating the Institutional Confluence of Indigeneity and Academia in Post-Tenure-Track
Frank Deer 173

11 An Incredible Journey: Passing Through the Gateway
Victoria (Tory) Handford 185

12 Potholes and Possibilities: Pursuing Academic Interests in the Era of the Corporate University
Greg Ogilvie 203

Section 4: Reflecting on the Tenure Journey: The Personal and Individual

13 Finding Energy From "Productive Anguish": Avoiding Descents into Tenure-Track Darkness
Lyle Hamm 227

14 Relationships, Associations, and Authority
Lee Anne Block 249

15 It's Not Me, It's the Process
Kathy Snow 261

16 Jill Revisited—Still Struggling With Mental Illness Within Academia Post-Tenure
Joan M. Chambers 275

17 In the Trenches
Greg Rickwood 281

18 Who Am I? Professional Identity on the Path to Tenure
Cam Cobb 293

Conclusion 307

Contributors 317
Index 324

Acknowledgements

We would like to express our gratitude, first and foremost, to the authors of this book. They were all involved in a related book *The Academic Gateway: Understanding the Journey to Tenure* (Sibbald & Handford, 2017). We were delighted when they agreed to participate in a book about their experiences of the time surrounding their tenure decision. Their willingness to continue with this project, a journey that began in 2013 and 2014, highlights this dedication. It has been a joy to grow with them, and continue to learn from them, through the preparation of this book.

Second, we would like to thank the University of Ottawa Press for supporting us early in the project. We have a relationship of constructive critique and support that fosters growth. The Press nominated the first book for the Foreword Indies Book of the Year award in the career category. What a delightful moment to see the efforts of the authors, the Press, and ourselves as editors, win a silver award.

In many ways, the project has developed some semblance of community. Some of the authors have gathered over dinners and chatted on the phone. Several authors have presented at conferences. While we have not met all the authors in person (yet), there is a sense that this book has fostered relationships and contributed to a degree of catharsis about the challenges faced in the early career stages of academia.

Lastly, we would like to acknowledge the financial support we have received for the production of this book. Specifically, we wish to express appreciation for significant funding from the Faculty of Education and Social Work at Thompson Rivers University. We also wish to thank Nipissing University for financial support. This book would not have been possible without their contributions.

Introduction

The tenure journey is a period featuring a heavy workload, one requiring a goal-driven personal effort to succeed. It is an intensive orientation where the candidate is scrutinized by people at all levels of the university to determine if he or she should be made permanent. It is easy to become blinkered because of this focus, but there is significant value in asking why the process is the way it is. Are there alternatives? Could the challenges be addressed by considering the larger context of the tenure-track period? Some view tenure-track as a rite of passage, something new faculty must endure simply because the established faculty endured it. Although flawed, this logic reveals that, on achieving tenure, many academics are dismissive of their experience, some even considering it a form of hazing of dubious value. What can be learned from looking at the experience of tenure-track and the period of time around receiving tenure? This book responds to that question by providing personal stories written by academics around the time of their tenure decisions.

Inspiration and Modelling

In producing a second book about experiences of early academics, we confess to drawing some inspiration from a British documentary series called *The Up Series*, which has followed a group of people since 1964. The documentary maker first interviewed the subjects as children at age seven (1964) and, subsequently, made new documentaries with the same individuals every seven years. We too are working with the same group—in our case the authors who wrote *The Academic Gateway: Understanding the Journey to Tenure*. *The Up Series* inspired us with the value of having a longitudinal collection of narratives of life in the tenure-track and the achievement of tenure.

We also attempted to learn from criticisms of *The Up Series* in editing this book, which we will keep in mind while we consider proposing a third book. One methodological criticism of the series was that individuals selected for the series were not as diverse as they might have been, which happened because there was no indication of the longevity the project would ultimately have (Davies, 2013). In our case, we feel we succeeded in our efforts to have a diverse sample. We have males and females, young and "seasoned," a large variety of cultural backgrounds, multiple language groups . . . in other words, we are reasonably diverse. Additionally, we have authors providing representation from every province in Canada. Our sample could be more diverse—we sought to have authors from all the larger and more prestigious universities—but did not have responses to the extent we hoped. In one case, we received a personal communication indicating that working with us would be seen as risky in terms of personal career goals in such institutions. So, we opted to work with those who were willing to share their narratives and were not overly surprised that our sampling generally emphasizes smaller and mid-sized institutions. As with *The Academic Gateway*, our authors are in the academic field of education. This limits the scope of the project. However, by focussing on one discipline there may be more representativeness than one might have thought. We do not spend time explaining faculties of education and how they differ from one another. Instead, the authors describe their experiences, which we believe resonate with faculty across many disciplines in the university.

Another criticism of *The Up Series* is the role and choices of the documentary maker who has been seen to have a post-modern influence on the end result. To address such concerns, in *The Academic Gateway* (Sibbald & Handford, 2017a), we chose to give the authors considerable leeway to speak about the experiences they chose. While this freedom had a side effect (the project missed out on some funding because it was not sufficiently theoretical), it avoided tainting the voices. However, we have developed the theoretical basis by using the first book to develop a phenomenological model of tenure-track experiences, which provides for theoretical benchmarking of our authors' collective development. That, along with revisions of the model based on subsequent critiques, provides a means to consider patterns rooted in theoretical considerations.

In developing the theory, we sought to provide a conceptual framework for understanding the varied experiences in the tenure-track. Theoretically, we understood that some who move into the academy experience a major upheaval that affects many aspects of their lives. We are examples of this, with Tory moving 4000 km and Tim moving 500 km, to achieve entry onto the tenure-track. Transitions include having to learn about a new city and workplace; the impact on family extends through all aspects of daily living. We felt that for many new academics the transition could be akin to a grieving process because they have suffered the loss of community, workplace cultures, and a general sense of place. A successful transition would see the grieving run its course, but it might persist in situations where joining the academy was not successful or continues to be "uncomfortable."

Our sense was that the transition into the academy could be traumatic. This is not simply a change of workplace because the process is a fully immersive stressful experience that can overwhelm and have repercussions that extend well beyond the workplace. The depth of impact new academics feel should not be dismissed lightly, nor glossed-over as part of a transitory phase. For that reason, we leaned toward using the Kubler-Ross model (Kubler-Ross & Kessler, 2005), which is intended for modelling grieving related to the end of life. It was our contention that in their first year or two in the tenure-track some academics face the challenge of processing the death of their previous way of living and of adapting to a new normal in all areas of their lives. While we do not believe all academics experience grief, we do believe the Kubler-Ross model facilitates the wide range of adaptations. Our vision of its application specifically involves cultural loss (Levy-Warren, 1987) during the transition into the academy.

The Kubler-Ross model entails five stages: denial, anger, bargaining, depression, and acceptance. Within the transition to the academy, denial captures the initial euphoria of having made it without being realistic about what working in the academy entails. Anger can arise as one looks for supports and discovers that universities generally provide few supports for faculty, whether the issues are academic or more personal in nature. Bargaining occurs during the coming to terms with the new workplace and how it functions. However, understanding the new place can lead to depressive moments as the reality that the academy is not necessarily the ivory tower that one thought it was. In many ways, depression reflects animosity toward policies or processes that are not as effective as their analogues in prior workplaces. Finally, acceptance is the key to becoming integrated within the academy because, for all the imperfections, universities are functional workplaces.

The second key element to the theory is the use of self-determination theory (Deci & Ryan, 2000; Broeck, Ferris, Chang, & Rosen, 2016). We do not suggest the entire theory is relevant to modelling the years in the tenure-track. However, we do suggest that any model of lived experiences in the tenure-track is about people who emphasize self-determination and that self-determination theory plays a key role. We contend that through graduate studies and into the tenure-track years, the personal capacity to demonstrate effort, agency and commitment are enhanced in a way suited to roles entailing competence (e.g., subject expertise), relatedness or connectedness to an environment, and autonomy or the ability to work with minimal guidance.

We anticipated that elements of self-determination theory would interact with the Kubler-Ross model if both were relevant to an individual. As an example, self-efficacy around agency and relatedness could be expected to decline temporarily if an individual moved to an unfamiliar geographical place. This is particularly relevant in the field of education, because it is provincially mandated in Canada and so a move to another province could lead to a loss of connections. We expect to find such a decline only in the short-term, because competence and resilience of these individuals will facilitate their finding ways to address their losses and needs.

We also expected interactions of self-determination and Kubler-Ross components around the beneficial aspects of the academy. For example, the bargaining phase of the Kubler-Ross model seems to fit quite well with autonomy in the face of having too many choices (Ivengar & Lepper, 2002) for research projects.

We have not set out to replicate *The Up Series* with academics, but consideration of the series did influence our thinking about the continuity between books. With that in mind we asked authors in this volume to consider the model of tenure-track experiences

(Sibbald & Handford, 2017b) as they wrote. The authors were under no obligation and, when some expressed concerns with aspects of the theory, we suggested they write what fit their experience rather than fitting their writing to the theory. The concerns gave us insight into two areas: first, they identified aspects of the theory that might not be effective as a model of tenure-track; second, it provided a benchmark to consider how the theory may need to be altered to address changes that have taken place as the academics gain experience in the academy and, particularly, earn tenure (and promotion). These insights are pivotal in understanding the place of the existing theory and highlight that the theory is a work in progress—it is not complete, but it sets this book up to allow for deeper thinking about what it means to be an academic.

Chapter Organization

With the exception of the literature review, chapters are organized according to an informal clustering using two dimensions (see Figure 0.1). We considered the chapters in terms of *perspective* and *change,* with each being along a continuum. The perspectives range from the individual to the institutional. Virtually all the chapters mention both, but we considered the overall emphasis in each chapter, and our impression of what they have said in relation to each axis. In the change dimension, we considered whether the chapter described an individual adaptation to the role (i.e., personal change) or identified or promoted any type of systemic change within the academy. Our impression of the scope of change was used to situate a "coordinate." We use small circles, rather than points, to represent individual authors because of the subjectivity used. Then we informally clustered the chapters to provide the reader with sequenced sections. It was a pragmatic approach, designed to create thematic groupings of chapters.

Given the subjectivity of this analysis, we concluded that saying which chapter fits within which oval (in Figure 0.1) is something academics could debate for quite some time! We purposely made the ovals large—the groupings are a suggestion, not rigorous. Regardless of the exact location of a chapter on this plot diagram, we do feel confident the clustering provides a sense of how authors identify their views of tenure and promotion. No one grouping is more accurate

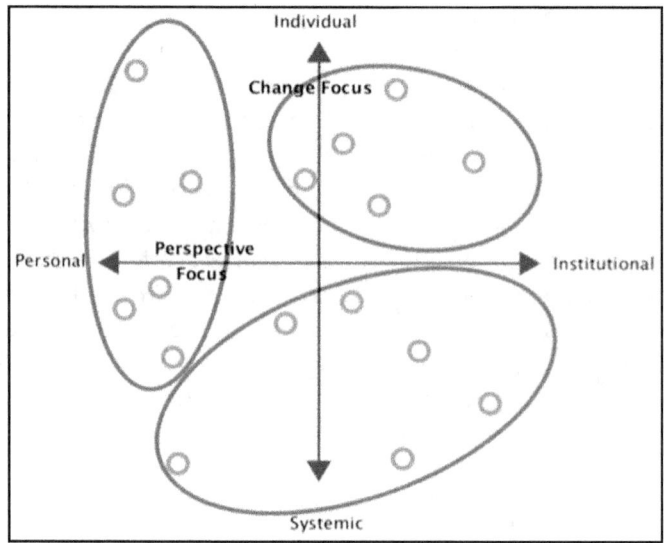

Figure 0.1. *Informal approach to chapter clustering within the book.*

or worthy than another; they are simply different views reflecting different experiences of the path into the academy.

As with *The Academic Gateway*, we provide a pragmatic order in each section. Although we ordered the previous book according to time spent in the tenure-track, in this book, the chapter order provides more insight into the interaction between authors and the academy. The achievement of tenure is approximately the same duration for each author; each chapter was written at different times over a period of a year and a half, meaning each was essentially written within six months of the author's tenure decision.

There is one exception to the chapter ordering. Manu Sharma took on the task of writing a literature review to provide some context based on the academic literature, which clearly needs to come first because it sets the stage for thinking about the other chapters.

References

Broeck, A. V., Ferris, D. L., Chang, C. H., & Rosen, C. C. (2016). "A review of self-determination theory's basic psychological needs at work." *Journal of Management*, 42(5), 1195–1229.

Davies, S. (2013). "Back to the future: The Up Series." *Dissent; Philadelphia*, 60(3), 8–12. DOI:10.1353/dss.2013.0057.

Deci, E. L., & Ryan, R. M. (2000). "The 'what' and 'why' of goal pursuits: Human needs and the self-determination of behavior." *Psychological Inquiry, 11*(4), 227–268.

Handford, V., & Sibbald, T. M. (2016, May). "Identifying issues on the journey to tenure." Presented at Canadian Society for the Study of Higher Education (CSSHE) 2016 conference, Calgary, AB.

Iyengar, S. S., & Lepper, M. R. (2002). "Choice and its consequences: On the costs and benefits of self-determination." In A. Tesser, D. A. Stapel, & J. V. Wood. eds., *Self and motivation: Emerging psychological perspectives.* Washington, DC: American Psychological Association.

Kubler-Ross, E., & Kessler, D. (2005). *On grief and grieving: Finding the meaning of grief through the five stages of loss.* New York, NY: Scribner.

Levy-Warren, M. H. (1987). "Moving to a new culture: Cultural identity, loss, and mourning." In J. Bloom-Feshbach & S. Bloom-Feshbach. eds., *The psychology of separation and loss.* San Francisco, CA: Jossey-Bass Inc.

Sibbald, T. M. & Handford, V. eds. (2017a). *The academic gateway: Understanding the journey to tenure.* Ottawa, ON: University of Ottawa Press.

Sibbald, T. M., & Handford, V. (May, 2017b). "A substantive model of the tenure-track Experience." Presentation at the Canadian Association of Action Research in Education (CAARE) portion of Canadian Society for the Study of Education (CSSE) 2017 conference, Toronto, ON.

Statistics Canada (2011). *Education in Canada: Attainment, field of study and location of study.* Retrieved from https://www12.statcan.gc.ca/nhs-enm/2011/as-sa/99-012-x/99-012-x2011001-eng.cfm

SECTION 1

The Review of Literature

Manu Sharma, who is quite early in her tenure process, wrote the literature review. When she wrote her chapter in *The Academic Gateway*, which she did with a colleague, Manu had a limited-term position. The good news is she is now tenure-track, tripartite. While she has experiences that are meaningful she is not far enough along in her journey to write about the period of time around her tenure decision.

Manu tells the academic story of tenure in a succinct systematic review of literature. She provides details of identified issues. The connection to existing literature also provides insight into the interpretive lenses that will help make connections to the reader's own environment.

CHAPTER 1

Are We There Yet? Understanding the Meanings of Tenure

Manu Sharma

Many tenure-track educators in post-secondary institutions see attaining tenure as the symbolic light at the end of the tunnel. Tenure is typically applied for and achieved in conjunction with promotion to the position of associate professor. On average, assistant professors in tenure-track positions work to establish themselves in research, teaching, and service for four to six years before earning tenure. This literature review provides insights on what this new status means for associate professors and the implications this has on their lives and their institution. It is important to note that the literature informing this review draws upon literature about tenure in a variety of disciplines such as, but not limited to, the arts, dentistry, radiology, law, and science. Each discipline has slightly different approaches to the process of tenure with respect to the average time it takes to become tenured and what kinds of publications are seen as acceptable for tenure approval. Moreover, every institution, and how each engages with different disciplines in the process of tenure, also varies based on its particular culture. Nevertheless, despite the variations in the tenure process based on discipline and type of institution, much can be said about the themes that arise from across this literature to help better inform educators about the tenure process.

In this literature review a brief history about the notion of tenure is presented, followed by the methodology used for the review. The chapter then describes the seven themes emerging from the current literature (2005–2017): (1) benefits of being tenured, (2) tenure connects to power in universities, (3) tenure allows for diversity in research publications, (4) tenure and gender politics, (5) tenure does not provide academic freedom or security, (6) tenure leaves associate professors without mentorship, and (7) tenure in different clinical disciplines. After presenting the seven themes this chapter also offers a brief discussion of the gaps and/or complexities that emerged from the literature, which provides an avenue for further research and consideration.

A Brief History of Tenure

The American Association of University Professors (AAUP) was founded in 1913 in the hopes of protecting faculty from public attacks on their academic thoughts and research (Peterson, 2007). As a result "... the inception of tenure [took place] in 1940 [by the] AAUP, [as] the case was made that 'the common good depends on the free search for truth and its free expression ... academic freedom applies to both teaching and research'" (Hueer, 1991, as cited by Ceci, Williams, & Mueller-Johnson, 2006, p. 555). Thus, by the 1940s AAUP formalized tenure to ensure academic freedom and job security (Franzoni & Rossi-Lamastra, 2017). Almost every college and university in the United States acknowledged and applied tenure in relation to faculty positions by 1970 (Bowden, 2009).

In a similar vein, the Association of American Colleges and Universities (AAC&U) affirmed faculty should have the freedom of discussion in the classroom but must be careful when addressing controversial topics unrelated to their discipline, and moreover, in their writing and speaking, recommended that academics steer clear of conflict that goes against the interests of their institution (Peterson, 2007). In contrast, Herbert and Tienari (2013) used the work of Bogue and Aper (2000) to explain how they understood tenure as a way to protect professors and provide due process for them regardless of political or financial agendas.

> Tenure of academic employment became popularized in the United States 'as an instrument to guarantee the independence of faculty in their search for truth, to assure them of due process, to offer a degree of employment security as a partial compensation for the relatively low salaries ... and to protect them from the

caprice of the politically and financially motivated, and the narrowness and meanness of colleagues who hold different views'.
(Bogue and Aper, 2000 as cited by Herbert & Tienari, 2013, p.158)

Although the above historical view of tenure paints a rather positive and supportive picture, current literature on what tenure means to associate professors challenges this very painting by giving voice to some of the confusion and mixed feelings they informally identify in relation to their new associate position status.

Methodology and Methods

The methodology used for this literature review is qualitative in nature. There were two searches completed in order to access the most current and relevant literature on what it means to be tenured as an associate professor. The first search was done using an American University data base that is housed within the Chalmer Davee Library data base, by entering the key words "academic tenure means" and applying the following filters "English language only, peer-reviewed, years of publication between 2005–2017, category of Education, and type of document being an article." This search yielded 23 documents. To determine what was relevant I did a close abstract read to ensure that the article was aligned with the topic of this literature review and focused on what it means to be tenured and not what difficulties arise when applying for tenure. As a result, this search yielded six relevant articles, which shared insight in the abstract on what tenure means in the context of higher education and often shared data of narratives and/or findings that demonstrated the complexity of what tenure means to faculty members.

To widen the scope of literature on this topic, a search was done in Google Scholar. The key words and categories used in this search were: in the field of title "associate professor" or "tenure", in the publication field "higher education", in the field of publication "accepting any kind of publication", in the field of limitations "without citations, non and track", and in the field of years of publication "2005–2017." This secondary search yielded 107 results. To narrow down the results, an additional abstract-by-abstract search was conducted to determine the relevance of the document to this literature review. When there was no abstract provided in the publication, a full read of the text was done to ensure that it also met the same relevant criteria mentioned above. There was one exception for the result that yielded a book by Chait (2009) where the table of contents was reviewed, and a relevant chapter was skim read to decide its applicability to this review. Ten relevant documents emerged following this filtering and analysis. The two searches provided a total of 16 relevant publications, which were used to ground this literature review (12 peer reviewed articles, one book chapter, and three magazine pieces).

Findings: Seven Themes in the Literature

The following section presents the seven themes that emerged from the 16 relevant literature pieces on what it means to be tenured as an associate professor.

1. Benefits of Being Tenured

Six out of the sixteen documents shared a common theme of highlighting the positive benefits of having attained tenure. Tang and Tang (2012) argue that professors enjoy the "love of money" in terms of pay satisfaction. They claim it is known that once assistant professors attain tenure they are also given financial reward by an increase in their salary. As a result, tenure signifies the benefit of financial reward, and this is seen as a welcomed outcome for most associate professors.

> Early in one's career, one has very little, or nothing, in terms of materials and possessions. One will need money to buy a new house, a car or two, raise one's family, send children to school, etc. up to a point. It is plausible that tenured Professors may have achieved some of the material goals in life. (Tang & Tang, 2012, p. 118)

Thus, Tang and Tang (2012) remind university administrators and state legislators ". . . that in order to attract, retain, and motivate university faculty, university administrators and state legislators do need to pay attention to external pay equity," in comparison to "comparable peer institutions" (p. 119).

According to Boardman and Ponomariov (2007), another benefit tenure creates is that it provides associate professors with greater access to larger applied and commercially relevant research grants, which may help them financially promote and achieve their research agenda. Many universities in the science disciplines now push for grants from institutions such as the Multidiscipline, Multipurpose, University Research Center (MMURC), the National Science Foundation's Engineering Research Centers, and the Science and Technology Centers, and often these larger industry grants are more accessible to associate professors (Boardman & Ponomariov, 2007). "Even those scientists with official license to conduct industry-related research devalue such research when they do not have tenure" (Boardman & Ponomariov, 2007, p. 63). Thus, tenure allows and promotes access to larger research grants to associate professors in the sciences.

In line with the benefits that arise from tenure status, Ceci et al. (2006) state that another benefit of tenure is providing associate professors the ability to exercise their power to "whistle-blow" on ethical violations they may have noticed: "Once tenured, Associate Professors are perceived to be somewhat more willing to 'ruffle feathers'. . ." (p. 568). However, Ceci et al. (2006) caution that there are complex situations in which 'blowing the whistle' may not take place if the associate professor feels uncertain about their promotion to full professor status.

> [A]ssociate professors with tenure were perceived as being only slightly more inclined to whistle-blow in the face of ethical violations, nor were they seen as being especially willing to assert their freedom to teach disfavored course or research unpopular ideas if doing so conflicted with the desires of those who will one day sit in judgment of them for promotion to full professorship. (p. 568)

Therefore, although there is an opportunity to call out unethical behaviours and actions in the academy, associate professors do not feel significantly more comfortable exercising this right.

With respect to job security and research topics of interests, Franzoni and Rossi-Lamastra (2017) believe that having attained tenure, research scientists have more job security than other job opportunities inside and outside the university. Moreover, Franzoni and Rossi-Lamastra (2017) contend, "[t]enured scientists generally enjoy modest job pressure as their work and productivity is not usually scrutinized. They can take leave from the department or buyout teaching without fear of losing their job or being displaced while away" (p. 691). This less stressful environment affords them freedom to research topics that they may not have endeavoured to investigate previously.

> Specifically, after tenure, it is reasonable to expect that a scientist becomes less risk-averse when selecting areas in which to conduct research. Indeed, tenure marks the passage from a period of considerable job insecurity concerning employment and career progression to a period of considerable job security and relatively predictable career progress. (Franzoni & Rossi-Lamastra, 2017, p. 694)

Based on these insights it is no surprise that other scholars such as Legg (2007) and Boardman and Ponomariov (2007) report that tenure is the aim of many educators and is often associated with economic and job security, making it ". . . the most broadly coveted prize that the traditional university reward system has to offer" (Boardman & Ponomariov, 2007, p. 53).

Concurring with this argument about the benefits of tenure, Peterson (2007) states "[o]nce the race is won (i.e., academic tenure attainment), unless one is terminated for cause, incompetence, moral turpitude, insubordination, or financial exigencies, one is a lifetime member of an elite group of faculty" (p. 357). Being tenured also gives one the gift of not having to retire at a certain age, which can be fulfilling to professors who wish to dedicate their lives to scholarship, university service, and teaching (Yoon, 2016).

Based on the literature that addresses this theme, there are several benefits to tenure such as a salary increase, access to larger research grants, ability to whistle-blow on unethical practices, job security, and no mandatory retirement.

2. Tenure Connects to Power in Universities
A second theme that emerged from the literature addresses how tenure gives power to faculty to influence the image and direction of their departments and the institution at large. According to Chait (2009), tenure "extends well beyond the terms and conditions of faculty employment to encompass, for instance, faculty status and institutional self-image" (p. 69). Tenured professors have the ability to make powerful decisions about who gets to be dean. They are also able to be on the hiring committees for new faculty, thus producing

leadership choices and developing the future direction of the university (Chait, 2009).

In the same line of argument, Yoon (2016) contends that "[m]ost universities, by virtue of being nonprofits, require faculty to evaluate and monitor university administrators and trustees. Tenure enables faculty to make good-faith decisions without recrimination" (p. 431). Some of these good-faith decisions made by tenured faculty can be exercised when tenured faculty ". . . sit in recruiting committees and have voting power in decisions to grant tenure to junior scientists. They appoint the dean and are pivotal in decisions about teaching, students' intake, lab or office space allocations etc." (Franzoni & Rossi-Lamastra, 2017, p. 694). Another example of the influential power tenured faculty have can be noted when senior faculty control what is deemed acceptable in a given field by virtue of editorships and board memberships (Boardman & Ponomariov, 2007).

Despite the aforementioned examples, it is argued by Chait (2009) that the amount of power and influence given to tenured professors depends on the type of institution where they are employed. For example, if they work at a research centered university or a prestigious private college they may have a greater voice in governance, which ultimately shapes the future of the institution. In other words, "[f]aculty at the tenure sites did have more power than colleagues under contracts, but neither approached the level of authority or the degree of self-direction professors have at more distinguished institutions" (Chait, 2009, p. 78). Consequently, Chait argues, it is important to consider the type of institution granting tenure, as it impacts the implications of how much power tenured faculty have on a personal and institutional level.

Another way of looking at the relationship between tenure and power is to ". . . think of academic tenure as a set of constraints on the discretion of managers (the administration) over various aspects of the academic enterprise" (Chait, 2009, p. 70). These constraints on administrators' decisions require the administrators to attentively listen, and do their best to persuade or channel the votes given by tenured faculty if they have a preset agenda (Chait, 2009). Thus, many administrators are aware of how influential tenured faculty members' decisions can be in terms of "shap[ing] institutional decisions through their actions in departments, colleagues, or the institution as a whole" (McPherson & Schapiro, 1999, as cited by Chait, 2009, p. 70).

Interestingly, Legg (2007) claims that from the perspective of high school students and potential faculty candidates applying to post-secondary institutions, one of the considerations taken into account is if there are any tenured faculty at that institution: "Students and other faculty might be attracted to an institution with tenured faculty because 'continuity and responsible leadership' are considered attributes of the tenure system" (Legg, 2007, p. 191). As a result, tenure is seen to be symbolic of creating sustainable leadership and providing institutions with a stronger public image and perception (Legg, 2007).

In summary, the relationship between post-secondary institutions and power accrued by tenured faculty is relational. Depending on the type of institution and their understanding of tenure, different levels of power can be exercised by associate professors. The literature illustrates that power is contained in: (1) decision making about leadership positions and the choice of new faculty entering the institution, (2) decision making on editorial boards about what counts as research that is noteworthy to publish or not, and (3) decision making about how the image and vision of the institution is sustained or changed in the future.

3. Tenure Allows for Diversity in Research Publications

Lin (2016) contends that academic tenure promotes research. In addition to research productivity, Yoon (2016) states tenured faculty feel increased comfort engaging with more diverse projects and research interests because of the job security they have attained. As a result of being able to exercise their freedom in research, tenured professors publish more frequently. According to Yoon (2016),

> [a]cross all publications tenured faculty publish more frequently, are cited with roughly the same frequency, and place in comparable caliber of journals. These productivity gains, however, largely disappear when excluding solicited publications. (p. 428)

It is important to note that when considering law faculty who are tenured, Yoon shares that "[t]hey publish more frequently while maintaining their citation counts and quality of journal placement" (Yoon, 2016, p. 429). As a result, tenured faculty overall do demonstrate productivity gains in their research publications and contributions to scholarly discourse.

However, Yoon contends that the type of institution must be considered when examining the scholarly research publications a tenured professor has, because "[f]aculty at higher-ranked institutions, all else equal, may find it easier to publish and place their writings at higher-ranked journals" (Yoon, 2016, p. 450). Moreover, another factor to be considered is the level of seniority a tenured Professor has. For example, a first year associate professor will not have easy access to higher-ranked journals when compared to a fourth year associate professor. The "[s]eniority, like institutional affiliation, may similarly bias our measures" (Yoon, 2016, p. 450).

Franzoni and Rossi-Lamastra's (2017) study suggests that research publication productivity needs to consider the diversification of research interests of the tenured faculty member.

> Using a panel of 562 scientists observed over 15 years, we found that achieving tenure is likely to be associated with a boost in diversification. This result seems to support the idea that scientists perceive diversification as a risky strategy that they are thus more likely to pursue under the relative job security of tenure. (Franzoni & Rossi-Lamastra, 2017, p. 705)

Their research study demonstrates that tenure allows for more diversification of research interests (Franzoni & Rossi-Lamastra, 2017), which then leads to greater increase in publications.

Faria and McAdam (2015) also contend that as long as the associate professor is able to demonstrate a range of research interests they will yield a higher number of publications. However if they have secured tenure only from their specialized doctoral dissertation, they will likely not be able to continue a productive level of publishing. This distinction between being specialized and dependent on one's doctoral dissertation for publication, in contrast to having more diverse research interests, is helpful as it demonstrates the longevity of productive research habits.

Thus, after attaining tenure, many associate professors permit themselves to conduct diverse research studies that may have been too risky to do prior to being tenured. The result of having diverse research interests, a desire to learn about them, and then publish on them helps with the increase in research productivity accomplished by tenured faculty.

4. Tenure and Gender Politics

A fourth theme that emerged out of the literature on what it means to be tenured is the role of gender and the implications it has for the associate professor. June (2009) shares that once women attain tenure and become associate professors, the path of further promotion is murky, difficult, and less travelled. She shares that the promotional path for female faculty is endangered due to a lack of mentorship, limited validation for service and supervisory work, and does not have a great deal of financial incentive.

The gender equity gap in promotional pay is not as high for women as it is for men, thus many female associate professors stay at the associate rank instead of pursuing full professor status (June, 2009). In other words, the range of financial increase from an associate professor status to a full professor status for female faculty is limited when compared to the financial range that is offered to male faculty. Thus, due to the lack of salary increase at promotion many female associate professors believe there is "... little incentive to aspire to and strive for promotion" (June, 2009). As for the issues of marital status and parental status, these did not change the statistics on women being promoted at a slower rate than men (June, 2009). Nevertheless, "[t]he report shows that women at doctoral institutions take two and a half years longer than men to reach full professor" (June, 2009). This finding is further supported by Buch, Huet, Rorrer, and Roberson (2011) who contend "... there appears to be a void at the next rank up, one that no doubt contributes to recent findings that many faculty—especially women—often get stuck at the rank of associate professor" (p. 39).

The other factor influencing the slow rate of female associate professors moving to full professor status is lack of mentorship. "Associate professors often have few devoted resources to tap as they try to move up. And female academics, in particular, often report that they have fewer opportunities for mentorship then men" (June, 2009). In light of this, June implies mentorship helps associate professors build the social capital they need to navigate unknown paths towards full professorship. A third factor beyond the lack of pay equity and mentorship is the gendered nature of the overloading of service work and supervisory duties on female associate professors.

> Women and minorities often "end up doing more committee work and more advisory work" that isn't credited fairly toward

advancement, said Ms. Maatz, whose organization has produced its own research on the obstacles female professors who seek promotion face. (June, 2009)

Thus, female and minority associate professors are asked to contribute disproportionately to service work with often-minimal validation or credit for it towards the path of full professorship. As a result, many female associate professors "... resigned themselves to a lifetime as an associate professor because they're engaged in activities that won't be 'rewarded' by their institution, such as working with students, preparing course materials, and doing research that involves the community" (June, 2009). Due to the high level of service and teaching female associate professors do, it has been argued that women write fewer articles after becoming tenured and that they are more often in lower ranking journals when compared to male associate professors (Yoon, 2016).

Female associate professors encounter many barriers, such as pay inequity, lack of mentorship, lack of validation of service and supervision, lack of time for research publications because of higher service demands and gender inequity with respect to the overall promotion process.

5. Tenure Does Not Provide Academic Freedom or Security

The literature describes having tenure status as not changing the level of academic freedom or job security that an assistant professor would have access to. Herbert and Tienari (2013) discuss how Aalto University in Finland is introducing a tenure-track system to its faculty. The negative implication of tenure systems according to Herbert and Tienari (2013) promotes an understanding of the relationship between tenure with senior management and how it can be harmful to any faculty member who is not supportive of the senior management team. The concern is a misuse of authority in turning down promotions, including from associate to full professorship, unless the applicants are in alignment with the senior management's agenda and goals. Herbert and Tienari (2013) argue that "tenure becomes a tool for realizing senior management strategic intent in the university" and thus it limits the agency and self-determination of future tenured faculty (p. 158). Given that the senior management agenda and the level of authority administrators may have, they can impose false marketing values in some institutions on all faculty. For example, some of these strategists who embody these administrative roles use the tenure system to steer and use authority to a point where

> [t]hey have taken the role of direction setting, and the direction of Aalto University clearly includes a new academic career system. 'Freedom to be creative and critical' is noted in the Aalto University values statement, but so far it is not clear where this value is put into practice. (Herbert and Tienari 2013, p. 165)

Due to this misuse of steering of university politics, many tenured faculty members have "told stories of elitism and cramping of creativity" (Herbert & Tienari, 2013, p. 170). Similarly, Williams and Ceci (2007) examine how some associate professors don't feel they have academic freedom because they fear not being promoted by their colleagues to full professor status and thus are not able to write or teach on topics that go against the views of their peers.

> Even now, having gotten tenure on promotion to associate professor, she does not feel comfortable undertaking the research. She reasons that once she has been promoted to full professor, she will finally be free to pursue the line of inquiry without fear of angering her colleagues. (Williams & Ceci, 2007)

As a result, Williams and Ceci (2007) contend that associate professors "... were more timid than [they] expected, rarely confronting departmental colleagues who disagreed with the content of their research and teaching." The worries that underlay the potential conflicts were about maintaining good relations with other tenured faculty to help with promotional opportunities in the future, instead of maintaining an ethical standard (Williams & Ceci, 2007).

> The muzzling effect of the current system of promotion in higher education—in which even tenured Associate Professors refrain from exercising academic freedom for fear of derailing their chances for promotion to full Professor—must be weighed against tenure's virtues, such as higher graduation rates and recruitment of a talented work force. (Williams & Ceci, 2007)

This "muzzling effect" does not give way to "academic freedom," which is supposed to arrive with tenure. "The truth is that most of us walk on eggshells until we become full professors. To quote one newly promoted 45-year-old friend, 'It's great to finally be able to speak my mind at work'" (Williams & Ceci, 2007).

Along the same lines as Williams and Ceci (2007), Bowden (2009) presents the argument that tenure does not guarantee security: ". . . tenure protection . . . is not necessarily a guarantee in that after a probationary period teachers 'should have permanent or continuous employment' not that they will have permanent or continuous employment as some sort of entitlement" (p. 21). Bowden (2009) claims that even though an associate professor has tenure it does not mean they cannot be terminated. He explains how the status of tenure is a privilege granted to professors by some post-secondary institutions to pursue their research and teaching interests but it is not an ". . . innate faculty right or even a legal right in-and-of itself" (p. 23).

Thus, some of the literature argues that tenure can potentially limit academic freedom, that tenure may not provide guaranteed job promotion to full professor, and finally, that tenure does not necessarily give job security that promises no termination. What makes this theme interesting is that it provides a different perspective and contrasts directly with the first theme that emphasizes the benefits of earning tenure.

6. *Tenure Leaves Associate Professors Without Mentorship*

Lack of mentorship for associate professors is touched on in theme four, which examines how tenure gets complicated for women. Picking up on this thread of mentorship, two further papers supported the claim of mentorship being crucial once an assistant professor gains the status of an associate professor. Wilson (2012) claims associate professors become isolated and overwhelmed by their new duties, and they desire mentorship that, usually, is lacking. She states candidly, ". . . once a Professor earns tenure, that guidance disappears, the amount of committee work piles on, and Associate Professors are often left to figure out how to manage the varying demands of the job—and fit in time for their research—on their own" (Wilson, 2012, para. 7). Wilson (2012) provides the example of David Harvey, a professor of history at the New College of Florida who shares during an interview: "As soon as you make tenure, you go from being one of the rising young stars of the department to being one of the workhorses" (para. 7). As a result, associate professors take on more service commitments but are still left unsatisfied with a lack of validation and appreciation for their work (Wilson, 2012).

Moreover, because the lack of mentorship is experienced alongside heightened isolation, many associate professors feel a mental anguish that makes them ponder ". . . a crisis of meaning, where they think: 'There has to be something more than writing research grants, publishing, and teaching'" (Wilson, 2012, para. 6). Consequently, such mental anguish sometimes manifests itself in unhappiness or depression, as there is a high level of uncertainty about what lies ahead. The few associate professors considering or seeking a new job because of anguish at their current institution find themselves locked in and unable to find another position: since they ". . . spend more of their time on service work, and less on their own research and writing, their ability to be competitive on the job market and move to another institution is diminished" (Wilson, 2012, para. 19).

To further the need for mentorship, Buch et al.'s (2011) research survey claims "associate professors felt that they were not receiving guidance from a mentor or administrator in charting their path to [full] professor, even while they also acknowledged not being proactive and intentional enough in their own career planning" (p. 42). Interestingly, these authors focus on the individual associate professor as an agent who must help him or herself. However, they understand that associate professors can ask for help but the guidance must come from senior full professor colleagues. In light of this, Buch et al. (2011) contend associate professors felt a need for criteria that were ". . . transparent, consistent, and fair, and that recognized the range of contributions needed to meet the diverse goals and broad mission of the institution" (p. 42).

Thus, the need for mentorship is clearly articulated as a resource that is lacking for associate professors. Moreover, it is apparent that the mental anguish and solitude that associate professors find themselves in after being tenured is felt as a negative consequence. In light of these findings it is essential to provide more support and mentorship to associate professors.

7. Examining Challenges With Traditional Tenure Expectations in Clinical Disciplines

The seventh theme arising from the literature review is about how tenure is often taken up differently in various clinical disciplines. In particular, dentistry and radiologic technology disciplines share challenges that associate professors experience once they are tenured. Peterson (2007) examines the dentistry discipline and argues that tenure should not be held to traditional values of publication and research grants, as the dental professors are required to be more hands-on with their teaching and mentoring of students. Associate professors in dentistry are often expected to teach their students about hand skills needed when operating on a patient, which means more time needs to be dedicated to supervising students as they learn the practical components of the profession (Peterson, 2007). Unfortunately, with politics meddling with post-secondary institutions, many associate professors [especially those in clinical disciplines] are asked to grapple with their service commitment to students' experiential learning while simultaneously gaining grants to sustain their work at the university, not having mentorship, and facing institutional norms that are resistant to change (Peterson, 2007).

Another discipline challenging what tenure means is radiological technology. In this discipline, "[a] majority of educational programs . . . are in settings where tenure for faculty is not traditionally offered" (Legg, 2007, p. 192). According to Legg (2007), the few associate professors in the radiologic technology discipline often have a small number of publications due to the demands of other hands-on activities such as the administrative roles, teaching and service that they must do. Part of the argument is that radiologic technology, like dentistry, demands more hands-on teaching and supervision which is often assigned to the associate professors and thus creates a lack of time for them to compete for research grants and produce timely publications. Finally, research on the narratives of associate professors who were contacted to inform both the dentistry and radiologic technology literature, present a concern about their clinical discipline losing its professional image because they are rarely able to meet the expectations of publishing in high ranking journals.

Thus, tenure status in both dentistry and radiologic technology seems to create perplexing and sometimes impossible expectations for associate professors to meet and consequently may have larger implications of challenging the level of "professionalism" attached to each of these disciplines.

Discussion of Gaps in the Literature Review

This literature review provides insights and different perspectives on how tenure is taken up by associate professors in different institutions and various disciplines. There are clearly a number of beneficial features of tenure but also several issues or areas of concern.

Theme four addressed gender differences and the impact on academic identity that have been found in higher education. However, this issue is not new:

> The AAUP has expressed concern about the lack of gender equity and considers it the responsibility of each institution to implement policies to reverse the situation. Although Title IX (disallowing gender discrimination) was passed in 1972, women are underrepresented in the tenure ranks and currently hold only 24 percent of full professor positions and 31 percent of tenured positions. (Peterson, 2007, p. 359)

Moreover, Peterson's research findings claim that "[t]he average salary for women at all institutions and across all ranks is 81 percent that of men. It has been said that 'we have structured an academic workplace for men of a bygone era' (Peterson, 2007, p. 359). Consequently, these findings demonstrate an awareness of inequity based on gender identity. The concern is that instead of fighting or creating alliances for gender equity in the tenure procedure, many women decide to settle with the lower ranking job and lower pay, while convincing themselves that this is just the way it is and making peace with it. Thus, the question of gender equity remains unanswered in the literature regarding the meaning of tenure.

There is a need for further research to understand and explore the different identity factors (e.g. race, sexuality, ability, ethnicity, social class) that make up the profile of tenured faculty because these can gravely impact the career trajectory of all levels of professors who may have many barriers throughout the promotional tenure process. Not much research has been done on the barriers and challenges that visible minority and marginalized faculty experience moving from associate professor to full professor and, thus, these voices are not represented in the aforementioned literature on what it means to be tenured. As a result, associate professors who identify with these barriers and challenges are subjected to the politics of the institutions they serve and consequently often remain suffering in silence and feeling isolated in the process of applying for full professor status. The statistics of the National Center for Education Statistics, according to which "men made up two thirds of tenured faculty in postsecondary institutions" and "White, non-Hispanics accounted for 85.1 percent of tenured faculty" demonstrate there exists a visible minority group that consists of visible minority and marginalized faculty (Legg, 2007, p. 191). This, then, begs the question: If one of the goals of post-secondary institutions is to be transparent about equity issues and to promote diversity with an asset-minded approach, why are the voices of visible minorities and marginalized faculty in academy and discussions around equity issues often missing? Can tenure and promotion committees, dominated by White and non-Hispanic people be trained by equity officers, on their respective campuses, to address the above equity concerns in a manner that is consistent with their institution's goals of equity and diversity?

Another gap in the literature, which was briefly presented in theme seven, is about how some disciplines, dentistry, and radiologic technology among them apply the process of tenure with various levels of rigor given the circumstances in which their associate professors find themselves. The question then becomes "... whether academic tenure is obstructing change by failing to adequately encourage the scholarship of teaching and learning, as well as promoting a discipline-based mentality that defies the need for discipline integration" (Peterson, 2007, p. 361). To better understand the challenges of tenure, more research needs to be done in different disciplinary areas that may or may not be able to assimilate traditional tenure procedures and responsibilities. Given that the nature of various disciplines has changed since the conception of tenure in the 1940s, alongside advances in technological tools that have occurred in fields of dentistry and radiologic technology, can the perimeters of tenure be reflective of more individual discipline needs? Furthermore, why does the standardization of traditional tenure procedures across campuses, regardless of discipline areas, need to be the precedent? Who benefits from this practice?

Thus, a more rigorous investigation on the aforementioned gaps in this literature review is needed in order to better comprehend diverse groupings of associate professors' lived experiences on what it means to be tenured.

Conclusion and Future Directions

It is evident, given the diverse themes that surfaced in this literature review, that there are multiple meanings and perspectives attached to tenure. This review provides insights on seven themes that emerged from the current literature (2005–2017) and identifies some of the complexities and gaps that need further consideration. The hope is that further research on this important topic will occur and contribute to building a positive and safe post-secondary institutional culture for all associate professors. This will only happen by addressing tenured professors' needs and reflections on what it means to be tenured in the twenty-first century.

References

Boardman, P. C., & Ponomariov, B. L. (2007). Reward systems and NSF university research centers: The impact of tenure on university scientists' valuation of applied and commercially relevant research. *The Journal of Higher Education, 78*(1), 51–70.

Bowden, R. G. (2009). The postsecondary professoriate: Problems of tenure, academic freedom, and employment law. *Academy of Educational Leadership Journal, 13*(3), 17–36.

Buch, K., Huet, Y., Rorrer, A., & Roberson, L. (2011). Removing the barriers to full professor: A mentoring program for associate professors. *Change: The Magazine of Higher Learning, 43*(6), 38–45.

Ceci, S. J., Williams, W. M., & Mueller-Johnson, K. (2006). Is tenure justified? An experimental study of faculty beliefs about tenure, promotion, and academic freedom. *Behavioral and Brain Sciences, 29*(6), 553–569.

Chait, R. (2009). Does faculty governance differ at colleges with tenure and colleges without tenure? In R. Chait, (Ed.) *The questions of tenure* (pp. 69–100). London, UK: Harvard University Press.

Faria, J. R., & McAdam, P. (2015). Does tenure make researchers less productive? The case of the 'specialist.' *Discussion Papers in Economics. DP, 5*, 14.

Franzoni, C., & Rossi-Lamastra, C. (2017). Academic tenure, risk-taking and the diversification of scientific research. *Industry and Innovation, 24*(7), 691–712.

Herbert, A., & Tienari, J. (2013). Transplanting tenure and the (re) construction of academic freedoms. *Studies in Higher Education, 38*(2), 157–173.

June, A. W. (2009, April 27). Not moving on up: Why women get stuck at associate professor. *The Chronicle of Higher Education*. Retrieved from https://www.chronicle.com/article/Not-Moving-On-Up-Why-Women/47213

Legg, J. S. (2007). Academic tenure in radiologic technology—revisited. *Radiologic Technology, 78*(3), 191–196.

Lin, Y. P. (2016). Academic tenure and the rising cost of higher education: An economist's point of view. *The Journal of Applied Business and Economics, 18*(4), 31.

Peterson, M. R. (2007). Academic tenure and higher education in the United States: Implications for the dental education workforce in the twenty-first century. *Journal of Dental Education, 71*(3), 354–364.

Tang, T. L. P., & Tang, T. L. N. (2012). The love of money, pay satisfaction and academic tenure: Professors in a public institution of higher education. *Public Personnel Management, 41*(1), 97–126.

Williams, W. M., & Ceci, S. J. (2007, March 9). Does tenure really work? *Chronicle of Higher Education, 53*(27): B16. Retrieved from http://chronicle.com/weekly/v53/i27/27b01601.htm

Wilson, R. (2012, June 3). Why are associate professors so unhappy? *Chronicle of Higher Education*. Retrieved from https://www.chronicle.com/article/Why-Are-Associate-Professors/132071

Yoon, A. H. (2016). Academic tenure. *Journal of Empirical Legal Studies, 13*(3), 428–453.

SECTION 2

Reflecting on the Tenure Journey: The Individual and the Institutional

While the authors in this section identify that change is primarily individual, they take a more institutional, rather than personal, perspective. This differs from the writers in Section Four who emphasize a personal perspective. It is worthwhile to consider that these authors are indicating active engagement in balancing their individual efforts with those of the institution. Within that effort, it is interesting to consider how academic freedom fits with adaptations one makes to be assimilated into an institution. At the same time, it is important to ask whether the adaptations are simply to fit into the institution or growing toward influencing the institution itself. In short, there may be balance but what is given and taken in order to sustain that balance?

Carmen Rodriguez's chapter "Of joys and sorrows: Lessons learned in applying for tenure and promotion" presents a significant effort to balance the individual and the institutional. The joys arising from fulfilling the role are clear, while the sorrows are presented as moments to understand and grow. The chapter's generosity in its understanding of sorrow may reflect the individual being more generous than the institution.

Margarida Romero's chapter brings to light her experiences related to leaving the academy in Canada in order to return to France and lead a university laboratory. In her chapter she describes how this journey occurred, and what she learned along the way. Her blend of individual and institutional is unique, particularly in light of the personal challenges she wrote about in *The Academic Gateway*.

Peter Milley had an unusual challenge in writing his chapter for this book. He proposed a model of experience in the tenure-track in *The Academic Gateway*, however, in preparing a chapter for this book he was asked to consider the theory presented in the introduction. This led to his considering two theories that do not reconcile easily (they seem to have different timeframes) and both have imperfections. The result is a detailed analysis of considerable depth.

Cecile Badenhorst speaks to finding a balance through the consideration of "Tenure life: Rhythms, time, and energy." Academics often speak about lacking balance and infringement between work and life outside of work. The option of flexibility in scheduling research and service time likely contributes to this, but Cecile very clearly has found a way to sustain a balance.

This section ends with the a chapter jointly written by **Sharon Penney, Gabrielle Young, Cecile Badenhorst, Heather McLeod, Sylvia Moore, and Sarah Pickett**. They were all part of the Memorial University Writing Group in *The Academic Gateway*. As editors we were challenged with how to handle the group when the requirement of authorship was to speak about the time around the tenure decision. That requirement did not fit those who have not sought tenure or those who are well established but contribute to the writing group. The compromise was a group of five authors who keep the spirit of shared writing alive and, once again, demonstrate the power of collaborating.

CHAPTER 2

Of Joys and Sorrows: Lessons Learned in Applying for Tenure and Promotion

Carmen Rodriguez de France

The words came as consolation, as balsam, at a time of disappointment and grief: *"Have you learned the lessons only of those who admired you, and were tender with you, and stood aside for you? Have you not learned great lessons from those who braced themselves against you, and disputed the passage with you?"* My partner reminded me of these words by Walt Whitman as I read my letter regarding the process I called my "TiPi" (Tenure-Promotion).

In the academic world, there are strictures and parameters within which one ought to operate in order to be considered commendable on being granted tenure and promotion. Within Indigenous spaces, this is sometimes an even more challenging process due to the inextricable relationship of one's work and one's service, which are still considered separate aspects of established academic duties. When promotion does not happen due to diverse circumstances, there can be a sense of loss, grief, and even disenchantment with the institution. Overcoming such "failure" can be an occasion to fall through the cracks or it can be an opportunity to revise and reframe one's commitment to oneself, to the institution, and to the members of the communities within which one works. During my study leave, I worked on the latter, trying to appreciate the feedback from the Appointment, Reappointment, Promotion, and Tenure (ARPT) Committee that did not grant me promotion, and finding some solace in the affirming letter from my dean who was able to perceive in my work my dedication to service, commitment to my scholarship, and my passion for teaching and learning. This chapter addresses ways in which I have been able to move past some of the stages identified by Elisabeth Kübler-Ross (1969) as part of the grieving process, which I experienced upon learning I had been granted tenure but not promotion.

A New Beginning

In the spring of 2015 I was given a three-ring binder to start collecting my documents to apply for tenure and promotion. The process was an exercise in tangibility for it allowed me to pay attention to the me "on paper," to imagine who I wanted to become. Beyond the practical representation as a holder of my being, those three rings represented my life as a scholar, based on the standards on which universities place accountability of their faculty members: one ring represented research; another represented teaching; the last related to the most important aspect of my life, service. These rings were also reminders of who I am outside of the academic world: I am a mother of three adolescents who, like me, are on the cusp of transition towards becoming something new. Not very different from whom they are right now and yet, close to exploring new life dimensions, emotions, and experiences.

Similarities and Differences
Like my children, Elisabeth Kübler-Ross was one of a set of triplets, though she was born almost 80 years earlier, in 1926. Her work on the process of dying and the natural outcome of death has been documented, cited, and, recognized around the world as part of the grieving process that most of us experience as part of the human condition when faced with loss. Her initial studies related to physical death but soon enough her findings were transferred to other realms of experience, and the concept of loss was related to divorce, illness, job, freedom, an amputation, and other forms of parting with someone or something, and where feelings (rational and irrational ones) emerge as a result of loss. Her monograph entitled "On Death and Dying," published in 1969, described five stages that capture the essence of knowing of an imminent loss; the stages are summarized as:

> Denial: the individual does not acknowledge the experience. Events seem unreal and distant from the present.

Anger: feelings of rage, frustration, and despair take the place of denial, and taking care of the individual becomes challenging.

Bargaining: the individual negotiates with death trying to delay it or postpone it.

Depression: the individual begins to understand that death is imminent, and begins to transition into accepting its certainty.

Acceptance: the person starts to prepare for death and starts to come to terms with it.

In her work, Kübler-Ross noted not everyone will necessarily go through all five stages, while Bowlby (1980) later stated "these phases are not clear cut, and any one individual may oscillate for a time back and forth between any two of them" (p. 85). Although seen as a superficial approach by some scholars (Silver & Wortman, 1980; Wortman & Silver, 1987, 1989, 1992; Osterweis, Solomon, & Green, 1984; Neimeyer, 2000; Jacobs, 1993; Corr, 2011; 2015), Kübler-Ross's work has been accepted, translated, and acknowledge as a good foundation to understand the process of death, grief, and loss. It has also been explored from the perspective of those who survive the death of a loved one and experience those five stages when grieving. Coping with loss varies from person to person and from experience to experience depending on stage of life, age, situation, context, and other factors that either allow or hinder an individual's ability to engage in a healing process. The complexity makes it a unique journey for each of us.

My journey towards tenure and promotion started with joy, and ended in confusion. For several months, I kept wondering if I should write a letter to the president of the university to explain my disappointment, not at being denied promotion but at feeling dismayed at the lack of clarity, professionalism, and transparency in the process. I learned I was entitled to submit a written response to the president according to a particular section of the Collective Agreement, which states that [the applicant] has the right to provide a written response to the Report sent to the applicant by the Chair of the University Academic Appointments Committee (UAAC). After consulting with loved ones, friends, relatives, and colleagues, I decided to send a letter expressing my disappointment, and offering feedback on how to possibly avert this happening to other applicants. I realize now that writing this letter was my way of accepting I had been part of an unclear and unfair evaluation, and that I needed to accept this 'failure.' However, I chose to identify failure as a situation in the hands of faculty members from the Tenure and Promotion Committee, as well as the UAAC, who omitted and neglected relevant information that would have made a difference in the way in which my application package was handled and discussed. I had hoped for respect and acknowledgement; both are values that reveal a true sense of collegiality, and are foundational to interactions.

Reframing

I grew up in a home where respect, love, and acceptance were (and continue to be) the foundation for relationships. In that home I learned to be of service; my parents modeled this behaviour for my siblings and me through their work as medical doctors. In that home I also learned to be considerate, patient, and most importantly, to always give people the benefit of the doubt; in other words, not to make assumptions. These teachings have served me well in my personal and professional life, although I sometimes wonder if not being judgmental is a useful trait, whether it is actually naïve. Upon reading the letter from the Committee, which stated I was granted only tenure but declined promotion, I could not help but feel some sadness thinking that my work was not worthy, and that what took so much care in putting together in the binder had been dismissed without proper care and respect for the work in which I take pride. This internal negotiation resembled the Bargaining stage from Kübler-Ross's model in that I was having a difficult time believing that my work had insufficient value and at the same time trying accept the Committee's decision.

Similar to how I engage with students' evaluations, I decided to put the letter away for several days and planned to re-read it at a time when I would be in a better emotional space, when I was in a better state of mind than when I received it. I could look at it when the winter weather eased a bit, which would give me an additional optimistic edge. While the letter remained in a drawer in my office, I was tempted more than once to retrieve it but I was determined to not allow that letter to define me, so I continued my work as usual. I reminded myself that I knew how to be efficient, how to be a good colleague, how to be of service, how to write book chapters and articles, and how to engage in research. Up to that point in time, I had dedicated ten years of my life to academia: five as sessional instructor and five in a tenure-track position. I felt I had a sense of what was expected of me but I also felt that those expectations could appear different for each applicant. I felt that it is similar to schooling: there was an explicit curriculum (or process) and a hidden one. Since the hidden one is out of view, it is challenging to assess or appreciate what is not being said or, in my case, not being considered. This, I was only able to absorb after reading the letter for the fourth time, and after the dean had asked me if I had requested the letters from the external reviewers who had offered positive comments with a few suggestions on how I could expand and improve my scholarship. It seemed that the Committee had omitted some of those comments focusing only on the suggestions and thus, producing a letter that did not include the various ways in which I had complied with the expectations.

Upon comparing the letters from the external reviewers to the letter I received, I could not help feeling sad and upset (similar to Kübler-Ross's description of the stage of Anger) at the realization that the focal point of my application seemed to have been what I was not doing, dismissing what I had accomplished throughout my career as a teacher and as educator, which had begun in México 32 years earlier.

To Be Indigenous
As a young woman living in México, my Indigenous heritage was seldom an aspect I considered when identifying myself. It was a taken-for-granted part of who I am so it was never necessary to mention it or to distinguish it as a feature of my identity given that most people in México share this same trait. However, upon arriving in Canada, and throughout my years residing here, my identity has shifted according to political stances and/or to regulations that are needed in identifying and grouping people. I arrived as an international student and moved to being an immigrant to now defining myself as a permanent resident, adding the identifier of being an Indigenous woman. This last characteristic has offered me opportunities to engage in Indigenous matters, collaborate and work with Indigenous people, establish reliable and honest relationships in Indigenous communities, and dedicate part of my life's work as an educator to informing others about the realities that Indigenous people face around the world. However, this characteristic (being an

Indigenous woman) has also hindered some opportunities to advance and be taken seriously within academia. As mentioned earlier in this chapter, in the academic world there are strictures and parameters within which one ought to operate in order to be considered commendable on being granted tenure and promotion. Within Indigenous spaces, this is sometimes an even more challenging process due to the inextricable relationship of one's work and one's service, which are still considered separate aspects of established academic duties.

Indigenous scholars (Antone & Dawson, 2014; Kuokkanen, 2007; Wilson, 2008; and Kovach, 2009) assert that Indigenous worldviews ought to be seen as integral to the expansion of bodies of knowledge across disciplines and within them. These scholars also remind us that Indigenous epistemologies open the doors to a wide range of possibilities for contributions beyond the academy seeking to disseminate knowledge in cross-disciplinary and interdisciplinary modalities, additional to serving in communities with whom one works. Not many people understand or appreciate education as a calling or as a profession aimed at service, often mistaking service for servitude. I have always felt proud in being of service, no matter how small or irrelevant it might appear. From writing letters of recommendation to working with Indigenous communities in diverse capacities, my life takes meaning in doing this work.

Teaching and research also enhance my life, but in ways that are different from service. I believe in the value of research and feel someone has to enact, implement, and apply the findings of rich research into the field, given that many scholars' contributions seldom move past the findings of their work. In thinking this way, my scholarship and applied forms of working, of which service is paramount, take the form of developing and delivering workshops, facilitating a book club, participating in international, national, and regional conferences and meetings, as well as expanding the body of knowledge through peer reviewed academic publications and other forms of writing accessible to a variety of audiences. This blurred image of where scholarship ends and service begins can be confusing to those unfamiliar with the holistic nature of Indigenous work inside an academic context. I have chosen to believe this confusion was in part what motivated the ARPT committee to dispense with the accomplishments documented in my tenure and promotion package, which in turn created confusion for me in understanding or appreciating the reasons for not being granted promotion;

there was no feedback nor was there a conclusive formulation for this outcome. While many of the observations within the UAAC's report were clear, there were others where the members' reasons for denying me promotion were unclear, inconclusive, and ill-informed given that they did not have/request all the necessary documents to assess important aspects of my application such as the Community Engaged Research Guidelines from the reviewing department, which were referred to by the ARPT committee and the dean. Further, even though the UAAC Report informed me that their votes were strongly in favor of granting me tenure, and strongly opposed to granting me promotion to the rank of associate professor, the reasons for arriving at such conclusions were not specific. There were also contradictory comments in some instances, and/or comments based on an already incomplete report submitted by the ARPT committee within the reviewing department. While citations were made, and with the exception of the last point in the Report pertaining to Service and Professional Activities, the UAAC report did not indicate how the dean's observations and recommendations were taken into consideration when concluding against my application for promotion.

It was then, after reading the UAAC's Report, that my partner's reading of Walt Whitman came as consolation and as balsam at a time of disappointment and grief:

> Have you learned the lessons only of those who admired you, and were tender with you, and stood aside for you? Have you not learned great lessons from those who braced themselves against you, and disputed the passage with you? (Leaves of Grass, 1867)

I knew I was supposed to thank him and feel gratitude for his compassion and reminder (which I did), but I also felt in need of expressing my frustration and disappointment at the process—and in need of feeling sorry for myself. Space and time were allowed for me to deal with the outcome. My partner reminded me of the need to celebrate my tenure, and to deal with the surprise of the promotion at a later time.

With this in mind, I tried to defocus on the negative and pay attention to my accomplishments and my worth, not necessarily dismissing the comments from the committee members who had reviewed my application package, but setting them aside for a while so as not to let them contaminate or pollute my soul. Some might think of this action as a denial of my reality, similar to what the first stage in the Kübler-Ross (1969) model describes: the individual does not acknowledge the experience; events seem unreal and distant from the present. However, for me, the experience was very real, very tangible, and very disappointing. One could say these feelings resembled the stage of depression within the model. I felt powerless, and unable to do much about this at that time. I felt the weight of failure, and tried to understand the experience of failure as both from within myself and within a system that had not valued my scholarship. Being able to separate the process from the person was the first step into acceptance. It took courage to compose a letter to the president, identifying the flaws in the process, and implying that better attention was needed in this important step on the tenure-track pathway. Writing the letter was my way of letting go of the surprise and disappointment, and to carry on with my responsibilities and my work.

It is my hope that with unwavering support from my mentors and other Indigenous colleagues, as well as with the help from the people of the various communities in which I work, my journey towards learning the language of the academy continues to be a rewarding experience.

To Be Continued

Across the university, there are non-Indigenous colleagues who are respectful allies and support Indigenous academics who continue to navigate the complexities of an institution rooted in Euro-centric conservative values that are often in conflict with Indigenous worldviews. Scholar Shawn Wilson (2008) describes the position that non-Indigenous academics (and others) can adopt when supporting, advocating for, and relating to Indigenous values and beliefs. Wilson describes such individuals as "Indigenists," affirming that his experience as a man will never allow him to appreciate a woman's experience but that this ought not to stop him from being a "feminist," meaning that he will forever support and advocate for the principles and values for which feminism stands. Similarly, he invites non-Indigenous people to think of themselves as "Indigenists," meaning that one does not have to be Indigenous in order to advocate for, respect, and acknowledge Indigenous principles and values.

Within the university, the field of Indigenous education is growing and expanding; we are now a department within the Faculty of Education, with all the rights and responsibilities this entails.

We are currently in the process of adopting some of the guidelines for tenure and promotion that have been of benefit for Indigenous scholars at various universities across Canada. Said guidelines for example, allow candidates for tenure within a department of native studies at one of the universities to proceed along three different paths depending on the nature of their scholarly work. Candidates declare at the time of appointment, which path they wish to follow. These paths were outlined at a CAUT conference as a) Candidate with conventional academic background; b) Candidate with traditional Aboriginal knowledge background; and c) Dual Tradition Scholar. What follows is a summary of what each pathway entails.

Conventional Academic Scholar
This refers to those individuals whose program of research and inquiry is in accordance with the principles of the western academy and whose effort is based mostly reflected in the publication of written peer-reviewed material.

Traditional Aboriginal Knowledge Scholar
Within this pathway, traditional Indigenous knowledge is described as not usually gained through university study but rather as a knowledge of the rites of passage, language and traditional customs, rituals, and teachings of a particular group of Aboriginal people or peoples. Knowledge would have been acquired though active and lengthy participation in particular cultural structures and processes. In many cases, individuals would have studied with a knowledgeable elder who would have facilitated their advancement.

Dual Tradition Scholar
This pathway aims at recognizing, supporting, and encouraging scholars who wish to combine conventional academic and traditional Aboriginal approaches to scholarship and teaching. These approaches are informed by principles and methods appropriate to an exploration of traditional Aboriginal knowledge and western academic disciplinary tradition.

While it is not clear whether or not we will adopt these same classifications, I believe that in some ways, this possibility could present me with opportunity and challenge: opportunity to apply for promotion next spring, trusting that my colleagues will appreciate, acknowledge, and respect my work; and challenge to recognize that a negative outcome is possible if they believe that the worth of my work needs further evidence.

As I continue to appreciate and accept the reality of this point of my professional life as an Indigenous female academic, and continue to learn how to navigate the institutional waters, I am encouraged to move forward by the words of late Ojibway writer Richard Wagamese:

> We carry the embers of all the things that burned and raged in us. Pains and sorrows, to be sure, but also triumphs, joys, victories, and moments of clear-eyed vision. People give us those. People cause flames to rise in our hearts, minds, and spirits, and life would not be life without them. (p. 27)

References

Antone, E., & Dawson, T. (2014). 'But how do I put this dream catcher into my teaching dossier?' Learnings and teachings from one faculty member's tenure experience of documenting community-based teaching and learning. In C. Etmanski, B. L. Hall, & T. Dawson (Eds.), *Learning and teaching community-based research: Linking pedagogy to practice* (pp. 287–387). Toronto, ON: University of Toronto Press.

Bowlby, J. (1980). *Loss*. New York, NY: Basic Books.

Bowlby, J., & Parkes, C. M. (1970). Separation and loss within the family. In E. Anthony (Ed.), *The child and his family* (pp. 167–216). New York, NY: Wiley.

Corr, C. (2011). Strengths and limitations of the stage theory proposed by Elisabeth Kubler-Ross. In K. Doka & A. Tucci (Eds.), *New perspectives on dying, death, and grief* (pp. 3–16). Washington, DC: Hospice Foundation of America.

Corr, C. (2015). Let's stop 'staging' persons who are coping with loss. *Illness, Crisis & Loss*, 23(3), 226–241.

Jacobs, S. (1993). *Pathologic grief: Maladaptation to loss*. Washington, DC: American Psychiatric Association.

Kovach, M. (2009). Being Indigenous in the academy: Creating space for Indigenous scholars. In A. M. Timpson (Ed.), *First Nations, first thoughts: The impacts of Indigenous thought in Canada* (pp. 51–73). Vancouver, BC: University of British Columbia Press.

Kübler-Ross, E. (1969). *On death and dying*. New York, NY: Macmillan.

Kuokkanen, R. (2007). *Reshaping the university: Responsibility, Indigenous epistemes, and the logic of the gift*. Vancouver, BC: University of British Columbia Press.

Neimeyer, R. (2000). Searching for the meaning of meaning: Grief therapy and the process of reconstruction. *Death Studies, 24*(6), 541–558.

Osterweis, M., Solomon, F., & Green, M. (1984). *Bereavement: Reactions, consequences, and care.* Washington, DC: National Academy Press

Silver, R. C., & Wortman, C. B. (1980). Coping with undesirable life events. In J. Garber & M. Seligman (Eds.), *Human helplessness: Theory and applications* (pp. 279–375). NewYork, NY: Academic Press.

Wagamese, R. (2016). *Embers: One Ojibway's meditations.* Vancouver, BC: Douglas & McIntyre.

Whitman, W. (1867). *Leaves of Grass.* Self-published.

Wilson, S. (2008). *Research is ceremony: Indigenous research methods.* Black Point, NS: Fernwood Publishing.

Wortman, C. B., & Silver, R. C. (1987). Coping with irrevocable loss. In G. VandenBos & K. Bryant. (Eds.), *Cataclysms, crises, and catastrophes: Psychology in action* (pp. 189–235). Washington, DC: American Psychological Press.

Wortman, C. B., & Silver, R. C. (1989). The myths of coping with loss. *Journal of Consulting and Clinical Psychology, 57*(3), 349–357.

Wortman, C. B., & Silver, R. C. (1992). Reconsidering assumptions about coping with loss: An overview of current research. In S. Filipp, L. Montada, & M. Lerner (Eds.), *Life crises and experience of loss in adulthood* (pp. 341–365). Hillsdale, NJ: Erlbaum.

CHAPTER 3

Starting From Scratch After Tenure to Run a New Lab in France

Margarida Romero

Academia is not the easiest professional arena. In past centuries, academic jobs have been a profession in which individuals could have time for reflection and conducting in-depth research with a certain freedom. Nowadays faculty are part of the overloaded professionals under the pressure of competitive funding and research outcomes. Despite academia no longer being the bohemian position of the last centuries, it remains a prestigious and coveted job. The gateway to reach tenure is a long process in which up and downs challenge our perseverance (Romero, 2017). Once we reach tenure, we obtain a form of stability. In this chapter I will describe my life after tenure, from starting to feel like a tenured professional and the transition to running my own lab. After years of ups and downs, I was expecting to enter a certain comfort zone after tenure. Meanwhile, an unexpected opportunity to run a new lab led me to quit my nearly reached comfort zone to again enter the uncertainty of moving into new professional challenges in another university. I will describe the challenges of moving from being a tenured associate professor (*professeure agrégrée*) within an established research lab in Canada to running my own lab as full professor in France. Challenges are part of the adventure that will be described in this chapter; bringing insights to researchers who are transitioning to full professorship positions or who consider the possibility of running a lab.

Moving to Advance

In a context of highly supportive families and deficient youth opportunities, like those in southern Europe, there is an important ratio of young adults living with their families, while there is also a high number of young adults migrating to third countries. In Spain, families create cocoons of support that are hard to leave if you do not have a good alternative. I wanted to explore beyond my family, my community, and city, which is why I decided to enrol at Barcelona University. Moving from my hometown, Reus, a small city of 100,000 citizens, to Barcelona, a dynamic city of near two million inhabitants, was a big challenge. This initial move from a small city to a cosmopolitan metropolis was the most challenging because it was the first time. The 100 kilometres move between Reus and Barcelona required that I effectively cut the umbilical cord; after this initial move, all subsequent (inter)national ones have been relatively easy to conduct. Our jobs—my partner and I—have taken us to Barcelona, Paris, Nîmes, Barcelona again, Québec City, and Nice. We haven't lived in one place consistently for more than four years in the last twenty; nor did I continue in any position more than this time. I have never been fired but I often feel heartbroken when quitting a position due to parting with students, colleagues, projects, and partnerships that I was required to leave behind to continue in a new position. My last move has also been challenging and the mourning process has just begun to finish, while I enter the acceptance phase of the process. My new position, as director of a new research lab, is the most challenging work I have ever had. Sometimes I doubt my ability to achieve the objectives of my new position and I wish I could go back to my previous role. In the next section I describe this last move both from the perspectives of the professional career and my personal and family life.

A Research Nomad Quitting the Comfort Zone Again and Again

After initiating my research career at Université Autonoma de Barcelona (UAB) in a quite precarious way, I was unsatisfied and worried about my survival possibilities in a Darwinist environment. After two miscarriages, I was ready to quit academia; I needed to move from the side of researching to the side of caring. I decided to resume my studies in psychology to help myself and to facilitate helping others. I defined a transition period of two years to move into a new job as psychologist while finishing my graduate studies in psychology. In reality, I was not actually ready to quit academia, but I was ready to move to another planet or the next galaxy if I had received an offer from there. I did not apply elsewhere but I got an email to apply to Université Laval (Québec). Apply I did and, in 2013, I landed an assistant professor position. After a noisy Skype interview, I never imagined being selected for the position. But I was selected, and I was feeling lucky to have been part of a fairy tale selection process. My faith in the academy was restored and I moved to my new university without hesitation. Very rapidly, I married my long-term partner before moving to another continent for this next position. Adapting from Barcelona to Québec was an exciting challenge; not only was the weather totally a contrast—the paradisiac Mediterranean weather of Barcelona becoming the more severe Canadian winters of Québec—but social and academic cultures were very different. Despite my enthusiasm for a new professional challenge in North America my parents tried hard to dissuade me about the move. The move required an important investment, a salary downgrade and considerable paperwork to address the immigration procedure. Moreover, once the decision to move was established, I became pregnant without having planned for it. From a rational point of view, moving from our comfortable apartment in Barcelona and the supportive family network to an unknown context was not the easiest move. We were supposed to arrive in December but immigration papers took longer than expected and we arrived in April.

Announcing to my new colleagues that I was pregnant, without even having started to work, was a source of anxiety. When we finally got the authorisation to move to Canada I was five months pregnant. We landed and arrived at an empty flat with three pieces of luggage and a one-metre cube container of our most emotional stuff: a paella, some photos, books and records, and a few clothes. Starting from scratch, when we had enjoyed a very comfy life in Barcelona was not easy, but it was definitively an enriching experience of material detachment and a way to learn to live with the essentials. I was supported by some colleagues and started contributing to my academic duties. I started supervising graduate students and preparing the course I would start teaching after my maternity leave. I took only a session of maternity leave to ensure my maternity was not too disruptive to my new employment situation.

I was in a new country with no family, no solid network of friends, and a very high level of pressure to start a new position while starting my new motherhood role. Thinking about this in retrospect, I have compassion for myself for surviving this crazy period. I was only moving one day after another in the best way possible and trying to smile while being supportive to students when they delayed their assignments for what seemed questionable causes much of the time. For example, being supportive of a delay due to a hockey match when you are sleeping few hours in a day from time to time is one of the best ways to strengthen your emotional regulation superpowers. It is an understatement to say the first year was difficult: life was terrible, almost hell, and I was not much of a shoulder for students to cry on. My family wanted me back, my husband was not excited about our new life—he was depressed by the winter weather—and I started to think that we had made the worst no-return-point decision in our life. For my husband it was my fault, and he was right: I pushed him too much for this move while trying to ignore all the efforts made by my family to prevent the move to the other side of the Atlantic Ocean. I was reminded of being pushy while taking care of our brand-new baby. Hormones and culpability mixed into tearful evenings. My family was emotionally distant and kept reminding me about their no-go advice and the move.

While I was realizing my dream of having a live and healthy baby, and trying to ensure development and success in my new tenure-track position, my dearest ones were trying to make me to reconsider the Canadian move. They suggested returning to Barcelona even without employment. They wanted me to quit my new position and rethink the family support I would have in Barcelona. And what about my work? For the first time in 35 years, this was not the point in the eyes of my so future-perspective-oriented family (Zimbardo & Boyd, 1999). My dearest ones were highlighting the non-academic opportunities I could try when returning to Barcelona while pushing on the culpability button of being too career oriented... Looking at how some of my new colleagues had succeeded to find a balance between their family and professional life in a highly syndicated and protected environment helped me to resist the pressure to quit. But more than ever, I was baby-oriented. For every decision I thought about my baby. In the first instance I could be by her side giving her the best possible caring context for a good starting point of her life. Canada, despite my family not being there, was the best place to raise her and permitted my having time to be with her in her early years and develop a proximal development parenting relationship in a child-oriented society. In Barcelona, working parents spend less time with children and abuse the kindergarten services to ensure they respond to professional Darwinist pressure. I had lost two pregnancies while in Catalan and was feeling, with all my heart, that returning to Barcelona was not a safe move for my baby and me.

In this context of family tensions and conflicting desires to live here or there, I had to find the deeper inner forces to continue to do my best to be accepted in my new position. Two years later I began to emerge from the stressful period and started to see improvements. One day, after some family tensions and tears, my Terrible Two brought me her teddy; I hugged her while crying. This was an awakening moment: I decided to be stronger and to make sure it would not be repeated. I was resisting too much against the tensions and decided that I would not accept being blamed for the Canadian move. I started to be more assertive and make sure that my husband understood that I would not move back to Europe until our daughter was a toddler and, even then, only if I had the possibility of landing a tenure-track position.

The tension continued but I was stronger. At the professional level, my efforts started to go smoothly with respect to my responsibilities for courses, research projects, and supervisions. After three years, I started to be accepted and good collaborations started to emerge with few difficulties. Québec is a relatively small research community. When you arrive into the community and are probationary you need to prove your value. If you are doing well, the community starts to exchange ideas about possibilities to integrate you. After two years I started being accepted by the community, which helped make everything go smoothly. I was thriving and publishing, not only research oriented work on the creative uses of technologies (Romero, Lille, & Patino, 2017), intergenerational game-based learning but also creating a children's book which was in the intersection of my research interests, societal and parental commitment. *Vibot the Robot* (Romero & Loufane, 2016), despite being a children's book, is one of which I am quite proud. It was hard to create and to edit because research and child-oriented publishing are so different. Children's books are much more difficult in the art of ensuring the reader understands the message through a minimum of information and illustrations. When Resnick, the creator of Scratch, complimented the metaphors within the book I was in heaven. It was not only children, teachers and parents who appreciated the book but also the research

Figure 3.1. *Minister of Education Proulx (middle) with* Vibot the robot, Dansereau (AQUOPS, left) and me (right).

community around Scratch were complimenting it. In Canada, the book has been printed in 3000 French units and 2000 English units.

While the educational community was increasingly accepting me, this acceptance was transforming the outlook of my colleagues. Some were happy to see that I was succeeding to integrate and develop research partnerships; others were considering my new opportunities as a challenge to the status quo of research in the department and started to behave in less-supportive ways. I got the feeling that whatever I did, challenges and tensions would arise. My success or failure appeared to activate tensions from one aspect or another because of the exigency to be even more subordinate to local colleagues while being competitive. It was an impossible equation to solve. I was recruited on my performance but I was asked to do less once I started my new job. I tried to solve this tension with love, acceptance, and a lot of invitations to be a grant co-researcher, a research paper co-author, or a book co-editor. I tried my best to be social—I cooked *paella* for my colleagues and tried to attend most of the social events. I spent hours drinking bad coffee and remaining at my desk with the door open for everyone to show up.

While some colleagues were not supportive, other colleagues in education technology (edtech) thrived as we worked together. I also enjoyed the many graduate students with whom I worked. My coffee machine was running constantly, filling many cups for colleagues and students whom I loved collaborating with. I felt like part of my department but also part of its internal historic problems. The department had once consisted of around 20 professors in edtech. In the last two decades our numbers were dwindling, and we were down to four colleagues. I was the only one under 60 years old and the only one who was not planning her retirement yet. The department was not supporting the educational technology field or programs and I had the feeling that I was recruited for the impossible task of trying to maintain the edtech field at a minimum. I tried to raise awareness about the mid term risks of not recruiting other colleagues. With the program director of the edtech program, we tried to convince our colleagues, the dean, and the larger university community of the importance of further developing the program through the recruitment of other colleagues. But we failed to ensure having any additional positions in the edtech field.

The mockery from some colleagues intensified when I considered not voting for the strategic recruitment plan; some intimidation followed. From a rational perspective, intimidation could be understood as a social mechanism for ensuring power and subordination in the workplace. I was not assertive enough and I was seeking acceptance from the very beginning of my new position. If I could go back in time, I would act more as a peer and less as the new young-sorry-to-start-pregnant colleague desperately-wanting to be part of the gang. I really wanted to be part of the early career colleagues I admired—as parents-researchers having time to run and party—but I would rather seek senior protection for navigating the department and not showing too much my desire to belong.

Looking back, I would be less intimidated had there been greater peer support (Salmivalli, Kärnä, & Poskiparta, 2011), from my senior colleagues. Being an outsider with no mentor, and wanting to join a new department, can be risky if you do not have a senior mentor to help navigate the jungle and its different species.

From Québec to Nice

After four years at Université Laval (Québec) I received a message from my thesis director informing me about a position to be opened in France. He wrote "The university is looking to create a new education-focused lab and wants to recruit a professor to run it." Wow! I was so happy to be informed about this position and decided to apply. But it sounded too good to be true, and the first exchanges with a leader at Nice informed about the significant challenge creating a new lab from scratch would be in a difficult context. Surviving difficulties, being part of my superpowers, made me confident that I can deal with the challenges of this position. But the definitive point for making the decision was the excitement of my family in Spain on the idea of being closer and my husband's thoughts about the idea of quitting the seven-month winter of Québec for the French Riviera. Thinking about my daughter, I was not sure moving to France would be the best move in terms of education, but familial love will probably compensate for the limits of south European traditional educational systems that are less learner-centred than the North-American ones. I prepared my application in a way that focused not only on teaching and research quality, but also on the way I was successfully adapting to different challenges within my career and how this perspective helped me to empathize with colleagues needing to be put back on track to be part of a team. I stressed my commitment to well-being and belonging when creating a new research team, and reuniting colleagues who were following separate paths within the last years. I acknowledged the challenge of being one of the younger members of the team and landing at a French university I did not know in terms of internal politics. I knew the job was not a piece of cake, but I knew I was ready for it. I went through the longest selection process I have ever gone through. While preparing for the position, I started writing the lab research program after studying my new colleagues' profiles. My husband, my family, and I really wanted this position. The pressure on my shoulders was at its maximum again. I got the feeling I was prepared, and when I got confirmed as the selected person for the position I was pinching my arm to make sure I was not dreaming it.

Running a lab is a significant challenge and a rare opportunity in academic life. The transition, I thought, would be easy, except that I was no longer allowed to direct my doctoral students at Université Laval if was moving to a new position . . . a shock for both them and me. In a context where there are some cases of intimidation, leaving them made me fear the worst. One of the reasons why I decided to keep 10 percent of my role during the first year of transition was to ensure I could be protective towards my students, but also so that I could fund them with the CoCreaTIC project to ensure they would finish the project properly. During this transition, finding a new director for my doctoral students became one of the top priorities. The transition has been smoother than expected and, since my move to France, I have returned three times a year to follow-up and finish my research engagements and supervise PhD candidates. Some colleagues and graduate students have been to Nice for short research stays (some for weeks, others up to three months) since I started my new position. These research stays have been really valuable not only for ensuring the quality of transition with the projects and supervisions I was finishing at Université Laval but also for capitalizing on this collaboration into new international projects. In June a student successfully defended his PhD dissertation. Two other students are finishing their doctorates, and they continue to advance correctly despite not having me at their shoulders every week. Moreover, our research lab, the Laboratoire d'Innovation et Numérique pour l'Education (LINE) is doing a partnership with Centre de Recherche et d'Intervention sur la RÉussite Scolaire (CRIRES) at Université Laval for a yearly joint workshop, which will begin next March.

From a family perspective, returning to Europe has been a blessing. We can meet our families more often than before and, as a daughter, I can be there to help my ageing parents when they need it. My husband is more than happy to live in Nice; he wanted to leave Québec and was desperate about moving even before having the opportunity to move to Nice. In retrospect, it would have been possible to proactively apply to different positions, but a combination of a busy workload and the appreciation of the child-oriented society in Québec prevented me from seeing this possibility clearly and made me hopeful that we would find our balances as a family in Québec.

Running a New Lab in the Field of Educational Sciences

Running a new lab is not easy where labs are created within a project-oriented culture such as in INRIA. But at the university level, starting a new lab with no resources is especially challenging and time consuming. From the human resources perspective, laying the foundation that will encourage the lab members to collaborate is something that takes time to ensure everyone is engaged in the process and not only a surface follower. It took me a lot of time to engage the colleagues in the discussion of the lab research program. I invested the first weeks in my new role meeting everyone and listening to them. Sometimes, it took the form of a group therapy, for healing past experiences in a prior lab (which had been closed by the university); in subsequent meetings, we could start entering the research arena. In other cases, the exchanges flowed from the first minutes. In a few cases, colleagues share the minimum, which is understandable considering their experiences. I tried to develop my research lab leadership with the values from my years at Université Laval (Romero et al., 2017): communication, helping each other, tolerance, pleasure, engagement in collaborative activities, freedom (from an epistemological, methodological, technological and all other perspectives) and diversity, among other values. Values and mission definition are not usual in south Europe, and some colleagues go through it as a loss of time because "work is work" and "we're not at work to be friends, just working." The tenure-track career in France brings early career focus on one's own research because only this aspect of contribution is evaluated to achieve the professorship level. Professorship positions are scarce and power networks within the stabilised disciplinary fields are at his maximum because each field (CNU) has the possibility, or not, to ensure the potential advancement in the career. Entering the power networks within our field will be a challenge for the next years.

As a leader, I wanted to ensure my colleagues understood they could rely on me. Once I developed a sense of trust, the main challenge was to co-create a shared project to unify the different areas of expertise and interests of the different lab members. At this point, the lab is three years old and has just succeeded in its first periodic evaluation. We have succeeded to lead a highly competitive project schema within the Agence Nationale de la Recherche (ANR) and be partners on two Erasmus+ projects. I'm proud of having succeeded in the emergence of this new lab and having reunited colleagues to collaborate on an exciting research agenda on the creative uses of technologies, including computational thinking, problem solving, and creativity. Survival skills developed during my early career have been foundational to develop the strengths and perseverance I have today when running a lab, but also to support and have empathy for colleagues who are going through difficult moments.

Priority Changes From Postdoc to Tenure and Research Direction

During my early years as a researcher, it was very important to ensure I could contribute individually to a team. To do this, I had to consider my strengths and, above all, to ensure I did my job well within the organization at its different levels: the research team to which I was attached, and the training programs on which I was working. To earn tenure, one had to receive good evaluations for both research criteria (contribution within a research team) and by the contribution and quality of teaching. My future was at the departmental level and it was important to follow the directions already defined by the research team as well as the training programs. It was also important to consider the strategic directions of the faculty, the university, and its research ecosystem at the national level. However, my ability to influence at this level was very limited: it was to identify trends and decisions that could have influences on my research team and on the training program. However, my integration success as a permanent teacher was not as important as in my prior positions. My future was in the hands of my most immediate peers making it necessary to play local. In a simple way, it was necessary to be a good soldier so that my colleagues collegially accept my progress and I could obtain permanence.

Despite the awareness of local issues, I was too independent in these early years before tenure. I had to pay for this independence and I am sure that if I had been a better soldier, more obedient and more aligned with the powers in progress, I would have had fewer difficulties during my journey. When I look back, I wonder how much it could have been easier to step after a senior colleague to get his or her protection until tenure, but I was not fully aware on the need to be on a follower way of thinking. By choosing to navigate the jungle without a senior mentor protection, my journey was more complicated, but also more exciting. In all the cases, the collegial process that allows you to move from the post-doc stage to tenure is extremely complex. To enter the academic gateway, both individual values and ability to develop research and teaching goals are important. At the same time, is important to ensure that colleagues in the research laboratory centre and training programs feel that they are contributing enough to the collective project. These processes lead us to a certain submission to the powers established within the research and training teams. At the same time, these formal and informal powers at different levels play with the decision-making powers over the permanence of new colleagues. In some cases, there is competition between different candidates aspiring for the same permanent position, which leads us to an over investment in the team-oriented contributions and alignment to existing powers.

Once tenure is obtained, we can afford to distance ourselves slightly, but we must be careful not to lose the key supports needed to develop our research activities. From my prior experiences I know how important is to be part of the social networks of influence and prevent these networks from attacking individuals as a possible threat for their resources or status quo. Investing in networking and colleagues takes time, but it is necessary. At the same time, research funding proposals are a key for the development of the lab. Similarly, we are a research lab and designing and developing appropriate research projects must be one of our priorities. How to achieve all these objectives in a harmonious work life balance? Well, I am still trying to find the best way and probably will continue that search until retirement.

References

Romero, M. (2017). Surviving and thriving in the first years of tenure-track: A journey through France, Spain, and Québec. In T. Sibbald & V. Handford, (Eds.), *The academic gateway: Understanding the journey to tenure* (pp. 145–158). Ottawa, ON: University of Ottawa Press.

Romero, M., Lille, B., & Patino, A. (Eds.). (2017). *Usages créatifs du numérique pour l'apprentissage au XXIe siècle* (Vol. 1). Québec, QC: Presses de l'Université du Québec.

Romero, M., & Loufane. (2016). *Vibot the robot*. Québec, QC: Publications du Québec.

Salmivalli, C., Kärnä, A., & Poskiparta, E. (2011). Counteracting bullying in Finland: The KiVa program and its effects on different forms of being bullied. *International Journal of Behavioral Development, 35*(5), 405–411.

Zimbardo, P. G., & Boyd, J. N. (1999). Putting time in perspective: A valid, reliable individual-differences metric. *Journal of Personality and Social Psychology, 77*(6), 1271.

CHAPTER 4

Transitioning to the Academic Tenure-Track at Mid-Career: Exploring Adaptive Responses Through the Lenses of Resilience, Grieving, and Institutional Logics

Peter Milley

From outside the academy, the job of a fulltime professor looks rewarding and privileged; and it is.[1] Since transitioning to a tenure-track position as assistant professor in 2013 from a career in the federal public service, I have come to appreciate the university provides for self-direction on research and knowledge production as well as a community of interesting, committed people. However, this positive impression emerged very slowly through a challenging career transition (see Milley, 2016). It is an impression similar to the majority of fulltime professors in Canada who report having considerable decision-making influence over their research activities and collaborations (Metcalfe et al., 2011).[2] Professors tend to report being satisfied with their jobs, especially after obtaining the position of full professor, which can take a decade or two (Weinrib et al., 2013). Only a small fraction of one percent of the population in Canada become fulltime professors implying it is a position of privilege.

One such simile of academic privilege was offered during a symposium in 2016 on the challenges and opportunities of being novice professors. At the event, an experienced professor in the audience asserted that academic work is like having a sweet tooth and being able to stuff full one's mouth with chocolate cake every day. By cake, he seemed to be referencing the "brain candy" available in a professor's job: new knowledge, fascinating projects, engaged students, and interesting people. At the time, however, an alternative metaphor sprang to mind: that of being force-fed chocolate cake, along with the unpleasant images of this. I was not quite three years into a professor's job and still felt overwhelmed with the sheer number and variety of tasks, long hours, competitive culture, and constant evaluation by administrators, peers and students. Similar to tenure-track professors in other universities (Brown & Sherry, 2010; Hill, 2004; Hirschkorn, 2010), the job and my overall response to it frequently left me feeling unwell, mentally and physically. But the tenure clock was ticking. I only had another two years to prove to my peers, administrators and myself that I had what it took to be accepted as a 'real' professor by making tenure, a sentiment other novice academics also experience (Aitken, 2010; Archer, 2008; Gleich, 2016).

Looking back at the chocolate cake incident, with the benefit of two additional years and a formal application for tenure behind me, I see that I had been chasing an "illusive sense of a secure self through 'careering'; a frantic and frenetic individualistic strategy designed to moderate the pressures of excessive managerial competitive demands" in contemporary universities (Clarke & Knights, 2015, p. 1865). My persistent, instrumental focus on establishing a long-term career in academia led me to behave in the ways colleagues, peers, administrators, and, more vaguely, the organization seemed to expect. I had been striving to deliver the results they seemed to want, but to some extent had lost touch with the intrinsic value of finding meaning in the work.

My choice of the word "seemed" is deliberate. The signals and messages I received about expectations tended to be anecdotal, multifaceted, and inconsistent. The language in the collective agreement was also not particularly helpful in this regard, given its necessarily broad reference to achieving a "good" record of research, teaching that "meets expectations," and "satisfactory" provision of service (Association of Professors of the University of Ottawa, 2019a). With hindsight, I have come to think of these messages and signals about performance expectations as noise that I could have blocked out if I'd had more self-confidence at that stage. Doing so would have allowed me to establish realistic goals, clearer priorities, a feasible and healthy way of working, and the conviction to say "no" when encouraged to have another piece of cake. However, my ever-expanding agenda that was partly of my own making and partly fed to me, ended up draining the optimism and joy I had felt when I started the job (Milley, 2016). Similar to other novice professors (e.g., Hellsten, Martin, McIntyre & Kinzel, 2011), my idealistic sentiments about academia had vanished.

Over the last five years of being on the tenure-track, I have learned the job of a fulltime professor does not necessarily reflect public perception. Nor does it reflect the idealized image I had as a graduate student in the early 2000s, an image reflected in what Berg and Seeber (2016) recently resurrected in their book *The Slow Professor: Challenging the Culture of Speed in the Academy*. That ideal remained in my mind as I pursued a career outside of academia; while significant changes in universities took place that intensified workloads and performance accountabilities (Fredman & Doughney, 2012; Gopaul et al., 2016; Hartman & Darab, 2012; Weinrib et al., 2013). In fact, the role is multi-faceted, competitive, and involves its fair share of managerial "administrivia," the latter increasing over recent years as administrative support staff have been replaced with online systems that offload tasks to end-users, including professors (Newport, 2019). Recent survey results based on a large sample of Canadian professors revealed they worked an average of 50 hours per week. In this same study, 45 percent of professors reported a deterioration in working conditions over the course of their careers, 42 percent reported their jobs producing considerable strain (Weinrib et al., 2013), and 75 percent reported the pressure to raise external research funding had increased since their first appointment (Gopaul et al., 2016). Other observers have found that early-career professors and professors at research-intensive universities work more than the average, which resonates with my experience. For example, until my fifth year, I worked most evenings and weekends, booked the majority of my annual leave days so that I could "legitimately" put an out-of-office response on my email and send my regrets for official committee meetings and other obligations while I tried to make progress on research projects or course preparation.[3] By now, I have found some healthier strategies for managing the workload, many of which other assistant professors in similar circumstances kindly shared. I am also grateful for the mentoring and coaching resources my university made available.

In retrospect, I can see that adjusting to the pragmatic realities of the job involved a search for adaptive strategies to remain healthy, something I noted early in my journey (Milley, 2016). The career transition also involved a process of grieving, something I did not explicitly recognize until I read Handford's (2016) account of her career transition to a professor's job. She observed "change involves grieving what was lost, which transitions into anger about what is lost . . . embracing the new . . . and, finally, incorporating what was lost and what is new as a lived experience, transforming oneself into a new whole" (p. 203). This description resonated: having felt a sense of loss, I had tried to suppress or ignore the emotions associated with it for fear of becoming alienated or being perceived as a bit histrionic.

Looking back, I can now see the grieving process in my case was associated with two distinct senses of loss. The first pertained to the career transition, such as losing a community of colleagues, a sense of efficacy and competence, and job security. This was short-lived, as I will describe below. The second pertained to the loss of an idealized vision of the nature of a professor's work and the role of universities. This latter sense of loss took longer to process. Although I knew little about what a professor's job entailed, I had studied the role of universities as part of my doctoral research. In that work, I drew on ideas about the university from Jürgen Habermas' critical social theory perspective (Habermas & Blazek, 1987), which presented them as a place for deep conversations and meaningful debates, critical reflection, and contributions to society. I thought that the work of professors, especially in a Faculty of Education, would focus primarily on these substantive objectives. What I discovered is that the work can accommodate these purposes, but it is also full of instrumental concerns and tasks that can overwhelm and displace a focus on substance (Newport, 2019).

Research Goals and Methodology

I wrote this chapter a few months after making an official request for tenure and at five-and-a-half years on the tenure-track. It updates a personal narrative I produced at 18-months into my challenging mid-career transition from a job outside of academia to an assistant professorship in educational administration (Milley, 2016). That previous narrative drew on concepts about resilience (Holling, 2001; Holling & Gunderson, 2002; Masten & O'Dougherty Wright, 2010) to assess my responses to a period of significant change in terms of whether they supported or hindered a healthy, functional career transition. At that time, I described an uneven adaptation to the three main roles of a professor's job, including a successful transition to the teaching role, a difficult adjustment to the research role, and a promising foray into the service role. Drawing on Holling (2001) and Patton (2011), I identified four "maladaptive traps" that could lead to negative outcomes and outlined potential strategies for avoiding them. I also assessed the status of my protective systems of resilience (Masten, 2001) and outlined strategies for strengthening them by focusing on supportive relationships, improving aspects of my self-regulation, and finding positive meaning in the work. I concluded that in terms of resilience my overall transition was following a "recovery pattern" (Masten & O'Dougherty Wright, 2010, p. 221) consisting of an initial decline in adaptive functioning followed by an upward trajectory towards a positive level.

The process of writing that chapter left me feeling cautiously optimistic for a healthy transition if I followed through on the strategies I identified to avoid some of the traps. However, my caution at that time was warranted. As the opening section of the current chapter suggests, my subsequent journey continued to be quite challenging professionally and in terms of well-being, even as it continued to pursue a recovery pattern. The challenges endured for so long that I decided to build this chapter directly from my previous one in terms of theory and methods and to continue the personal narrative it offered. The idea was that this would allow for an internally coherent longitudinal perspective.

In what follows, I have extended the theoretical perspective of my previous chapter to incorporate a stage theory of grieving (Jacobs, 1993; Maciejewski, Zhang, Block, & Prigerson, 2007). I link these stages (i.e., disbelief, yearning, anger, depression, acceptance) to specific phases in Holling's adaptive cycle model (i.e., release, reorganization, exploitation, conservation) to illuminate how the career transition involved both adaptive learning and grieving. I also draw on research about grieving (Boerner & Jopp, 2010) to highlight the individual and collective factors that support adults in coping with loss.

Similar to my earlier chapter, this one also works in the spirit of autoethnography to communicate personal experience as a means of deepening understanding (Ellis & Bochner, 2000) of the process of becoming a 'full-fledged' academic by earning tenure. I narrate my personal experience while viewing it through a theoretical lens and triangulating it with findings from other relevant studies. Data sources consist of professional artefacts (e.g., curriculum vitae, planning documents, instructional and assessment materials, research proposals, manuscripts) and records from a self-interview conducted in the fall of 2018, two months after submitting my official application for tenure and promotion. This interview was based on four questions: What have you been doing and experiencing in the transition, especially with respect to tenure? What are your successes and challenges and how are these related to your sense of wellbeing? What responses seem to alleviate or exacerbate problems? What strategies have you implemented since your previous reflections at 18 months into the tenure-track, and how have these served you professionally and in terms of well-being?

Resilience Theory: On Functional Adaptation Through Adversity and Grief

I use two specific research-based models of resilience to explore my adaptations along the tenure-track. The adaptive cycle from Holling's (2001) and Holling and Gunderson's (2002) ecological theory and Masten's (2001) concept of protective systems of resilience from developmental psychology. These models are complementary, with the former emphasizing how resilience is affected by cycles of change precipitated by "disturbances" and the latter focusing on the psychological and social factors that promote resilience. Both models also account for what happens when there is a lack of resilience. In the case of ecology, the focus is on whether one's responses are maladaptive (Holling & Gunderson, 2002); while, in the case of psychology, a lack of resilience is associated with a decline in adaptive functioning (Masten & Obradovic, 2008). Both of these models were introduced in my previous chapter (Milley, 2016). I only briefly discuss them here while adding a theoretical layer by describing stages of grieving and factors for weathering loss.

The Adaptive Cycle: Phases of Adaptation and Maladaptive Traps

The adaptive cycle provides a heuristic model for analyzing adaptive dynamics associated with change (Patton, 2011). The phases include: (1) growth and exploitation, (2) conservation, (3) release, and (4) reorganization. The transition from (1) to (2) consists of a relatively slow, incremental process of growth and accumulation of capital (e.g., the consolidation of expert knowledge and skills, and social and reputational capital). The transition from (2) to (4) usually begins with a disturbance (e.g., a career change, a professional setback such as

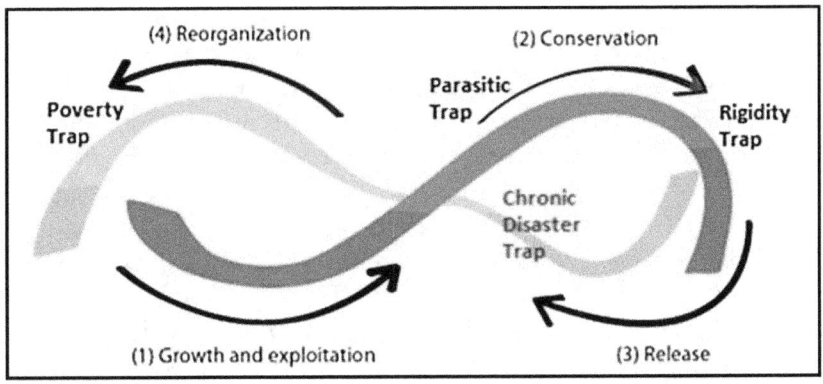

Figure 4.1. *The adaptive cycle. Phases and the maladaptive traps.*

a loss of research funding, or a budget crisis in an organization), creating the need for rapid response and change. If someone lacks anticipative capacities (e.g., foresight, access to information, planning) or adaptive capacities (e.g., agility, support networks), the transition from (2) to (4) may cause someone to experience a regime shift (e.g., a decline in health status), the outcome of which is unpredictable.

Four traps can make any journey through a cycle of change maladaptive: first, rigidity traps can develop in Phase 2 if too much emphasis is placed on control and stability (i.e., doing the same old things), smothering inventiveness and initiative (Holling, 2001); second, chronic disasters can arise during Phase 3 if too much emphasis is placed on short-term crisis management without a sense of overall direction (Patton, 2011); third, poverty traps can appear during Phase 4 if a lack of diversity (e.g., in ideas, skills and networks) diminishes options to support renewal (Denhardt & Denhardt, 2010; Holling, 2001); and, fourth, parasitic traps can emerge during Phase 2 that eat away at the capital accumulated through a cycle of renewal and reduces the capacity to deal with other pressures for change (Patton, 2011). Figure 4.1 illustrates the cycle, phases and traps.

Multiple adaptive cycles coexist in different aspects of one's experience (e.g., adapting to research, teaching, and service roles). These cycles operate at small scales (e.g. teaching a new course) and large scales (e.g., transitioning to a new career in academia). The journey through each cycle takes place at a different rate (e.g., quickly adapting to teaching a new course, more slowly adapting to academic culture). Each cycle is interlinked, with cycles at smaller scales providing inputs (e.g., innovations, lessons learned) to support change at larger scales. Cycles at larger scales tend to move more slowly, but problems arising at larger scales can create cascading effects that disrupt adaptive functioning at smaller scales (Holling, 2001).

Protective Systems for Resilience to Adversity
From the perspective of developmental psychology, Masten and O'Dougherty Wright (2010, pp. 225–228) have identified some protective systems that encompass individual capabilities, social supports, and safeguards of resilience rooted in communities and cultural systems. These include

- close relationships that provide for emotional security, learning, and positive socialization;
- access to knowledge about what is happening, what to expect, and what to do and the capacity for reflection, planning and action with longer-term objectives in mind;
- motivational systems that promote agency and mastery and through which people develop a sense of competence and self-efficacy;
- self-regulation skills that allow for the control over attention, impulses, emotion, stress reactivity, behaviour, and active engagement in the definition and pursuit of goals; and
- meaning making processes that allow for faith, hope, and optimism and the realistic appraisal of events, experiences and future possibilities.

An individual's resilience can be promoted by restoring, or mobilizing, these protective systems (Masten, 2001).

Stages of Grieving Losses
The idea that people's response to loss entails a hypothesized progression through a series of stages has been widely accepted by lay people and clinicians as a model for reflecting on grieving as a process (Maciejewski et al., 2007). Numerous models have been put forward over the years.[4] I draw on Maciejewski et al. (2007) empirically examined model that adjustment to loss progresses through the following stages, which are presented sequentially while recognizing that they may be overlapping and that the process and timing

related to them is not the same for everyone: disbelief, yearning, anger, depression and acceptance.

I use the model heuristically to prompt reflection on the sense of loss and slow progress towards acceptance that I experienced in the career transition and journey towards tenure, but recognize there are important limitations of using the model for this purpose. In particular, the model was developed and studied in the context of bereavement associated with death, a more profound experience of loss than career transition. In addition, there is scientific debate about the validity of stage theories as an accurate explanation of grieving.[5] While the technical application of a grief model may not be a perfect fit for understanding grief-like responses to significant life changes not involving bereavement or traumatic loss, the generalized idea may be useful for reflections that help move forward through such changes.

Resilience Factors for Weathering Experiences of Loss

Following Boerner and Jopp (2010, pp. 133–138), there are intrapersonal and interpersonal factors that support resilience in the face of loss. Coping and emotional regulation are also implicated. At the interpersonal level, individuals who are physically and mentally healthy before the experience of loss tend to be more resilient. In addition, if one tends to form secure attachments with other people this can also support resilience. The personality traits of extroversion, optimism, self-enhancement, and low neuroticism also appear to play a role in resilience during the experience of loss. At the interpersonal level, social support from family, friends and colleagues is particularly significant in the face of loss, and lack of such support is linked to less resilient trajectories. In terms of coping with loss, patterns arising while processing grief are significant. In particular, continual thinking and talking about the loss and not confronting the new reality is associated with less resilient trajectories. Finally, in terms of emotional regulation, higher emotional flexibility (the ability to suppress or enhance emotional expression) is associated with better resilience. An important part of regulation is to not let negative emotions take over to the extent that experiencing positive moments become impossible. Resilient people can have both negative and positive affect as they cope with loss. This also means they may be more enjoyable as social partners, which helps sustain their social support networks.

(Counter)balancing Institutional Logics

I have also framed this account with inputs from neo-institutional theory (Friedland & Alford, 1991; Thornton, Ocasio & Lounsbury, 2012). In particular, I draw on the notion that a variety of institutional logics, each comprised of distinctive assumptions, values, norms, beliefs and rules (Thornton & Ocasio, 1999, p. 804), compete for our attention in contemporary academic settings, complicating how we make sense of our experience, make decisions, and take action. Four such logics that seem to be prominent in contemporary education are

- Professional—aimed at increasing individual educator's sense of responsibility as well as collective expectations among groups of educators by conferring authority for decision-making and the use of professional judgment onto them and having them share in addressing and maintaining professional standards.
- Bureaucratic—aimed at increasing the control over and scrutiny of educator's work by establishing systems, procedures, rules, and regulations and ensuring compliance with them is monitored and assessed.
- Market—aimed at increasing the performance and reputations of individual educators and the organizational units by enhancing competition among them, increasing the pressure exerted by "clients," promoting entrepreneurial attitudes and skills, using performance measurement and management techniques.
- Communal—aimed at building a sense of reciprocity, connection, and belonging among organizational members and the broader community that increases mutual aid, support, and social cohesion (Bridwell-Mitchell & Sherer, 2017; Dulude & Milley, 2018).

These logics provide organizing principles, the "raw materials and guidelines" by which we "produce, reproduce and provide meaning to [our] social reality" (Hallett & Ventresca, 2006, p. 213) in and beyond universities. They provide frames of reference that condition the vocabulary we use to motivate action and to express our sense of self and identity (Thornton, Ocasio & Lounsbury, 2012, p. 2). We continually seek to find an appropriate balance among these competing logics as we elaborate upon them through our thinking and action, even as they guide and structure that thinking and action. One or more logics may be dominant organizationally, but as individuals we may attempt to contest them or to counterbalance them with other logics (Haveman & Gualtieri, 2017).

In what follows, I use this neo-institutional perspective to foreground how the pronounced bureaucratic and market-oriented features of contemporary universities triggered the sense of loss I experienced during my adaptation because I had anticipated, somewhat naively or idealistically, a career that was predominantly anchored in professional and communal values.

Personal Narrative: Context

My previous chapter on this topic (Milley, 2016) describes my stance towards a personal narrative on this topic, the institutional context for that narrative, and my gratitude to my university, administrators, colleagues, mentors, collaborators, and students for their support. I will not repeat that material because it provides a largely accurate portrait to this point in time, apart from two significant developments in the institutional context that have arisen since the previous chapter. I highlight those developments here.

First, in 2015, the Government of Ontario altered the format and funding of teacher education programs, doubling the number of semesters for coursework while reducing the per capita funding to universities offering the programs (Ontario College of Teachers, 2015; Ontario Ministry of Education, 2013). For many faculties of education in the province, including mine, the change in program format negatively affected enrolment as potential candidates adjusted their plans and expectations in light of the longer period of training required to become a teacher. The reduced provincial funding meant that most faculties delivering the programs needed to look for cost efficiencies over the long term. In my case, this resulted in a 50 percent increase in the class sizes to reduce the number of sections of the courses I teach in the Bachelor of Education program.

Additionally, funding per enrolled student in graduate programs is higher than for undergraduate programs (Ontario Ministry of Training, Colleges and Universities, 2015; Ontario Confederation of University Faculty Associations, 2015). Given this, faculties of education could seek to make up revenue shortfalls in their undergraduate programs by expanding enrolment in their graduate programs while exercising similar cost-saving measures by increasing average class sizes, among other strategies. This logic emerged in my faculty, where a push was made to migrate more courses online to attract students from outside the region while training and allocating more teaching assistants to support professors with online and/or larger classes. These organizational responses require faculty to teach larger groups, whether in-class or online.[6] In my case, having access to resources offered through the university's Teaching and Learning Support Services was helpful. My impression was the changes stimulated a degree of internal competition among professors. This is because the changes brought forward the need for us to think about managing our appeal, or brands (Jillapalli & Jillapalli, 2014), so that our courses would fill up to the minimum level to avoid cancellation or to the threshold at which we might receive the much welcomed support of a teaching assistant to support delivery. This sense of competition was not entirely new as one already needed to manage one's reputation because the university makes a centralized inventory of official evaluation results of professors' past teaching and courses available to students. My experience in this context led to feeling significant upward pressure related to my teaching workload. This increased workload was distressing because for the majority of my time on tenure-track, my teaching workload had already been hovering just below the level at which, according to a study conducted by the Ontario Council of Vice Presidents (2014), professors in Ontario universities have difficulty producing even a single research publication.[7]

Second, starting in my third year on tenure-track, my university embarked on an ambitious agenda of improving many administrative services by using online applications and commercial software (Association of Professors of the University of Ottawa, 2018, 2019b). While support manuals for using these online services were available in a centralized Internet portal, I experienced an increased responsibility for learning the rules, procedures, and steps to follow, and for doing the required data entry. Sometimes this added work felt infuriating especially when more pressing and core tasks needed attention. More recently, the Government of Ontario made changes to tuition fee policies that are forecast to reduce the university's revenues by approximately 3 percent (Association of Professors of the University of Ottawa, 2019c). As a result, the dynamics of workload impacts of fiscal management will continue.

Personal Narrative

In light of the first three sections of this chapter, I turn now to my narrative, which describes the personal strategies I used to adapt to the three main roles of an academic career (i.e., research, teaching, service) and assesses the strengths and weaknesses of these in supporting a functional career transition and journey along the tenure-track. This narrative also describes how two grieving processes transpired during my adaptation, and how one of these processes was triggered by an unanticipated preponderance of bureaucratic and market logics shaped a job that I thought would be predominantly guided by professional and communal logics.

Adaptive Responses, Maladaptive Traps, and Grieving Processes
In this section, I use the adaptive cycle model to analyze my progress with respect to the three main roles of a professor's job (teaching, research and service), taking into account maladaptive traps and grieving processes discussed in the theoretical section above. From the outset of my journey to tenure in 2013, my plan had been to engage in all three roles, but to emphasize teaching in year one, to ramp up research in year two, and to deepen service commitments in year three.[8] Implicitly, I thought this would get me to some kind of healthy balance by year four or five, after which it would need to consolidate what I had accomplish into the dossier that would constitute my application for tenure. As part of this process, I thought it was prudent to bear in mind the convention that teaching and research should each account for 40 percent of one's workload, with service constituting the other 20 percent.

Adaptation to the Teaching Role
By 18 months on the tenure-track, my transition to the role of teaching courses had gone relatively smoothly because it used curriculum design and delivery skills from my previous career (Milley, 2016). The transition has continued to be smooth since that time. The adaptation to this role was accelerated by the fact that each semester of teaching constituted a cycle of learning and feedback that was shorter than, for example, those related to most of my research projects. The externally imposed structure of the teaching role also forced me to learn quickly, in contrast to my adaptation to the research role, which hinged largely on my own decisions and intrinsic motivation, apart

from the prompts of an annual performance review and two contract renewal processes.

The two main challenges I experienced in the period after that first 18 months in the job included

1. the growth in class sizes which has led to a heavier workload and a search for effective teaching strategies for larger groups of students and efficient methods for assessing and evaluating their learning;
2. taking on the official supervision role of graduate students at the Masters and Doctoral levels which added a new dimension to the workload and entailed a steeper learning curve than expected.

I addressed the class-size challenge by using the university's online learning platform, even for classroom-based courses, to host weekly content modules and all the other important course elements (e.g., syllabus, course readings, assignment descriptions, assessment rubrics, exemplars, info on conducting literature searches using library databases, announcements). This strategy seemed to improve communication with students and allowed them increased autonomy. I also became more assertive in advocating that teaching assistants be assigned to my courses, and was grateful for the ensuing support from the administration. To my surprise, however, it took almost two years to find an effective way of working with these assistants. They were assigned after courses started and could not help with preparation tasks; and, in most cases for graduate courses, they did not have knowledge of the specific subject area being taught, so having them support delivery was also frequently a conundrum. To deal with the lack of subject area knowledge, I took to designing most of my graduate courses around generic learning outcomes such as analytical skills and the expression of ideas. This allowed most teaching assistants to support the assessment and evaluation of student work, especially when combined with criterion-referenced assessment tools, exemplars of past work and feedback, and inter-rater exercises whereby we compare, discuss, and reconcile our individual assessments on the same sample of student work to enhance reliability.

With respect to the challenges of supervising the programs and thesis research of graduate students, I remain on a significant learning curve because of the long timeline for each adaptive cycle (i.e., a minimum of two years for Master's students and four years for doctoral candidates). In 2015, I began supervising two Master's students and two doctoral students, and in subsequent years I took on four more Master's students. Looking back, my plan for supervision was too ambitious. It produced an unforeseen added workload in terms of the reciprocal relationships that take place between professors in terms of serving on thesis committees. I needed a dozen colleagues on the committees of my students and, because reciprocity lies at the heart of collegiality, I quickly found myself serving on more than a dozen of my colleagues' students committees. This rewarding work helped teach me about supervision by watching how more experienced colleagues went about it, but the distraction of too many disparate graduate student projects made me feel like I was in a chronic disaster trap. In retrospect, I should have sequenced my supervisory obligations in a more step-wise fashion. I have since adjusted my approach by carefully vetting the interests and backgrounds of potential candidates to ensure the compatibility of our research interests and working styles and, now, take on no more than one new supervision per year.

Phases of Adaptation and Grieving in the Teaching Role
I consider myself to be in a conservation phase in my adaptation to the teaching role, and at the acceptance phase in a grieving process. The latter came on early and lasted until fairly recently. It was associated with the loss of an idealized vision of what it meant to be an educator in the university context. The unexpected dominance of market-oriented logics, instead of the professional logic I anticipated, precipitated that sense of loss. For example, the profit seeking strategy of increasing graduate program enrolments while keeping costs down through increased class sizes conflicted with my sense of professionalism of maintaining academic standards. The increased class size led to a more pronounced bureaucratic logic than anticipated, when I found myself designing and delivering my courses with a strong managerial mindset emphasizing efficiency, predictability, standardization, and control. In another example, the market-oriented logic of making teaching evaluations available confronted my professional understanding of assessment and evaluation as supporting professional learning. This particular practice also conflicted with the communal logic because it increased competitive pressure while reducing reciprocity and cohesion.

I yearned for a sense of authentic connection with the students, a communal logic that was undermined by the fiscal emphasis of the teaching and learning environments. At times, I would attend my prescribed office hours awaiting potential visits or calls from students, but few ever came, which was depressing—until I realized it gave me time to work on research. Then they would write emails at all hours or at the last minute before assignments were due, and I would find myself getting angry (at what seemed to be unrealistic demands) all over again. Of course the situation was not their fault; everyone seems to have busy lives now. I have gained a more realistic handle on how to find an appropriate balance of logics in the teaching role. In particular, I look for professional meaning in the work of the students rather than seeking it in face-to-face conversations. When I do have the chance to meet with them in traditional classrooms, I try to use group facilitation techniques to build some degree of community and reciprocity among them and with me. I suspect my acceptance of this state of affairs will lead me on a new adaptive cycle in teaching because I will need to continue finding ways to express my identity and ideals as an educator in this context of competing logics.

Adaptation to the Research Role
At 18 months into this role, my adaptation was proving to be difficult. I was finding the research methods and skills used in my career in the federal public service did not mesh with academic research standards and culture. The 10-year gap between my PhD completion and debut on the tenure-track also created certain barriers (Milley, 2016). At that time, I determined I was in an early phase of reorganization in a cycle of adaptation. I articulated six strategies to make short-term gains in building a track record of academic research productivity while building towards a longer term, sustainable research agenda. I was worried about falling into two maladaptive traps: the first being the threat of chronic disaster associated with having too many disparate projects to manage; the second being a poverty trap in terms of lacking the time and resources to "exploit" projects by turning them into scholarly publications—in other words, the trap of not publishing and thus perishing. Looking back, the interpretation helped propel me through the career transition and yielded the desired results; however, I only made it through these traps along the way through the brute force of overworking. This pattern of

behaviour tended to have a negative affect on my wellbeing. It also resulted in bouts of anger, sadness, and cynicism.

Despite getting publication results, the use of multiple strategies did not help me progress to the point of becoming a scholar with a long-term program of research working in an identifiable field of knowledge with a related community of academics. I have defined and committed myself to two main streams of research (administrative ethics; social innovation in education), and am through an initial exploitation phase on one in terms of publishing results (Milley, 2017; Samier & Milley, 2018). The challenge ahead is to remain confident about this research agenda, while remaining open to opportunities for other interesting projects but without falling into the traps I encountered over the last five years.

Phases of Adaptation and Grieving in the Research Role
I see myself at the tail end of a reorganization phase in my adaptation to the research role. In terms of the grieving process with respect to this role, it largely stemmed from the sense of loss with respect to self-efficacy, competence, and recognition of peers during the transition from being one kind of researcher in the federal public service to being a much different kind of researcher in the university (Milley, 2016). This grieving process came early. It started with shock and disbelief that I had to let go of my professional identity and skills; it was followed by a yearning to return to my previous employer and career, then by frustration and anger that while I could not go back, nor could I find a way forward; then to depression about the whole situation. This cycle dissipated with the publication of two or three peer-reviewed publications, which confirmed that I could begin letting go of the past.

To a more limited degree, there was some grieving associated with the loss of an idealized vision of what it meant to be an academic researcher. Of particular note was the significant emphasis on research productivity, which seemed even stronger than the directive to "publish or perish." The logic behind this push was perplexing: on one hand, it signaled some professional beliefs and values that research publication is a core part of a professor's responsibility to their organizations, research communities, and even the broader community and society. On the other hand, the focus on both volume and quality, frequently communicated with indicators such as number and type of publication, quality of publication venues (e.g., impact factor journals), dollar values and sources of external research funding, resonates within a market logic that aims to increase the performance and reputations of individual researchers by enhancing competition among them. On the other hand (again!), the use of information from these productivity indicators in organizational systems and processes to monitor professors' work and ensure compliance with regulations and standards articulated in policies, resonates within a bureaucratic logic. I had anticipated a preponderance of a professional logic when it came to the research role, and that research quality would be the main goal, and quality would be assessed by one's peers as part of the collegial process of maintaining professional standards. Certainly that logic exists. However, it sits in tension with the market and bureaucratic logics that also structure and shape what constitutes an effective academic researcher, which is the standard for earning tenure at my university.

I went through a period of shock and disbelief upon my arrival in the university when I was confronted with the palpable sense of pressure to get results on the research front quickly and frequently. I was also surprised at the degree of image and reputational management work that I perceived was necessary as an academic, especially in a social media age. A market logic made these aspects of the work come to the fore. Most of all, I was destabilized by the amount of organizational evaluation and review conducted on one's research record—for example, I had at least twelve official reviews in five years[9], not because anything seemed wrong with my work, but because that is the official way the organization functions, following a bureaucratic logic. I would like to say that I have come to accept the mix of logics structuring and shaping the research role, and that I have adjusted my vision of what it means to be an academic researcher; but that would be premature. Perhaps because I am still struggling to feel competent as an academic researcher, I find that I occasionally become frustrated about the contradiction between the long time it usually takes to produce and publish quality research and the apparent need for speedy results. Other times, I get somewhat depressed, even cynical. I suspect these are normal feelings under the circumstances and may not be part of an ongoing grieving process.

Adaptation to the Service Role
At 18 months into tenure-track, I had sensibly stuck to my plan of moving slowing into the service role given that teaching and, especially, research were the most important personal and organizational

priorities (Milley, 2016). However, near the end of my second year I failed to uphold boundaries when administrators or colleagues would approach me with requests for service. I soon found myself caught up in numerous regular service activities. Examples include being a member of the labour-intensive university's Research Ethics Board and the Faculty Equity Committee, serving as the designated leader of a group of professors teaching core curriculum in the teacher education program, acting as the Faculty's liaison to the undergraduate students' association, regularly chairing oral hearings for thesis defenses, conducting evaluation projects for community organizations, and peer reviewing publications. These commitments were all interesting and rewarding, but their volume and variety proved overwhelming at times, especially during teaching semesters or when research deadlines loomed. I found it difficult to say no to requests, in part, because I felt the work would be interesting and, in part, because the university community benefits from each professor's commitment to service—so it was both my moral and organizational duty to commit.

Phases of Adaptation and Grieving in the Service Role
Although I have made it through numerous adaptive cycles on specific service obligations and taken a break from most such obligations over the past year, I see myself in a reorganization phase of an overall adaptive cycle in this role. In terms of a grieving process, it was much more minor than with respect to the other two roles, and I went through it quickly. This minor sense of loss is related to an idealized vision of the work that is based predominantly in professional and communal logics—in other words, service is part of our individual responsibility as professors, and it aims to build a sense of reciprocity in university and academic communities that increases mutual aid, support, and social cohesion—that can be thwarted when some of those serving do so only to comply with the convention or rule that they must serve (a bureaucratic logic). This latter kind of logic was not shocking. It is something I also witnessed in my previous career in the public service, and I have been guilty of indulging in it myself. But in a putatively collegial organization, I thought this behaviour and the logic behind it was going to be less evident. What it means for organizations, however, is that certain individuals tend to bear a much heavier service load than do others.

Overall Adaptation to the Roles of a Professor

Figure 4.2 illustrates the relationships between the adaptive cycles related to my teaching, research, and service roles and the overall cycle of my adaptation to the tenure-track. The dynamics with respect to my career transition indicate I have reached a stable point with respect to teaching and am consolidating with respect to research, while sitting in a bit of a holding pattern with respect to service and trying to figure out which service obligations to (re)commit to. This scenario implies a successful career transition, but it also indicates that career development will involve a "release and reorganization" phase in teaching, an "exploitation and conservation" phase in my research programs, and the need to select service commitments that provide substantive personal and organizational value. Beyond my gratitude to colleagues, administrators and students for making this transition rewarding, I want to acknowledge the numerous organizational supports offered at the university, such as early-stage research funding, coaching and mentoring, teaching technology support, and membership in the Centre for Research on Educational and Community Services.

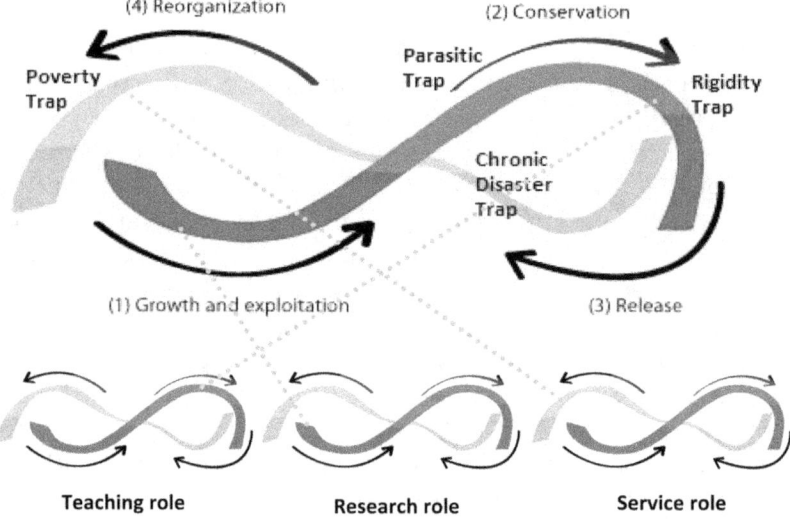

Figure 4.2. *The adaptive cycle. My current state of overall adaptation to the job of a professor.*

Overall State of Grieving Processes

Figure 4.3 illuminates how, according to my theorizing, one moves through the phases of an adaptive cycle while also moving through phases of grieving. The figure also indicates that, at 18 months, I was at the acceptance phase of a grieving process related to my career transition. It also indicates that, at that same time, I was still at a yearning phase with respect to the grieving process related to the loss of my idealized vision of what it means to be a professor and what the nature of a university is, at least in its current incarnation. At the time of writing my previous chapter (Milley, 2016) I was yearning to return to my previous career, even though it was no longer an option. As my analysis here suggests, I reached the acceptance stage of grieving the loss of this vision between my fourth to fifth years on tenure-track, after going through bouts of anger, frustration, depression and cynicism.

If the foregoing analysis about my processing of a sense of loss of an idealize vision is correct, the question that arises as to why it took a fairly long time to cope with it. Following Boerner and Jopp's (2010, pp. 133–138) work on resilience factors for weathering

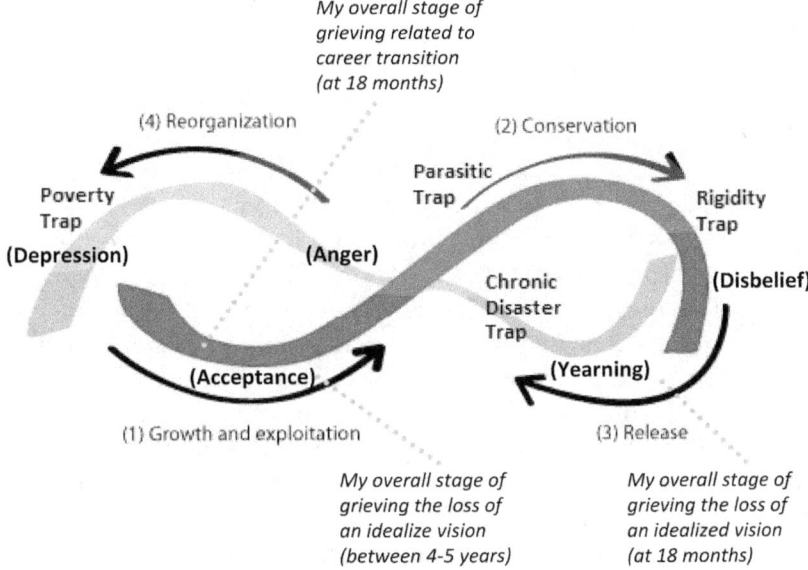

Figure 4.3. *The adaptive cycle. Moving through phases of adaptation while grieving.*

experiences of loss (see the theory section above), a few possible areas to explore further present themselves. First, of the four personality traits that appear to be associated with resilience to loss, I suspect I only exhibit one (low neuroticism) and not the other three (extroversion, optimism, self-enhancement). Second, in terms of a grief process, I tended quite regularly to seek out people with whom to talk about the loss—often others in similar circumstances such as other novice professors—to avoid patterns but not to confront the new reality. I suspect this kept reinforcing the yearning, frustration, and anger. Third, at the interpersonal level, I have been lucky to have, and am grateful for, ongoing social support from family, friends, and colleagues, even if through overworking and conscious avoidance I frequently truncated social contact with them such that they would only see me when I was feeling positive or at least able to suppress negative emotions.

Closing Thoughts: The Journey as a Search for Balance

The foregoing theorizing and narrative reveals that a journey to tenure can entail a multi-faceted search for balance. In my case, a part of this search involved letting go of some of my (naïve) idealism about what it meant to be a professor and to adopt a more realistic vision of and pragmatic stance towards the job and the workplace, which I likened to a process of grieving. The journey also required a search for equilibrium among the three roles of a professor's job (and manifold tasks associated with each of them) while also balancing my responses to the mix of institutional logics that underpin and shape the nature of the job and workplace. I have tried to show in this chapter that these roles and logics interact with, and to some degree constrain, the agency professors have to shape important aspects of their work based on their beliefs, values, identities, skills and practices. I feel it would have been helpful at the outset of my journey to have a better grasp of how the dynamics between roles and logics affect choices professors make. As a result, I have developed a list of what professors tend to focus on, either consistently or situationally, depending on their goals.[10] I have also included hints at the types of strategies professors using each focus might gravitate towards, and the prominent institutional logics shaping their work.

The hope is that novice professors might use this information heuristically to guide their reflections about what to focus on and

Table 4.1

Professors' Consistent or Situational Foci, With Related Strategies and Prominent Underlying Institutional Logics

	Research	Teaching	Leadership and/or service	Reputation and/or engagement	"All-in"
Goal	Demonstrate a robust research trajectory	Demonstrate quality and innovation in teaching	Demonstrate leadership qualities and collegiality	Demonstrate reputational and/or social capital	Demonstrate full commitment
Related strategies	Seek to reduce teaching and service workloads Continually apply for funding Recruit excellent grad students who can contribute to the research Publish frequently and/or in quality journals	Find synergies and efficiencies by conducting research on teaching and concentrating service commitments on educational programs	Seek to reduce teaching workload Obtain an official administration position	Master social media and other communication tools Conduct networking, workshops and events for practitioners or other targeted audiences Collaborate on research projects with practitioners or other targeted audiences (using workshops and events as sites for data collection)	Modulate through each focus situationally based on exigencies and priorities over time Work harder and longer hours
Prominent underlying logic(s)	Professional and market	Professional and communal	Communal and bureaucratic	Market and communal	All (shifting balance)

how to modulate their strategies as they proceed along the tenure-track, while expressing their beliefs, values, interests and identities and remaining clear on meeting the criterion placed upon them for success. In my case, for example, because of previous experience as an educator and administrator, I gravitated first to a focus on both teaching and service. These areas also resonated within my preference for working within professional and communal logics. However, I underestimated at the outset what it meant to work in a large, research-intensive university, which required that I adopt a significant research focus. Although I could (and do) identify with the professional logic underpinning this role, it has taken considerable effort to develop the skills and practices to work within this logic. This combination of foci meant that I quickly found myself working long hours with a nearly all-in focus. Because of the negative impacts on wellbeing of this situation, it became necessary over time to rebalance and modulate my foci based a more coherent professional identity, clearer priorities and a better understanding of the cycles of work related to roles, and a commitment to upholding boundaries. Admittedly, this remains a work in progress, as does my selective use of strategies identified in Table 4.1.

In my experience, a clarification of focus and identity has strengthened my "protective systems" of resilience (Masten & O'Dougherty Wright, 2010, p. 222). It has helped me to establish close, mutually supportive professional relationships with a circle of colleagues who share common interests and outlooks. It has had a calming effect emotionally and in terms of overall workload. This has led to a better functioning mind, one that is not distracted by a sense of near chronic disaster described at various points in the narrative. Clarity of focus has also helped to induce a more positive set of emotions to find substantive meaning in the work. It is my hope that the foregoing reflections will be of some value to those who find themselves in similar circumstances.

Endnotes

1   Non-tenure-track professors working on short-term contracts and without the protections and benefits afforded tenured professors now make up more than 50 percent of the academic workforce in Canada. The working conditions for these types of professors are much worse than they are for tenure-track and tenured, fulltime professors (see Pasma & Shaker, 2018).

2   Weinrib et al. (2013) report, however, that Canadian professors have negative impressions of "top-down managerial processes and low levels of academic involvement and influence over institution level decision-making processes" (p. 98).

3   Newport (2019) captures well the dysfunctional dynamic around service obligations in contemporary academia: "For many professors, service has transformed from an important duty to a serious problem. This is due, in large part, to the haphazard manner in which the obligations tend to be distributed. A typical approach to service is to say "yes" to a fire hose of incoming requests until you become so overcommitted that you retreat in desperation to catch up. Those whose personalities can tolerate it sometimes deploy a more extreme strategy in which they shirk these responsibilities, risking the disapproval of colleagues in exchange for peace and quiet."

4   According to Maciejewski et al., (2007): "Bowlby and Parkes were the first to propose a stage theory of grief for adjustment to bereavement that included four stages: shock-numbness, yearning searching, disorganization-despair, and reorganization. Kubler-Ross adapted Bowlby and Parkes' theory to describe a five-stage response of terminally ill patients to awareness of their impending death: denial-dissociation-isolation, anger, bargaining, depression, and acceptance . . . [and] Jacobs synthesized and illustrated the hypothesized stage theory of grief, in which the normal response to loss progresses through the following grief stages: numbness-disbelief, separation distress (yearning-anger-anxiety), depression-mourning, and recovery (p. 716)."

5   I use a stage theory of grieving as a heuristic model to support relatively brief reflections in this chapter on the sense of loss associated with making a career transition, recognizing that such theories have come under critical scrutiny for their scientific or clinical validity. For example, authors argue the Kubler-Ross model from which stage theories tend to be derived was not scientifically developed and has been misapplied to contexts other than the experience dying and death (Friedman & James, 2008). Jacobs (2016) observes "a model of grief as a multidimensional process . . . that evolves over time is more realistic and accurate than a model of several stages" (p. 8).

6   Gopaul et al. (2016) report data from a survey of Canadian professors that revealed average enrolments in graduate courses at the Masters level of 9.8 participants. In my case, the average enrolment in the 11 graduate courses I have taught over the last five years was 30.

7   The Ontario Council of Academic Vice Presidents' (2014) study found that professors responsible for an average of 4.13 courses and 192 students in a year were "research inactive"; while those with 3.32 courses and 151 students were "research active" (p. 7). In the 2018–19 academic year, my workload was 5 courses and 190 students.

8   This pattern is reflected in surveys of Canadian professors, which shows novice or "junior" faculty doing more teaching and senior faculty doing more research (Ontario Association of Academic Vice Presidents, 2014).

9   Reviews took place annually by the Dean and the Tenure and Promotion Committee, twice for the renewal of my employment contracts at years three and five, and five times when I applied for internal research funding.

10 These categories are based on my personal observations of the many professors I have now met on my journey at and beyond my university. However, the idea was inspired by Gopaul et al.'s (2016) study that showed 80 percent of Canadian professors were invested in their teaching and research roles, but 54 percent of this group leaned toward research, while 26 percent favoured teaching.

References

Aitken, A. (2010). Becoming an academic: Professional identity on the road to tenure. *Journal of Educational Thought, 44*(1), 55–68.

Archer. L. (2008). Younger academics' constructions of 'authenticity,' 'success,' and professional identity. *Studies in Higher Education, 33*(4), 385–403.

Association of Professors of the University of Ottawa. (2018). Update—Campaign on the issue of workload. Retrieved from http://www.apuo.ca/campaign-issue-workload/

Association of Professors of the University of Ottawa. (2019a). Collective agreement. Retrieved from http://www.apuo.ca/collective-agreement/collective-agreement/

Association of Professors of the University of Ottawa. (2019b). Update on the issue of workload. Retrieved from http://www.apuo.ca/update-on-the-issue-of-workload/

Association of Professors of the University of Ottawa. (2019c). Ford government's post-secondary education sector announcement. Retrieved from http://www.apuo.ca/ford-governments-post-secondary-education-sector-announcement/

Berg, M., & Seeber, B. (2016). *The slow professor: Challenging the culture of speed in the academy*. Toronto, ON: University of Toronto Press.

Boerner, K., & Jopp, D. (2010). Resilience in response to loss. In J. W. Reich, A. J. Zautra & J. S. Hall (Eds.), *Handbook of adult resilience* (pp. 126–145). New York, NY: The Guildford Press.

Bridwell-Mitchell, E. N., & Sherer, D. G. (2017). Institutional complexity and policy implementation: How underlying logics drive teacher interpretations of reform. *Educational Evaluation and Policy Analysis, 39*(2), 223–247.

Brown, W. I., & Sherry, J. G. (2010). When the tenure road is rocky: Toward integrated selves and institutions. *Journal of Educational Thought, 44*(1), 147–161.

Clarke, C. A., & Knights, D. (2015). Careering through academia: Securing identities or engaging ethical subjectivities? *Human Relations, 68*(12), 1865–1888. doi:10.1177/0018726715570978

Denhardt, J., & Denhardt, R. (2010). Building organizational resilience and adaptive management. In J. W. Reich, A. J. Zautra & J. S. Hall (Eds.), *Handbook of adult resilience* (pp. 333–349). New York, NY: Guildford Press.

Dulude, E., & Milley, P. (2018). Towards an understanding of the institutional complexity leaders' face in making data-informed decisions about equity. Paper presented at the bi-annual conference of the Commonwealth Council of Educational Administration and Management, 13–16 November, St. Paul's Bay, Malta.

Ellis, C., & Bochner, A. P. (2000). Autoethnography, personal narrative, reflexivity. In N. K. Denzin & Y. S. Lincoln (Eds.), *Handbook of qualitative research,* 2nd ed. (pp.733–768). Thousand Oaks, CA: Sage.

Fredman, N., & Doughney, J. (2012). Academic dissatisfaction, managerial change and neo-liberalism. *Higher Education, 64*(1), 41–58.

Friedland, R. & Alford, R. R. (1991). Bringing society back in: Symbols, practices, and institutional contradictions. In W. W. Powell & P. J. DiMaggio (Eds.) *The new institutionalism in organizational analysis* (pp. 232–263). Chicago, IL: University of Chicago Press.

Friedman, R., & James, J. W. (2008). The myth of the stages of dying, death and grief. *Skeptic (Altadena, CA), 14*(2), 37–42.

Gleich, J. (2016). Write first, ask questions later: publishing and the race to tenure track. *Cinema Journal, 55*(4), 133–138.

Gopaul, B., Jones, G. A., Weinrib, J., Metcalfe, A., Fisher, D., Gingras, Y., & Rubenson, K. (2016). The academic profession in Canada: Perceptions of Canadian university faculty about research and teaching. *Canadian Journal of Higher Education, 46*(2), 55–77.

Habermas, J., & Blazek, J. R. (1987). The idea of the university: Learning processes. *New German Critique, 41,* 3–22.

Hallett, T. & Ventresca, M. (2006). Inhabited institutions: Social interactions and organizational forms in Gouldner's patterns of industrial bureaucracy. *Theory and Society, 35*(2), 213–236.

Handford, V. (2016). From there to here. In T. Sibbald & V. Handford (Eds.), *The academic gateway: Understanding the journey to tenure* (pp. 203–214). Ottawa, ON: University of Ottawa Press.

Hartman, Y., & Darab, S. (2012). A call for slow scholarship: A case study on the intensification of academic life and its implications for pedagogy. *Review of Education, Pedagogy, and Cultural Studies, 34*(1–2), 49–60.

Haveman, H., & Gualtieri, G. (2017, September 26). Institutional logics. *Oxford Research Encyclopedia of Business and Management*. Retrieved from http://oxfordre.com/business/view/10.1093/acrefore/9780190224851.001.0001/acrefore-9780190224851-e-137

Hellsten, L. M., Martin, S. L., McIntyre, L. J., & Kinzel, A. L. (2011). Women on the academic tenure track: An autoethnographic inquiry. *International Journal for Cross-Disciplinary Subjects in Education, 2*(1), 271–275.

Hill, N. R. (2004). The challenges experienced by untenured faculty members in counsellor education: A wellness perspective. *Counsellor Education and Supervision, 44,* 135–146.

Hirschkorn, M. (2010). How vulnerable am I? An experiential discussion of tenure rhetoric for new faculty. *Journal of Educational Thought, 44*(1), 41–54.

Holling, C. S. (2001). Understanding the complexity of economic, ecological, and social systems. *Ecosystems, 4*(5), 390–405.

Holling, C. S., & Gunderson, L. H. (2002). Resilience and adaptive cycles. In L. H. Gunderson & C. S. Holling (Eds.), *Panarchy: Understanding transformations in human and natural systems* (pp. 25–62). Washington, DC: Island Press.

Jacobs, S. (1993). *Pathologic grief: Maladaptation to loss*. Washington, DC: American Psychiatric Association.

Jacobs, S. (2016). *Traumatic grief: Diagnosis, treatment, and prevention*. New York, NY: Routledge.

Jillapalli, R. K., & Jillapalli, R. (2014). Do professors have customer-based brand equity? *Journal of Marketing for Higher Education, 24*(1), 22–40.

Maciejewski, P. K., Zhang, B., Block, S. D., & Prigerson, H. G. (2007). An empirical examination of the stage theory of grief. *Journal of the American Medical Association, 297*(7), 716–723.

Masten, A. S. (2001). Ordinary magic: Resilience processes in development. *American Psychologist, 56*(3), 227–238.

Masten, A. S., & O'Dougherty Wright, M. (2010). Resilience over the lifespan: Developmental perspectives on resistance, recovery, and transformation. In J. W. Reich, A. J. Zautra & J. S. Hall (Eds.), *Handbook of adult resilience* (pp. 213–237). New York, NY: The Guildford Press.

Masten, A. S., & Obradovic, J. (2008). Disaster preparation and recovery: Lessons from research on resilience in human development. *Ecology and Society, 13*(1). Retrieved from http://www.ecologyandsociety.org/vol13/iss1/art3/

Metcalfe, A. S., Fisher, D., Gingras, Y., Jones, G. A., Rubenson, K., & Snee, I. (2011). Canada: Perspectives on governance and management. In W. Locke, W. K. Cummings, & D. Fisher (Eds.), *Changing governance and management in higher education* (pp. 151–174). Dordrecht, Netherlands: Springer.

Milley, P. (2016). Transitioning to the academic tenure-track at mid-career: exploring adaptive and maladaptive responses to challenges and adversity. In T. Sibbald & V. Handford (Eds.), *The academic gateway: Understanding the journey to tenure* (pp. 179–198). Ottawa, ON: University of Ottawa Press.

Milley, P. (2017). Maladministration in education: Towards a typology based on public records in Canada. *Educational Management Administration & Leadership, 45*(3), 466–483.

Newport, C. (2019). Is email making professors stupid? It used to simply crucial tasks. Now it's strangling scholars ability to think. *The Chronicle Review*. Retrieved from www.chronicle.com/interactives/is-email-making-professors-stupid

Ontario College of Teachers. (2015). Looking at enhanced teacher education. Retrieved from https://www.oct.ca/-/media/PDF/Enhancing%20Teacher%20Education/Enhanced_Teacher_Education_EN_Digital.pdf

Ontario Confederation of University Faculty Associations. (2015). Making sense of the funding formula for Ontario universities. Retrieved from https://ocufa.on.ca/general/making-sense-of-the-funding-formula-for-ontario-universities/

Ontario Council of Academic Vice Presidents. (2014). Faculty at work: A preliminary report on faculty work at Ontario universities 2010–2012. Retrieved from https://cou.ca/wp-content/uploads/2015/04/OCAV-Faculty-at-Work.pdf

Ontario Ministry of Education. (2013). Modernizing teacher education in Ontario. Retrieved from https://news.ontario.ca/edu/en/2013/06/modernizing-teacher-education-in-ontario.html

Ontario Ministry of Training, Colleges and Universities. (2015). Overview of the current university funding model: Opening briefing. Retrieved from http://www.tcu.gov.on.ca/pepg/audiences/universities/uff/uff_overview.pdf

Pasma, C., & Shaker, E. (2018). *Contract U: Contract faculty appointments at Canadian universities*. Ottawa: Canadian Centre for Policy Alternatives. Retrieved from https://www.policyalternatives.ca/publications/reports/contract-u

Patton, M. Q. (2011). *Developmental evaluation: Applying complexity concepts to enhance innovation and use*. New York, NY: Guildford Press.

Samier, E. A., & Milley, P. (Eds.). (2018). *International perspectives on Maladministration in education: Theories, research, and critiques*. New York, NY: Routledge.

Thornton, P. H., & Ocasio, W. (1999). Institutional logics and the historical contingency of power in organizations: Executive succession in the higher education publishing industry, 1958–1990. *American Journal of Sociology, 105*(3), 801–843.

Thornton, P. H., Ocasio, W., & Lounsbury, M. (2012). *The institutional logics perspective: A new approach to culture, structure, and process.* Oxford University Press on Demand.

Weinrib, J., Jones, G. A., Metcalfe, A. S., Fisher, D., Gingras, Y., Rubenson, K., & Snee, I. (2013). Canadian university academics' perceptions of job satisfaction: ". . . The future is not what it used to be." In *Job satisfaction around the academic world* (pp. 83–102). Dordrecht, Netherlands: Springer.

CHAPTER 5

Tenured Life: Rhythms, Time, and Energy

Cecile Badenhorst

These are the facts: I started working at Memorial University in July of 2011. I filed for tenure in September 2016. A year later, in September 2017, I became officially tenured. When reflecting on the transition from being non-tenured to tenured, it is tempting to tell a linear narrative of progression where one moves smoothly from a state of angst and insecurity to one of confidence and well-being. However, the lived experience is much more complex.

In this chapter, I articulate that complexity by using the concepts of rhythms, time, and energy to describe the continuities and discontinuities as I progressed from tenure-track into a tenured position. I am aware, as I write this, that autobiographies are fictions or technologies of the self, in Foucault's words (Michelson, 2011). Writing about oneself is "an exercise in self-creation by human beings who are as much the products of their own narratives as their referents" (Michelson, 2011, p. 5). Autobiographical narratives, while inherently expressions of experience, are essentially constrained by the way we construct the context in which the narratives are told. We set up the specifications for the narratives and then produce partial representations of self-hood where only some stories are told. While conscious of these potential and inevitable constraints in writing narratives of the self, like Cancienne and Snowber (2003), I agree that it is important to "notice the details of our lives and access the nooks and crannies of our experiences and perceptions" (p. 248). They suggest attentiveness is something we do with our body as well as our minds: "an act of 'bodily attending,' a way to represent the physicality of the textures around us: sound, gesture, smell, sight—the vowels of the physical world. Therefore, writing becomes not just a recording of details but a process by which we are awakened to the details of experience" (Cancienne & Snowber, 2003, p. 248). In this way, writing "becomes an interaction between knowing and being, ontology and epistemology, and the ordinary and the extraordinary" (Cancienne & Snowber, 2003, p. 248).

By focusing on rhythms, time and energy, I explore this "bodily attending." Time, particularly time-pressure, definitely became a major feature for me over the tenure-track years and it seems to be "a prominent and pervasive feature" among academics generally (Ylijoki & Mäntylä, 2003, p. 55). Rhythms help capture the flow and stoppages that occur over the cycles of the years. The concept of energy is useful because it helps explain the nuances of the parts of the job I love and find energizing and the parts that are exhausting and draining. All three are intricately interwoven and help provide a language to describe the transition to tenure.

Rhythms, Time, and Energy

Rhythm is the patterned recurrence of movement (Lefebvre, 2004). Biological rhythms have both continuity and variability as beings adapt to their environment. These rhythms are also intimately connected to time. The human body, for example, is organized around a specific and finite time structure and our many biological clocks keep track of our complex molecular rhythms. Outside of the body, cyclical time draws attention to the cyclical rhythms present in our world: the rising and setting sun, the waxing and waning moon, the ebbing and flowing of the tides, or the growth and withering of life in the changing seasons. These patterns last for a period and then return to restart, repeating over and over with familiar regularity. Linear time, however, compresses these rhythms into in a single time-dependent direction. As we move along this time-line, there is no going back (Pirani & Smith, 2013). While cyclical time is often rooted in the rhythms of the earth, linear time emerges from social practice and human activity. Energy comes into play with the qualitative experiences of time and rhythms. Waiting for the dentist, for example, may be five minutes on the clock but hours in terms of the impact on emotions in the body. Similarly, Noonan (2015) describes the hard-pressed, time-pressured "money-time" in academic contexts as compared to the unstructured, open-ended slow "thought-time" academics need to produce scholarly work. Each requires and produces different energies.

These varied conceptions of rhythm, time, and energy are always interacting in multiple layers on the academic "self" and in the relationships one has with others. While we watch our mechanical clocks, we also note the rising and setting sun with accompanying energies. This layering can create conflictual relationships with time, rhythms and energy, and we are sometimes faced with compromises and disturbances as we navigate our way through the ritual practices of life (Lefebvre, 2004). In the sections that follow, I observe the key areas of academic work—teaching, service, and research—through the lens of rhythms, time, and energy to show the compromises, disturbances, and areas of synchronicity that I have observed.

Teaching
Teaching has a rhythm and a time structure because we teach over semesters and in specific time-slots. Faculty and students are invigorated at the beginning of the semester and the pace is fresh. Over the course of the semester, the rhythm slows, energy wanes, before surging at the end of the semester as final tasks are completed in time to meet the deadlines. There's a cyclical rhythm of assignments arriving at certain times, being marked and sent out again (Ylijoki & Mäntylä, 2003). Once the semester is over, there is a release of tension and a relaxation of pace. I am fond of this flowing and ebbing of the school semester; it is a comfortable and familiar rhythm for me.

However, before joining the faculty at Memorial, I had not taught online. Online teaching, which makes up the majority of my courses, created a discordant rhythm for me. The geographical nature of the dispersed communities that our program serves is immanently suited to the online environment. Indeed, our program was experiencing a drop-off in numbers when I first joined and I was part of the decision-making process to transfer all our face-to-face classes to the online environment. Once the transition had taken place student numbers began to increase again. Delivering the entire program online was a good decision for our unit, and it met our students' needs.

While I enjoyed the challenge of creating optimal learning environments online, I found the rhythms of online teaching challenging.

Online "teaching" involves checking the course material, reading student posts, emailing students, replying to emails, and marking. Since there is no set structure of blocked-out classroom time with online teaching, I found I shifted my teaching time into the evenings or weekends. Weekdays were spent in meetings, service, supervising students or the administration of research projects. These activities, because of the physical presence of students and colleagues, took precedence during this time. I found myself filling my days with activities but then still having to "teach" in the evenings. The parts I really enjoyed about teaching, such as building relationships, getting to know students, telling stories, and responding to student needs by changing my teaching plans in situ are largely absent in the online environment. This also had an impact on my personal energies. I found the personal contact, the material space of the classroom and the embodied experience of the desks, the board and students in the face-to-face classroom energizing, and I usually feel stimulated after teaching.

Online teaching does not create the same conditions of energy renewal for me. Over my six years on the tenure-track I found my enthusiasm for teaching waned, something I had never experienced before. Possibly this is the result of standardization and conformity that characterizes online learning management systems or it may have been caused by the toll of large classes which take time and energy. Overall, my enthusiasm for teaching decreased and I have had to strive to develop online courses that contain originality and creativity, and that I enjoy teaching. Like Lupton (2013), I view teaching as an art that involves aesthetics for myself as well as my students. I have actively sought out face-to-face teaching to regain that buzz I used to get from teaching. Since getting tenure, I have noticed that I am more mindful of my energy levels with regard to teaching. I find I cannot work all day and then teach in the evenings as well. I began to create spaces in my weekday calendar, marked off in red, which allocated time for specific tasks such as reading discussion posts or grading. After penning "teaching time" in my daily calendar, I was determined not to relinquish this time to meetings or other work and I have largely kept to this schedule. I still grade on weekends and in the evenings, but prioritizing my online teaching has helped to even out some of the discordant rhythms and energies of teaching.

Another related area where I have felt conflicting rhythms is with supervision. Prior to coming to my current faculty position,

I had worked in a graduate school and managed a large doctoral program. Consequently, I was familiar with supervising both master's and doctoral students. On joining Memorial, I immediately took on two doctoral students and a number of master's students. Although I enjoy these interactions with students, I found the time commitment to be enormous in addition to all the other components of a faculty job. Meetings, reading written work, reading source documents and all the administration around students, especially doctoral students, with comprehensive exam committees and various other committees took up an extensive part of my work week. Like teaching, the meetings took place during the day but reading written work was completed in the evenings and on weekends. As students came closer to submitting final drafts, reading theses often meant days of solid work devoted to supervision. Everything else would become backed up, and I would be panicked and frenzied trying to get on top of things again. Early in the tenure-track process, I found that supervision, while enjoyable, could become overwhelmingly draining as students finished their theses unexpectedly at the same time and when supervision requirements overlapped.

As I came closer to tenure, and particularly after receiving tenure, I made the decision to reduce the number of students I supervise to manageable levels. Now, I try to stagger student projects so that one might be in the beginning stages while the other is completing. This allows me to gather the energy required to get each student through what is usually a hectic final phase of thesis reading and editing. The decision to limit my supervision was a difficult one because I enjoy the stimulus of working with students, particularly doctoral students, and I am often sorely tempted to take on new students. Their projects are always interesting and if I get to know a student, it is hard to say "No."

This is a challenge I continue to face, but it has been a good decision and has allowed me to develop some regularity in energy and time commitments. Overall, some aspects of teaching drain my energies and I have to actively protect my time, while other aspects are fulfilling and rewarding.

Service
Of the many aspects of faculty life, the nebulous zone of service is one that is often hard to capture. There are many responsibilities where the tasks are not visible yet take up considerable amounts of

time. These include writing reference letters for students, supporting colleagues when they apply for awards, responding to queries about programs, supervision and funding, and so on. In my case, I became Chair of my unit in my second year on the tenure-track, which is an unusual circumstance. While interesting, this role involved multiple tasks like meetings, decision-making and constant monitoring of program requirements and delivery. Tasks included receiving and making phone calls to solve problems, responding to emails from administrative staff, assessing equivalency in courses and programs completed at other universities, making decisions (and filling in the forms) for program renewal, new course development and old course upgrading, advising on teaching allocations, and so on. Each task on its own was a small matter that took up minutes of time, however, all together, they could be a full-time job, even with the superb administrative support received. It requires ongoing effort to remain mindful that being Chair does not become a dominant rhythm in my working life. Being available and accessible through email and cell phones 24/7 creates dangerous expectations and requires determined resistance to manage (Menzies & Newson, 2007). Training myself to respond to a 12/5 week has taken considerable effort but I am determined to keep these boundaries in place.

The more visible service work I perform centres around my core area of research—graduate student writing. Here I regularly deliver workshops on thesis writing, writing for publication, overcoming procrastination, and many more topics. I get requests to deliver workshops from departments across campus, the Writing Centre, the School of Graduate Studies, the Graduate Student's Union, and of course, in my own faculty, Education. Although these workshops are time-consuming, I find them invigorating and they give my energies a boost. I think this is partly because they provide me with face-to-face teaching experiences. Consequently, I often over extend myself by booking more workshops than I have time to accommodate. Yet, this is not an area of work that I want to curtail. Even now as I think about these workshops, I can feel the rush of energy through my body, I find them fulfilling.

Other service work involves playing a role on faculty committees. In contrast to delivering workshops, I find this work largely draining. I chair several committees and the endless discussions—which result in few decisions, along with the drama of entrenched tensions—are wearying. Search committee work can be extremely time consuming and fractious, particularly in the neoliberal university where the stakes are high and resources are becoming increasingly scarce. Long, unfocussed meetings consume energy, both emotionally and intellectually. With time at a premium, I often feel I am wasting time during these meetings.

The final band of service is a partially visible area. This involves reviewing: reviewing papers for journals, and reviewing student and faculty grant applications. As the tenure-track years ticked away, I noticed an increase in requests from journals to review papers. This is an area where I could easily say "No" and conserve my time. However, surprisingly, I enjoy reviewing papers. Reviewing grant applications is less invigorating but there is something stimulating about reading new research ideas and projects. All in all, reviewing spurs me to think about my own writing and research projects. Finding a balance is the key here: Just the right amount of commitment to reviewing to stimulate but not so much that it becomes exhausting. As with teaching, the challenge is finding a way to meet workplace service needs while at the same time not depleting all my energies.

Writing and Research
Writing and research takes up a large percentage of my time: More than 40 percent when I'm not teaching, and much less when I am. My research time is clawed back, snatched from other priorities and conducted in frantic moments in between other tasks. Writing, at times, seems like hard labour; at other times it is satisfying creative expression. In the neoliberal environment, time is often compressed so that research is performed at a frantic, frenzied pace and writing is focused on producing a product. This accelerated pace is often caused by externally imposed obligations, which insist on a shorter time span (Ylijoki & Mäntylä, 2003). This results in long working days and fragmented time as one tries to get a range of tasks done.

Like other universities in Canada (see Acker & Webber, 2016), all faculty members are under pressure to complete grant research projects within tight timeframes and with the accompanying audit culture of accounting and reporting. There is not much time for creativity or deep thinking. This time-pressure is exercised structurally within institutions through mechanisms of start-up grant deadlines of three years and other grant time-spans only lasting a year or two. Additionally, new scholars are given incentives to apply for grants.

For example, within the SSHRC framework, new scholar applications are pooled separately, increasing applicants' chances of success. The consequence of these incentives is that new scholars are encouraged to apply for multiple grants during the tenure-track years. This was certainly true in my case. I applied for several grants not expecting to achieve success in as many as I did. The outcome was juggling different grant projects at the same time with the same deadlines. I often felt overwhelmed and harried as a result. Post-tenure, I no longer feel the pressure to apply for multiple grants. This slowing down of the pace has allowed me to think through my research objectives more carefully and to select specific grants that would be most appropriate.

In terms of the writing process, before tenure I felt pressure to publish single-authored papers. I like writing on my own, but the papers where I have worked with partners have proved to be especially stimulating, motivating and productive. In one partnership (with Dr Heather McLeod), the process has been organic and stress-free. Heather and I have worked on empirical and conceptual projects together and I enjoy the slow, non-competitive nature of our collaborative work. In more current contexts, where competition is normalized between academics (Davies, 2005; Archer, 2008), this type of working relationship is relatively rare. For example, in our most recent co-authored paper, we began by talking about an issue on an autoethnographic theme over coffee one morning. That conversation stimulated me to see if there was literature on the topic, and I began collecting papers. Over the next couple of months, whenever we met, we would discuss the issue a little further and think about it more deeply. Then a call for papers for a book collection appeared in our email, the theme seemed immanently suitable, and we thought about submitting an abstract. If it was not accepted, we had nothing to lose, we thought.

It was accepted, so we moved into the next phase, which was collecting data and pulling the paper together which happened easily and collaboratively with each of us writing different sections. We stimulate each other and, for me, I feel I produce much better writing with her than I would have on my own. With this paper, particularly, I felt I was in an almost constant state of excitement while writing. Here I experienced the timeless flow of time (Csikszentmihalyi, 1990); time seemed to fall away and I could work without consciously noticing the ticking of the clock. This kind of nomadic rhythm is upbeat and buoyant while at the same time slow. It is the pace I want to cultivate in my future work, and the one I work best at. I want to disengage with neoliberal practices that create discordant structured, fast-paced time (Ulmer, 2016), and post-tenure, I aim to involve myself in a culture of research/writing that is non-competitive. Writing in partnerships has also been a connecting experience for me where I feel a sense of belonging. These partnerships have created the conditions for me, as Neimanis suggests, to: "experience ourselves less as isolated entities" (Neimanis, 2012, p. 96).

Finding a regular writing practice is one of the most challenging tasks of academic life and is especially a process of balancing rhythms, time, and energy. One tries to tame the dissonant jarring rhythms of the frenzied to-do (must-do) list, into some kind of order to create space to think and to write. I am reminded of Latour and Woolgar's (1986) metaphor of noise and signals. They argue that we construct texts out of a cacophony of noise. When you begin a writing project there is always jarring noise. Finding the clear note of the signal is part of the writing process. This process itself is not an individualised solitary act. It involves a series of micro-negotiations between place, selves, texts, and the details of writing, as well as imaginary audiences and live readers. Finding your way through "the noise of a thousand thoughts" involves "sorting, picking up, enclosing" (Latour & Woolgar, 1986, p. 247) the signal. I have a better writing rhythm now post-tenure. I'm slowing down, thinking more, working more collaboratively, and writing with more intention but it is still a struggle to maintain a balance with all the other clamouring tasks.

Bodily Rhythms

Over the past seven years, I have really begun to notice my bodily rhythms. At the start of my tenure-track journey, I was already in my late forties. My children were teenagers and I was still very much a mother. Days were filled with work, household tasks, and teenager activities. Now I am facing an empty nest as my children have moved out and begin lives of their own. I have noticed two things happening. First, having children in the house forced me to find balance and family time. I prioritized them and couldn't work long hours. Now that they are no longer around, I have found myself at my desk far longer. Second, as I get older, my body cannot cope with the enforced hours hunched over a keyboard. In the summer after I submitted my tenure folder, I needed physiotherapy for jaw, neck, and shoulder tension, something that continues to plague me. My body is slowing down. This is a natural cycle, one I need to be mindful of, and pay attention to.

One of my often-used phrases both prior to and post tenure is "I'm exhausted." This reflects an embodied time-energy, something I often ignore. I noticed that I talked about exhaustion more than my colleagues and began to question why I always felt so tired. Widerberg (2006) asks "How tired is it 'normal' to be? Is everybody equally tired?" (p. 106). There is a substantial literature on academic overwork and distress (Acker & Armenti, 2004; Barcan, 2018; Brunila & Valero, 2018; Gill, 2010; 2014; Menzies & Newson, 2007; Mountz et al., 2015). Over the tenure years, one gets trained in certain ways and it becomes normal to have too much to do. We learn to do more in less time, and to stop talking to each other because it seems to be a waste of time. With technology such as laptops, we can work at home, whether ill, at leisure or entertaining. As Widerberg (2006) suggests: "When it is normal to have too much to do, it is likely that it is also normal to be tired and worn out" (p. 115). This is what Brunila and Valero (2018) call a "public secret" in academia: "a kind of taboo that nobody mentions and that all hide, so that the apparent vulnerability and precarity of the individual do not become revealed in the 'wrong way'" (p. 77). Feeling exhausted then becomes taken for granted and more dangerously, if you are not worn out, this is often perceived as indicating a lack of commitment. Tiredness becomes a theme that we do not question. This is particularly so for women who are still expected to be "good girls" who need "to do everything properly, and to have the needs of others as their first priority" (Widerberg, 2006, p. 115).

Yet within this realm of overwork and distress, I have also experienced strong threads of satisfaction. How is it possible to be exhausted, overworked all the time, and yet feel some satisfaction? Barcan (2018) argues that the notion of "vocation" (p. 108) (a call to serve) provides insight into this paradox. Academics tend to have a sense of social mission: "vocation is a concept and way of experiencing the world in which passion, satisfaction, duty, and sacrifice are woven" (Barcan, 2018, p. 116). Vocation is characterized by self-sacrifice as an ethic, and by shame if we cannot cope. There are deep temporal investments in vocation—essentially we are talking about "forever" here. Feeling exhausted certainly characterized a good portion of my pre-tenure years, and even now, it's a familiar state. I am becoming more cognizant of how damaging the notion of vocation is as I fund myself to go to conferences and sacrifice personal and family time by working overtime and not taking leave. While I am aware that there is a strong structural architecture that keeps the idea of the academic vocation in place, I am more determined than ever to resist this machinery and not to let the rhythms based on social structures eclipse my natural bodily rhythms (Menzies & Newson, 2007).

Concluding Thoughts

McAlpine and Amundsen (2011) suggest we construct our academic identities over time from doctoral work to pre-tenure to tenure through the integration of three areas: intellectual (scholarly interests), networking (personal and work connections), institutional (structures and processes), and how these interweave in different ways over time. The intellectual strand includes how one sees oneself as a scholar and the contribution to a field. It "leaves a trail of artefacts, e.g., publications, citations, papers, course/curriculum design" as times marches forward (McAlpine & Amundsen, 2011, p. 179). Networking includes relationships formed through research collaborations, teaching, and work colleagues. The institutional thread includes the context and environment that supports or hinders an individual. It is in this strand where much of the judgment and measurement, so central to our work these days, can be found. I find this conceptualisation of identity-formation over time a useful one. I can see how each strand can be a source of tension as well as satisfaction.

For me, the intellectual and networking areas provide the most fulfillment while the institutional thread is one where I feel I am always fighting for time and resources. McAlpine and Amundsen (2011) assert: "What is essential in this environment is endurance and resilience, the capacity to adapt positively and successfully to, and to bounce back from, adverse circumstances by negotiating one's intentions, and sustaining socially positive relationships" (p. 180). My goal, post tenure, is to work with people whose company I enjoy and to produce intellectually satisfying products within reasonable time frames while at the same time having a life outside of academia.

Common narratives of the pre-tenure to post-tenure path assumes a normative progression, a coming-of-age, in a sense, yet this path is rarely coherent or straight-forward (Wiessner, 2005). I would like to write that life after tenure has changed in significant ways; I feel more confident, able and successful; and, post-tenure life is stress-free as the benefits of academic freedom kick in. As I write this, our collective agreement is on the bargaining table and post-tenure review is an issue administration is keen to see realised. The university is under severe fiscal austerity and we are once again being told to do more with less. The insecurity and stress-levels have not disappeared but the concepts of rhythm, time, and energy have allowed me to show the complexity and messiness of academic life.

Some activities, while productive, are draining. Others that are seemingly insignificant are energy-boosting and satisfying. In some cases, I have managed my time well and in others, I am still struggling to find a way through. There is a tendency for some aspects of the job to dominate and others to be subsumed. It is a fine balance to find some sort of equilibrium and peace in the face of all the demands the job requires and my own personal needs and values. But one thing I have learned is that it is important for me to feel a sense of belonging, of companionship, of aesthetics, of value in the work I do. Just keeping my head above the water is not enough.

References

Acker, S., & Armenti, C. (2004). Sleepless in academia. *Gender and Education*, 16(1), 3–24.

Acker, S., & Webber, M. (2016). Discipline and punish: The tenure review process in Ontario universities. In L. Shultz, M. Viczko. (Eds.), *Assembling and governing the higher education institution* (pp. 233–255). London, UK: Palgrave Macmillan. DOI 10.1057/978-1-137-52261-0_13

Archer, L. (2008). The new neoliberal subjects? Young/er academics' constructions of professional identity. *Journal of Education Policy*, 23(3), 265–285.

Barcan, R. (2018). Paying dearly for privilege: Conceptions, experiences and temporalities of vocation in academic life. *Pedagogy, Culture & Society*, 26(1), 105–121. DOI: 10.1080/14681366.2017.1358207

Brunila, K., & Valero, P. (2018). Anxiety and the making of research(ing) subjects in neoliberal academia. *Subjectivity*, 11, 74–89. https://doi.org/10.1057/s41286-017-0043-9

Cancienne, M. B., & Snowber, C. N. (2003). Writing rhythm: Movement as method. *Qualitative Inquiry*, 9(2), 237–253.

Csikszentmihalyi, M., (1990). *Flow: The psychology of optimal experience*. New York, NY: Harper Collins.

Davies, B. (2005). The (im)possibility of intellectual work in neoliberal regimes. *Discourse: Studies in the Cultural Politics of Education, 26*(1), 1–14.

Gill, R. (2014). Academics, cultural workers and critical labour studies. *Journal of Cultural Economy, 7*(1), 12–30. DOI: 10.1080/17530350.2013.861763

Gill, R., (2010). Breaking the silence: The hidden injuries of neo-liberal academia. In R. Ryan-Flood & R. Gill, (Eds.), *Secrecy and silence in the research process: Feminist reflections* (pp. 39–55). London, UK: Routledge.

Latour, B., & Woolgar, S., (1986). *Laboratory life: The construction of scientific facts.* Princeton, NJ: Princeton University Press.

Lefebvre, H. (2004). *Rhythmanalysis: Space, time and everyday life.* (S. Elden & G. Moore, Trans.). Paris, France: Continuum.

Lupton, M. (2013). Reclaiming the art of teaching. *Teaching in Higher Education, 18*(2), 156–166. http://dx.doi.org/10.1080/13562517.2012.694098

McAlpine, L., & Amundsen, C. (2011). Making meaning of diverse experiences: Constructing an identity through time. In L. McAlpine, C. Amundsen. (Eds.), *Doctoral education: Research-based strategies for doctoral students, supervisors and administrators* (pp.173–183). Dordrecht, Netherlands: Springer.

Menzies, H., & Newson, J. (2007). No time to think: Academics' life in the globally wired university. *Time & Society, 16*(1), 83–98.

Michelson, E. (2011). Autobiography and selfhood in the practice of adult learning. *Adult Education Quarterly, 61*(3), 3–21.

Mountz, A., Walton-Roberts, M., Bonds, A., Mansfield, B., Loyd, J., Hyndman, J., Basu, R., Whitson, R., Hawkins, R., Hamilton, T., & Curran, W. (2015). For slow scholarship: A feminist politics of resistance through collective action in the neoliberal university. *ACME: An International Journal for Critical Geographies, 14*(4), 1235–1259.

Neimanis, A. (2012). Hydrofeminism: Or, on becoming a body of water. In H. Gunkel, C. Nigianni & F. Soderback. (Eds.), *Undutiful daughters: New directions in feminist thought and practice* (pp. 85–100). New York, NY: Palgrave Macmillan.

Noonan, J. (2015). Thought-time, money-time and the conditions of free academic labour. *Time & Society, 25*(2), 213–233.

Pirani, B. M., & Smith, T. S. (2013). *Body and time: Bodily rhythms and social synchronism in the digital media society.* Cambridge, UK: Cambridge Scholars Publishing.

Ulmer, J. B. (2017). Writing slow ontology. *Qualitative Inquiry, 23*(3), 201–2011.

Widerberg, K., (2006). Embodying modern times: Investigating tiredness. *Time & Society, 15*(1), 105–120. DOI: 10.1177/0961463X06061348

Wiessner, C. A. (2005). Storytellers: Women crafting new knowing and better worlds. *Convergence, 38*(4), 101–119.

Ylijoki, O., & Mäntylä, H. (2003). Conflicting time perspectives in academic work. *Time & Society, 12*(1), 55–78.

CHAPTER 6

Women Reflect on Remaining an Academic: Challenges and Supports

S. Penney, G. Young, C. Badenhorst, H. McLeod,
S. Moore, and S. Pickett

This follow-up employed a collaborative autobiographical methodology to understand the journey of six women, each becoming an academic. Since last writing together on this topic, four of the coauthors achieved tenure, one individual transitioned to a tenure-track position, and one remains in a contractual position. Self-determination theory served as a theoretical framework and a lens for this project (Deci & Ryan, 2000; Ryan & Deci, 2000; Ryan, 1982). The data collected included self-reflections, group sharing, probing, theme development, and group writing (Chang, Ngunijiri, & Hernandez, 2012). Five broad themes emerged: first, tenure as a dream—as an end goal and as a relief from the pressure to publish, and how tenure has provided choice and control over their work life; second, gaining confidence—being able to have autonomy, speak out, and be political; third, associated costs with remaining in an academic career—loss of place, loss of relationships, and loss of professional identity; fourth, work-life balance and health a continued struggle—guilt surrounding loss of time for family, friends, and self; and guilt associated with taking the time for family, friends and self; and, fifth, supports—relationships, mentorships, joint projects, and the faculty's writing group. This project examined the experiences of six women, the supports and guidance they received, how they navigated their new responsibilities, and their continued struggles to manage work-life balance while maintaining wellness.

A collaborative autobiographical methodology (Chang, et al., 2012) was adopted to explore the experiences of six women pursuing academic careers, who are members of the Faculty of Education Writing Group at Memorial University, in St. John's Newfoundland. The authors, who are at various stages of their academic careers, provided self-reflections about their careers in academia, which provided specific emphasis on maintaining wellness, and how changes have taken place in terms of autonomy, intrinsic and extrinsic motivation, and "choice" throughout their careers.

In previous group publications (Penney et al., 2015; Young, Penney, et al., 2017), and group explorations of wellness (Young, Kilborn, et al., 2017), analysis of the personal reflective narratives uncovered themes, which focused on striving to have work-life balance, personal and professional costs associated with being unwell, and the impact of academic work on families. As academics in various stages of our careers, we offered personal suggestions for being well in academia, such as choosing to engage in work and leisure activities that are enjoyable and maintaining relationships. We also provided recommendations that can be implemented at the institutional level, specifically focusing on strategies to: provide clear promotion and tenure processes, examine workload expectations, promote wellness, and facilitate mentorship (Young, Kilborn, et al., 2017). Emphasis was placed on how writing groups can be used to support wellness in academia (Badenhorst, et al., 2013; Penney, et al., 2015).

It is important to examine the experiences of academics as they move from early to mid-career. Mid-career faculty fill essential instructional, program development, administrative, and citizenship roles at their institutions (Baldwin, Lunceford, & Vanderlinden, 2005). They form a bridge between faculty generations by mentoring new colleagues and assuming leadership duties as their senior colleagues move toward retirement (Baldwin & Chang, 2006). Mid-career faculty are key players as their institutions adapt to continuous educational changes and austerity measures. They can be either allies or stubborn opponents as their institutions adjust to financial pressures, reporting responsibilities, and competitive pressures such as revision of programs to meet the needs of increasingly diverse students and integration of new educational technologies.

Theoretical Framework

Self-determination theory (Deci & Ryan, 2000; Ryan & Deci, 2000; Ryan, 1982) was used as a framework. Self-determination theory examines both internal and external motivations, as well as the three basic psychological needs of competency, autonomy, and relatedness. Ryan and Deci (2008) suggested that these three basic processes are important; however, they are not equal, rather they privilege autonomy. Work environments that allow for autonomous self-regulation produce vitality, which in turn is a strong indicator of internal motivation and healthy employees. The implication is "vitality and energy are associated with better performance and persistence as well as psychological and physical wellness" (p. 714). Ryan and Deci suggest that autonomy plays an important role in developing inner resources. This means that organizations that support the psychological needs of their employees may show enhanced performance, persistence, and health. Self-determination, and specifically feeling autonomous in the workplace, predicts a number of factors including job satisfaction, motivation, wellness, mental health, and quality relationships (Skewes et al., 2017).

Self-determination theory has been used and studied across a variety of contexts including workplace and academic environments (Gagne & Deci, 2005; Skewes et al., 2017; Trepanier, Forest, Fernet, & Austin, 2015; Vansteenkiste, Lens, & Deci, 2006; Williams et al., 2014). Self-determination theory outlines two types of motivation: autonomous motivation and controlled motivation. Autonomous motivation is associated with tasks that individuals are intrinsically motivated to perform as well as tasks individuals have internalized as important. Controlled motivation is associated with tasks individuals may not wish to perform but do so because of external pressure or because they are coerced to perform.

Introjected regulation (first put forth by deCharms in 1968, as cited in Vansteenkiste et al., 2006), refers to individuals performing tasks because the performance of the tasks is motivated by internal pressures like guilt or shame: "introjected regulations, which are a type of internal controls, can be primed by guilt-inducing strategies, shaming procedures, and the use of conditional regard" (p. 22). Human motivation is not simplistic. While internal and external processes may impact motivation, the coauthors felt coerced by both themselves and university structures such as promotion and tenure committees.

Methodology

Recruitment
The first two authors took the lead on this collaborative writing inquiry. In early March 2018, a group email invitation was sent

to all of the original coauthors (*Women reflect on becoming an academic: Challenges and supports*; Young, Penney, et al., 2017). Each was invited to write a follow-up self-reflection on their continued experiences in the academic environment. Two of the original co-authors moved away from Memorial University, and while alternative email addresses were provided, neither responded to the call for a follow-up reflection. The remaining individuals expressed an interest in contributing to a follow-up reflection surrounding their continued journey through their academic careers. Six of the original authors submitted narratives. A follow-up email was sent in June, inviting all those who had expressed an interest in participating, but had yet to submit their follow-up self-reflection, to do so. After the follow-up email was sent two individuals expressed an interest in providing their self-reflection and one asked that she be removed from further requests to participate. However, neither of the individuals who indicated a desire to submit actually provided their self-reflections prior to beginning this analysis, and time constraints prevented the remaining individuals from submitting their narratives.

Participants
Six women (between the age of 35 and 60), who were involved in the initial chapter (Young et al., 2017), agreed to participate in this chapter. Each of these women is a coauthor of this study, and all of these women remained involved with the writing group in the 2017–2018 academic year. The coauthors are primarily qualitative researchers and have varied backgrounds including Indigenous pedagogies, adult education, art education, counselling psychology, and special education. Since the last chapter submission four of the coauthors have achieved tenure, one transitioned from a contractual position to a tenure-track position, and one remains in a contractual position.

Data Collection
We employed a collaborative autobiographical methodology (Chang, et al., 2012) to understand the process of becoming an academic. Six women, between the ages of 35 and 60, used self-reflection surrounding their work in an academic environment and their journeys toward tenure or continued involvement in the academic environment as the primary source of data. The first two authors formulated questions to guide the self-reflections. These questions were formulated after

reviewing some of the theoretical literature on self-determination and research studies on middle career academics (e.g., Baldwin, & Chang, 2006; Baldwin, Lunceford & Vanderlinden, 2005; Deci & Ryan, 2000; Ryan & Deci, 2000). Each of the self-reflections was sent to the first two authors through email.

Data Analysis
The data used in this chapter was coded using an inductive thematic analysis approach (Braun & Clarke, 2006; Ryan & Bernard, 2003). The self-reflections were submitted to the first two authors as Word documents attached to their university email addresses. Each of the six transcripts submitted by the coauthors was downloaded to a folder and printed. The reflections were maintained on the first two authors' hard-drives, on password-protected computers. The printed copies were coded and the originals maintained. Each of the reflections was read and reread by the first two authors. Braun and Clarke referred to this process as "familiarizing yourself with your data" (p. 87). The first two authors used an old fashioned method, for according to Ryan and Bernard (2003), "looking for themes in written material typically involves pawing through texts and marking them up with different colored pens" (p. 88).

During the next phase of analysis, the first two authors extracted key statements from each of our coauthor's self-reflections. These key statements formed the beginning codes for the data. The first two authors then sorted and labeled these key statements. The first two authors met several times throughout this process to discuss the codes. The key statements were then analysed and coded in a table. This followed Braun and Clarke's second phase "generating initial codes" (p. 87). The first two authors examined the reflections for repetitions, for similarities and differences, and metaphors and analogies (Ryan & Bernard, 2003).

The next phase was "searching for themes" (Braun & Clarke, 2006, p. 87). During this stage the first two authors examined the key statements and started the process of searching for commonalities across the reflections. All of the coauthors examined the reflections for repetition. Then the first two authors sent the key statements (without codes) and the initial themes to the coauthors through an email attachment requesting their input or as Braun and Clarke stated "reviewing themes." This provided the opportunity to examine the data and to have alternative themes generated by the coauthors.

One of the coauthors responded and suggested that she felt the themes generated seemed appropriate to her and to carry on. With minor feedback from the coauthors, the first two authors finalized the themes and provided names for the themes based in the words of the coauthor's self-reflections, a process referred to as "defining and naming themes" (Braun & Clarke, 2006, p. 87). The coauthors followed the overall process for each of the four questions, and the themes that emerged from the data are addressed in this chapter.

The themes provided were derived from the four guiding questions posed to the coauthors. Most of the authors (with the exception of the second author) responded to the questions making the analysis related to each of the four questions fairly straightforward. The process for the second author, who wrote the reflection without regard for the four questions, was somewhat different. The first author reviewed the second author's reflection and coded the reflection into each of the four questions, then she met with the second author to review her initial coding. The first two authors reviewed the transcript statement by statement. A discussion ensued to determine which question was the best fit, with the second author having the final say. Some of the statements remained under the original questions and many were moved to different questions based on the second author's interpretation of the meaning. The authors also engaged in a process of poetic inquiry (Butler-Kisber, 2017), arranging key words from the reflections in the creation of found poetry. This

Table 6.1

Guiding Questions and Themes

Question	Theme
What pushed you or motivated you to keep going in your academic career?	Theme 1 *"Being tenured was my dream"*
What did you gain or lose along the way (in your academic career)?	Theme 2 *"I think I have "gained confidence"*
	Theme 3 *"I've achieved tenure but it comes at a cost"*
What challenges have you encountered since you wrote you last narrative in relationship to remaining in an academic career?	Theme 4 *"It's like 'tax season'"*
What supports did you receive within your academic career that helped you?	Theme 5 *"Friday night dinners (and support)"*

poetic interpretation was a shared process that followed an in-depth examination of each theme.

Results

"Voice": A Poetic Exploration of the Journey Through Tenure

> Acknowledged
> And accomplished
> by our knowledge and competence
>
> Privileged
> And passionate
> in our position and our work
>
> Stimulated
> And challenged
> By colleagues and students
> conversations feed our minds and souls
>
> Tenure-track and tenured
> Provides confidence
> Security and relief
>
> We have a purpose
>
> Challenged
> And conflicted by our expectations
> of ourselves and others
>
> Our guilt shows
> Pressured by ourselves
> Motivation ebbs

Theme 1—"Being Tenured Was My Dream"
Most of the six coauthors discussed motivating factors for staying within an academic work environment and provided a variety of perspectives including positive, negative, and some ambivalence. Some of the key statements that were extracted highlighted security, passion, purposefulness, pleasure, flexibility, and the ability to choose what to work on—whether that be creative work or research on topics of interest.

One coauthor noted she was motivated to stay within an academic work environment for the security it provided: "I was motivated to continue in my academic career and gain tenure to keep my employment." Others spoke of their sense of purpose in an academic environment: "I now have a more refined sense of myself as a scholar, what I hope to achieve, and what I have to do to reach those goals. I enjoy this life of teaching, reading, writing, and research, and there is a sense of purposefulness in it for me." Individuals spoke about their passion to pursue research collaborations on topics of interest or engage in creative endeavours and being able to share this knowledge with others: "I'm motivated by the people I'm privileged to work with, the creative endeavours I'm able to explore, refine and develop... the privilege of voice." Others spoke of the privilege of voice, and how their sense of advocacy and personal responsibility pushed them to take on new service endeavours: "After all, doesn't it feel good to be acknowledged as an expert in your field, and why wouldn't you want to 'help out' by serving as the keynote at a conference for educators?" Coauthors acknowledged that the flexible work environment kept them in academia: "I've gained a degree of flexibility. I can work from anywhere. I can work anytime (does not have to be 9–5). That is both a godsend and a problem because I feel like I am always on call." Upon achieving tenure, one individual expressed she was better at setting boundaries, allowing time to further extend her research agenda: "Once I received tenure, it was such a relief to be able to say "no" and only take on work I wanted to do... I wouldn't have spent the time on "creative" writing during my tenure-track years – this is the luxury of tenure."

"Somehow We Would Move Off the Treadmill"

Statements from coauthors' self-reflections highlighted the high cost of being in an academic work environment. Coauthors discussed the hectic work pace, with one individual noting that despite her prior assumptions, the pursuit of work-life balance remained elusive: "Everyone seemed to believe that once tenure was achieved there would be more time, that somehow we would move off the 'treadmill' and live in a more balanced life." Another individual echoed these statements stating, "Tenure is not what I expected. I had anticipated feeling free, having more free time, and being more in control of what I take on. NOPE!" One coauthor compared the academic work environment to a "pie-eating contest, in which the only reward is more pie." This individual noted, "They [non-academic friends] question why I place myself on the academic rat race, knowing full well that others will be interested in devoting more time and energy to their publication ranking, leaving me to try to run faster or feel at a continual loss." Several individuals questioned whether the choice to remain in an academic environment was worth the costs that are required to achieve tenure.

"Wondering If I Was Doing the Right Thing"

Several coauthors expressed a degree of ambivalence or uncertainty with respect to their place within the academic environment, with one individual noting, "I'm not sure that I would say I'm motivated in my academic career really." Some of the key phrases that were extracted from the self-reflections suggested that many of us have a degree of uncertainty about maintaining an academic career, and a sense of competing responsibilities. One coauthor noted, "I've achieved tenure but it's come at a cost. . . I navigated the murky waters of academia always wondering if I was 'doing the right thing' in regards to time devoted to writing amidst the webs of competing responsibilities." In responding to what motivated her to keep going in her academic career, one coauthor responded, "At this point I can't be certain. It could be that I've already invested the energy in achieving tenure, but I would say that maintaining a position at a university comes with multiple sacrifices." The concept of loss or sacrifice was portrayed in many of the reflections. Many of the coauthors relocated themselves and their families in pursuit of academic careers, and this added pressure to the pursuit of obtaining tenure: "I'd moved from the other side of the country in the second half of my career, therefore I felt after making such a big move that I couldn't have it not work out." Personal narratives conveyed that coauthors were "intensely focused on getting tenure," and upon achieving tenure, despite heavy workloads, student success motivated coauthors to remain in academia. "What motivates me? Well, I think when I saw my students walking across the stage! There was such a sense of accomplishment. But hidden within the accomplishment is a lack of understanding of all the balls that I juggle." She continued to note that students may not understand faculty workloads, and this may lead to "some resentment on my part." However, supporting student success and seeing their success in educational contexts motivated coauthors to remain in academia.

Theme 2—"I Think I Have Gained Confidence"
Several coauthors expressed that having tenure allowed them to speak out, and to be involved in institutional decisions with a degree of confidence and security. One individual commented that, "I'm more willing to speak out at Faculty Council . . . and I'm more focused on what I want to do than on what I 'should' do." Another coauthor noted, "I don't believe I would have been able to be in conflict without the benefit of tenure, but being tenured means I have been in the same position for a period of time and with that comes the politics of being in a university environment."

"Friends Who Encourage Me"
All of the self-reflections highlighted the importance of relationships with other faculty and staff within the university environment. In addressing the importance of relationships and collegial support, one coauthor felt, "The supports I've received are too vast to name—from colleagues and co-workers, my spouse, our children, friends and acquaintances." Another noted

> I am blessed to have a strong network of people who contribute to me developing my academic writing skills. These include colleagues in the faculty writing group, co-authors who bring much through sharing their skills, mentors who talk to me about my latest writing projects, and friends who encourage me to write more often.

Coauthors addressed the value of "colleagues who generously give of their time to answer my many questions and guide me in the workings of academic life." The key phrases extracted from the self-reports included words such as coauthors, mentors, generosity, people giving of their time, helping with writing and methodologies.

"Gained Access to Creative and Artistic Endeavours"
In addressing what they had gained in their pursuit of academic careers, one coauthor stated, "I've gained access to creative and artistic endeavours that had long been hidden in dormant parts of my being," while another noted that "I've gained new experiences, opportunities to work with folks that I'd never imagined." Upon progressing in their academic careers, most of the coauthors

discussed that they felt more in control of the projects and student supervision and what they decide to take on within the faculty. One individual noted she had gained "Autonomy to pursue topics that are of interest to me. Develop projects as I see fit and not necessarily someone else delegating the work." Coauthors expressed a degree of confidence and autonomy regarding their position with the Faculty of Education. One individual said, "In comparison to the unrelenting pressure to publish before I gained tenure, the last 2.5 years have been less stressful." Another echoed these sentiments saying, "I have cut back on student supervision so I feel like this is manageable now. I've decided to only take on one doctoral student at a time but the pressure is enormous to take on more."

Theme 3—"I've Achieved Tenure But it Comes at a Cost"
In addressing the pursuit of tenure, each of the coauthors discussed loss of time with family, friends, and their partners, along with the loss of time for themselves to pursue leisure, relaxation, and exercise. In describing the cost of the pursuit of tenure, one coauthor noted, "This career keeps me separated from my family. My children, husband, and parents all struggle with my absence. We can manage because they recognize the need on which my work is based and they value my contribution to it." Other coauthors were able to relocate with their families, but their absence continued to be felt. The statement of one individual rang true with others: "I've worked most weekends so I have not been able to go to the ocean. Take hikes with my partner, spend time at the ocean (it's minutes away from my house), it's taken for granted [because I am busy]."

"While My Friends and Family Remained"
Four of the six coauthors discussed moving themselves and their families to pursue their careers in the academy. One noted, "I moved my whole family to Newfoundland to pursue this career. My partner and I gave up a stable jobs so I could pursue this career, so not achieving tenure would have been extremely difficult for us." Coauthors discussed the loss of place they felt as they moved themselves and their families to an island on the east coast of Canada to take up their positions within an academic environment. They acknowledged the impact this transition had on themselves and their

families. One individual acknowledged that "Literature demonstrates that the transition into academia is generally a very isolating experience, as it is associated with a loss of collegial workplace ties and tenuous connections within the university environment provide far less support."

"But I Am Left Feeling Emotionless"

One of the coauthors discussed the loss of a marriage, along with the loss of potential children, while at the same time watching her young sister and brother expand their families. This individual noted that, "I became an assistant professor as a newlywed and will be promoted to associate as a 35-year old divorcee, who continues to wonder what the cards hold for me." She continued to note:

> I thought that when the dust had time to settle, and the heavy teaching responsibilities were behind me, that I would 'feel better' about achieving tenure or at least feel something. But I am left feeling emotionless, in fact, quite alarmingly, I wonder if I 'did the right thing.'

"I've Lost a Clear Career Path"

Two of the coauthors discussed loss of their professional identity. Interestingly, these two coauthors were both psychologists in their previous careers, where they had clear professional identities and expertise in health and school psychology. One noted:

> I've lost time, I've lost a clear career path, and I've lost further advancement as a practitioner. While I've kept up with my skill as a psychologist, this is in addition to the requirement for tenure, and in my case has predominately been "off the side of my desk."

The other lamented:

> When I worked as a psychologist (in my prior life) I felt skilled and respected. I was sought out for my knowledge and skills especially around children and children with mental health problems or illnesses. In short, I knew my way around this content area, not so much in the academic environment. I feel like I've lost skills that I no longer have to use.

Theme 4—"It's Like 'Tax Season'"
Key statements derived from the self-reflection question addressing challenges associated with remaining in an academic career focused on work-life balance, health, austerity, and the challenge to do more. One coauthor noted:

> I have tried to explain that teaching three courses online, amidst other work responsibilities, is like 'tax season.' But unfortunately, I am only fooling myself, for we both acknowledge that tax season seems to be every day, and I acknowledge that it is followed by the equally exciting 'conference season,' and the frantic paced start to the new year or 'scholarship applications / grant writing season.'

Connected to work-life balance, the coauthors focused on the guilt associated with the loss of time for family, friends, and relationships. They also focused on the guilt surrounding taking time for family, relationships, partners, exercise, and pets. One individual expressed that "I'm challenged to make it home for supper three nights a week, and to attend to my both of my children's academic needs for advocacy in the current education system." This sense of guilt was pervasive, as another coauthor felt that, "There is guilt associated with time when I don't get to walk our dog. I purchased him shortly after achieving tenure believing I would have the time to be involved with him. This has not been true."

"Challenged by the Scarcity"
While not uncommon in other geographical contexts, challenges that were raised included the province's budget reduction and financial support for our university. The impact of scarcity was reflected in the narratives, with one coauthor identifying that

> I'm challenged by the scarcity of the university at present, the ways we are consistently and persistently asked to do more, be more, provide more, with less. It reminds me of my visceral reaction to the 'lean in' notion. . . essentially the message is, you're not good enough as you are, so just 'lean in' a little and then everyone will see how worthy you are.

Others echoed these sentiments saying, "I thought I would feel more secure in my job after tenure, but the university is in financial difficulty so that insecurity is still around." Talks of austerity budgets lingered in hallways, as one individual felt

> Hallway conversations with colleagues have been laced with the heaviness of meeting conversations surrounding austerity budgets and implications for resources and staffing plans. While conversations with graduate students provide splashes of humour, there is always discernment in regards to how one can respond, given the complex power dynamics.

"Jealous of the Time and Energy Devoted to Academic Work"

Three of the coauthors discussed balancing their own workload and the needs of their students (including student's financial and mental health issues) as both enjoyable and challenging. One felt:

> My competency levels were soon put into question as I learned to navigate the development of online teaching shells and working with graduate students with complex mental health needs. Every experience seemed so new to me and so utterly different from what I was trained to do when I was in graduate school.

Reflections addressed the challenges associated with work-life balance. One individual asked herself:

> I wonder if others feel as I feel, a significant obligation to place students above my own work, including housework. This past week, I spent three days working on examining one of my student's thesis. Why? Because the student wants to go on vacation without have her thesis looming over her head.

Family members expressed resentment towards the amount of time taken away from family time and reallocated towards catching up on work. One narrative epitomized this sentiment, with a coauthor commenting:

> I soon came to realize that while academic merits may appeal to my grandmother, they are less appealing to significant others, who did not choose to marry the academy, and do not see me as a martyr for graduate students; but are rather suspicious and jealous of the time and energy devoted to academic work.

"I Would Not be Able to Work at This Pace for Much Longer"
Reflections addressed concerns surrounding maintaining an unsustainable pace of work. One coauthor perceived that "There were many times when I felt that health-wise I would not be able to work at this pace for much longer." Another felt that "I'm challenged by how exhausted I feel; how I work to resist guilt for going to spinning class (bike) four times a week, at 6 a.m., in an attempt at health, wellness and balance." Upon achieving tenure, coauthors strove to regain balance in their lives. One individual commented that "I'm very conscious of my health now and I'm trying very hard to be productive and healthy." While another lamented that "The summer after I got tenure I attended to my various health issues. I started gym and generally felt much healthier, but I find that when deadlines are due, I sacrifice all of that."

"Which of the Many Routes Now Open to Me, Do I Want to Take?"
Self-reflections highlighted that "Achieving tenure and taking a full sabbatical carry their own challenges." Coauthors reflected on the challenges associated with numerous ongoing research opportunities and responsibilities. One individual was optimistic stating, "I'm going on sabbatical shortly so hopefully this will change. Perhaps I can develop new habits and come back a more balanced person." Another fretted that competing graduate student requests impacted her ability to pursue individual writing goals and, because of this, "I'm riddled with anxiety, it's six months into my sabbatical and I have not accomplished what I had hoped to accomplish."

Theme 5—"Friday Night Dinners"
Coauthors addressed the supports helping them with their academic careers, and their narratives addressed the importance of relationships, mentorship, and working with co-authors in the writing group, and on joint projects. Narratives spoke to the importance of mentorship and close relationships with colleagues: "I can say 'I'm not coping' and know that I'll be heard, supported, and provided with some practical advice on how to move forward" and "We're able to laugh at some of the absurd aspects of the job which helps enormously."

In reflecting on the narratives, coauthors agreed that "As well as the supports to my academic career provided by family and individual friends, the single largest support for several years has been the Faculty of Education Writing Group." One individual noted that "We have the most fabulous writing group and without a doubt that has been the single-most positive contributing factor." Another shared that "I really doubt that I would have survived without the writing group. They provide release from the pressure cooker because we can talk openly and honestly and because we don't compete with each other." While the Writing Group has undergone many changes, and interest has increased and waned, in elaborating on the support provided by the Writing Group, one coauthor noted:

> The writing group has been a primary source of support, initially because it introduced me quickly to peers in a collaborative fashion. The relationships formed by being a part of this group branched out into Friday night dinners, and offers for childcare, to invitations to submit articles, forwards of publication calls from colleagues as my work came to their mind, suggestions for methods, offers to read a particular article I may be struggling with, support for taking a risk in a faculty meetings when sharing my ideas, collective advocacy, a forum for flushing out the politics of academe and the options for engagement, resistance, compliance, etc. In no short order these relationships have been my lifeline, the reason I stay and the motivation to carry on when I'm challenged.

Narratives addressed the benefits of contributing to group projects, as "Being able to work with colleagues in a supportive and extremely productive way makes the job so much more enjoyable." One individual felt "Learning from each other in the context of joint projects gave me insights into what colleagues in other areas of education value... I feel it assisted me to keep my eye on the larger picture." Narratives highlighted writing partnerships that developed out of the writing groups, which were described as "so much fun and extremely productive." Coauthors agreed that "This feeling of connection is so important." One succinctly stated what the others also identified: "The joint publishing has helped my CV and the socializing and support have provided a bright spot in my week." This individual continued:

> I feel extremely lucky to work in the Faculty of Education and truly enjoy coming to work... Although I do feel a huge release of pressure post-tenure, there continues to be huge pressure.

So, in a way, things have stayed the same—just shifted slightly. I'm not sure if these pressures are coming from me and my own expectations or whether they come from the job itself. I know I'm doing all I can to keep this job manageable but not succeeding at this at all.

Discussion

Mid-career faculty have been described as the keystone of the academic enterprise as they form a bridge between faculty generations by mentoring new colleagues and assuming leadership duties as their senior colleagues move toward retirement (Baldwin & Chang, 2006). Mid-career faculty have also been described as key players as their institutions adapt in a time of continuous change as they can be either allies or stubborn opponents as their institutions adjust to change (Baldwin & Chang, 2006). However, limited guidance and supports are provided to individuals in mid-career (Baldwin, Lunceford, & Vanderlinden, 2005). Recent scholarship on the early years of the faculty career has addressed orientation programs, mentoring, pre-tenure sabbaticals, and parental leave policies, as tools to ease the transition to academic life and enhance the performance of early-career faculty. However, there is no comparable empirical basis for policies and programs to support faculty in the middle of their academic career, leaving arguably the largest and most important component of the academic profession ignored both by scholars and policymakers (Baldwin, Lunceford, & Vanderlinden, 2005).

Self-determination theory (Deci & Ryan, 2012) views autonomy as the central factor in self-determination, taking priority over other psychological needs of relatedness and competence. Skewes and colleagues (2017) examined ways in which university faculty sought self-determination in the promotion and tenure process, as the promotion and tenure process occurs within a context that inherently limits autonomy, providing a unique opportunity to examine experiences of relatedness and competence when autonomy is constrained. Findings showed that men reported experiencing self-determination via informational competence whereas women approached self-determination through relational competence. These findings were supported by the current study, as individual narratives highlighted the benefits of relational support on the journey towards tenure. Creating a level playing field for faculty navigating the promotion and tenure process requires being attuned to different paths to self-determination, fostering relationships between faculty, and clarifying policies and procedures (Skewes et al., 2017).

Scholars have offered numerous approaches and best practices for mentoring faculty, many of which have provided valuable insight into the complex nature of the mentoring process. On average, young professors who receive mentorship have a more positive view on their work environment, manage their research more actively, and perform better in terms of acquired grants (Weijden, Belder, Arensbergen, & Besselaar, 2015). These findings indicate that it is important for universities to actively organize mentorship programs. Non-intrusive mentoring practices can help foster and sustain motivation (Lechuga, 2014), but more research is needed to shed light on how disciplinary cultures influence mentoring.

References

Badenhorst, C., Penney, S., Pickett, S., Joy, R., Hesson, J., Young, G., McLeod, H., Vaandering, D., & Li, X. (2013). Writing relationships: Collaboration in a faculty writing group. *All Ireland Journal of Teaching and Learning in Higher Education, 5*(1), 1001–1026. http://ojs.aishe.org/index.php/aishe-j/article/view/100/152

Baldwin, R. G., & Chang, D. A. (2006). Reinforcing our 'keystone' faculty: Strategies to support faculty in the middle years of academic life. *Liberal Education, 92*(4), 28–35.

Baldwin, R. G., Lunceford, C. J., & Vanderlinden, K. E. (2005). Faculty in the middle years: Illuminating an overlooked phase of academic life. *Review of Higher Education, 29*(1), 97–118.

Braun, V., & Clarke, V. (2006). Using thematic analysis in psychology. *Qualitative Research in Psychology, 3*, 77–101. doi:10.1191/1478088706qp063oa

Butler-Kisber, L. (2017). *Lynn Butler-Kisber defines poetic inquiry* [Streaming video]. Retrieved from SAGE Research Methods.

Chang, H., Ngunjiri, F., & Hernandez, K. C. (2012). *Collaborative autoethnography*. Available from https://ebookcentral-proquest-com.qe2a-proxy.mun.ca

Deci, E. L., & Ryan, R. M. (2000). The 'what' and 'why' of goal pursuits: Human needs and the self-determination of behavior. *Psychological Inquiry, 11*(4), 227–268.

Deci, E. L., & Ryan, R. M. (2012). Motivation, personality, and development within embedded social contexts: An overview of self-determination theory. In R. M. Ryan (Ed.), *The Oxford Handbook of Human Motivation* (pp. 85–107). Oxford, UK: Oxford University Press. http://dx.doi.org/10.1093/oxfordhb/9780195399820.013.0006

Gagne, M. & Deci, E. L. (2005). Self-determination theory and work motivation. *Journal of Organizational Behavior, 26,* 331–362.

Lechuga, V. M. (2014). A motivation perspective on faculty mentoring: The notion of 'non-intrusive' mentoring practices in science and engineering. *Higher Education: The International Journal of Higher Education and Educational Planning, 68*(6), 909–926. doi: 10.1007/s10734-014-9751-z

Penney, S., Young, G., Badenhorst, C., Goodnough, K., Hesson, J., Joy, R., McLeod, H., Pelech, S., Pickett, S., & Stordy, M. (2015). Faculty writing groups: A support for women balancing family and career on the academic tightrope. *Canadian Journal of Higher Education, 45*(4), 457–479. http://journals.sfu.ca/cjhe/index.php/cjhe/article/view/184396/pdf_52

Ryan, G. W., & Bernard, H. R. (2003). Techniques to identify themes. *Field Methods, 15*(1), 85–109. doi: 10.1177/1525822X02239569

Ryan, R. M., & Deci, E. L. (2000). Self-determination and the facilitation of intrinsic motivation, social development and well-being. *American Psychologist, 55*(1), 68–78. doi:10.1037/0003-066x.55.1.68

Ryan, R. M., & Deci, E. L. (2008). From ego-depletion to vitality: Theory and findings concerning the facilitation of energy available to the self. *Social and Personality Psychology Compass, 2,* 702–717. doi: 10.1111/j.1751-9004.2008.00098.x

Ryan, R. M. (1982). Control and information in the intrapersonal sphere: An extension of cognitive evaluation theory. *Journal of Personality and Social Psychology, 43,* 450–461.

Skewes, M. C., Shanahan, E. A., Smith, J. L., Honea, J. C., Belou, R., Rushing, S., Intemann, K., & Handley, I. M. (2017). Absent autonomy: Relational competence and gendered paths to faculty self-determination in the promotion and tenure process. *Journal of Diversity in Higher Education.* doi: http://dx.doi.org/10.1037/dhe0000064

Trepanier, S. G., Forest, J., Fernet, C., & Austin, S. (2015). On the psychological and motivational processes linking job characteristics to employee functioning: Insights from self-determination theory. *Work & Stress, 29*(3) 286–305. http://dx.doi.org/10.1080/02678373.2015.1074957

Vansteenkiste, M., Lens, W., & Deci, E. L. (2006). Intrinsic versus extrinsic goal contents in self-determination theory: Another look at the quality of academic motivation. *Educational Psychologist, 41*(1), 19–31.

Weijden, I., Belder, R., Arensbergen, P., & Besselaar, P. (2015). How do young tenured professors benefit from a mentor? Effects on management, motivation and performance. *Higher Education, 69*(2), 275–287. doi: 10.1007/s10734-014-9774-5

Williams, G. C., Halvari, H., Niemiec, C. P., Oystein, S., Olafsen, A. H. & Westbye, C. (2014). Managerial support for basic psychological needs, somatic symptom burden and workplace correlates: A self-determination theory perspective. *Work & Stress, 28*(4), 404–419. http://dx.doi.org?10.1080/02678373.2014.971920

Young, G., Kilborn, M., Arnold, C., Azam, S., Badenhorst, C., Godfrey, J. R., Goodnough, K., Lewis, L., Li, X., McLeod, H., Moore, S., Penney, S., & Pickett, S. (2017, July). Women reflect on being well in academia: Challenges and supports. Manuscript published in special issue on Fostering Health and Well-being in Education, in *Learning Landscapes*, 10(2), 335–351. http://www.learninglandscapes.ca/index.php/learnland/article/view/819

Young, G., Penney, S., Anderson, J., Badenhorst, C., Dawe, N., Goodnough, K., Hesson, J., Joy, R., Li, X., McLeod, H., Moore, S., Pelech, S., Pickett, S., Stordy, M., & Vaandering, G. (2017). Women reflect on their journeys toward becoming academics: Challenges and supports. In T. Sibbald & V. Handford (Eds.). *The academic gateway: Understanding the journey to tenure* (pp. 79–92). Ottawa, ON: University of Ottawa Press. https://www.jstor.org/stable/j.ctt1qft27z

SECTION 3

Reflecting on the Tenure Journey: The Systemic and Institutional

The authors in this section focus on systemic change with attention to the institutional perspective. They are in positions where they appear to see a need for institutional change. However, as readers it is necessary to consider what change they are looking for and whether it entails a change to address a specific issue or implies a need for a broad-based transformation of the academy.

A closer look at these authors, who are from both small and large institutions, reveals that many have held leadership positions, either within the academy or in other organizations. **Frank Deer** is a Canada Research Chair in Indigenous Education. **Onowa McIvor** and **Trish Rosborough** are both scholars working with Indigenous communities while called on to provide representation within their faculty and institution. Many people are engaged in efforts to reimage and refocus in a much more inclusive and comprehensive manner, but these scholars are leading change such as addressing the calls to action in the Truth and Reconciliation Commission of Canada report within their institutions. Among other roles, **Lloyd Kornelsen**, a high school teacher for many years, has worked at the provincial and national levels as a curriculum developer and a corporate consultant. Before working as a secondary school teacher, **Tim Sibbald** worked for a consulting firm writing industry reports. He is also a past-president of the Ontario Association for Mathematics Education. **Victoria (Tory) Handford,** a former school principal with six years' experience in provincial government organizations, currently coordinates a large graduate program and serves as the first vice-president for the Canadian Association for Studies in Educational Administration.

Another curiosity about the authors in this section is the timeliness of their response to the deadline. Without exception these authors submitted early and turned our editorial comments around quickly! We think their timeliness is driven by a desire to promote change within the institution. With the exception of Greg Ogilvie, there is a possibility their responsiveness to deadlines is informed by leadership experience, or it may simply reflect skill at multi-tasking. We leave it to the reader to consider whether there is any substantive reason explaining the observation.

This section begins with **Lloyd Kornelsen**'s chapter, "For academy's sake: A former practitioner settles in academe." Lloyd divides his chapter into three clear sections, competence, relatedness and autonomy, and strikes something of a balance between personal and institutional views, and individual and systemic views. His chapter speaks directly to the personal struggle navigating the differing views.

Onawa McIvor and Trish Rosborough's chapter, "Indigenous scholarship: What really matters and to whom?," presents some of the challenges that Indigenous scholars may face that other scholars do not. The perspective is both personal and systemic in perspective, but the systemic aspect is focused around specific aspects of the university and the academy.

Tim Sibbald's chapter, "Establishing balance to define a new normal," is situated in a balanced position, with personal and institutional views articulated and individual and systemic views included. His chapter is a direct exploration of his experiences interpreted through the lens of the theoretical model.

Frank Deer's chapter, "The mid-career Indigenous scholar: Navigating the institutional confluence of indigeneity and academia in post-tenure-track," addresses the need for a deeper institutional understanding of Indigenous cultures if they are to be effectively represented within the academy.

Victoria Handford's chapter, "An incredible journey: Passing through the gateway," looks at change as fundamentally a systemic consideration, that change is life, and it may not be either controllable or actually matter that much. Since the chapter suggests change is omnipresent it approaches it with a stance of *"On y va"* *("Let's go!")* and suggests moving forward with that spirit.

Greg Ogilvie's chapter, "Potholes and possibilities: Pursuing academic interests in the era of the corporate university," considers the larger political or philosophical place of the university. This speaks to a distinction between the academy as an ideal of independent thought and autonomy and the university as an instrument of societal influence that can be influenced through funding and other pragmatic mechanisms.

CHAPTER 7

For Academy's Sake: A Former Practitioner Settles in Academe

Lloyd Kornelsen

Four years into my appointment, one year following tenure-promotion, what has changed about my work and about me? In the first few years, working in a faculty of education, I was often angry and uncertain—angry that the knowledge (and rhetoric) of teaching and learning acquired from working as a high school teacher for 24 years was not considered on par with the knowledge (and rhetoric) produced by education academe, and uncertain that my claims for scholarly recognition, based on those 24 years, were actually worthy of academic merit.

Today I am more confident. I have a more nuanced appreciation for the symbiotic relationship between field and academy—respecting what each, field and academy, necessarily and uniquely, offer the other. I still believe that knowledge and the epistemological orientation derived from teaching practice is undervalued and poorly understood in much of education academe. This awareness motivates and informs much of my work today. However, I teach, administrate, and write with greater confidence, humility, and less deference (dare I say more joy?). Realizing that that I am not alone, I am freer to pursue the issues that most enliven my sense of academic purpose.

The Oxford English Dictionary (2018) variously defines "settle" as becoming calmer or quieter; falling or come down onto a surface; turning one's attention to or applying oneself.

A sense of "settled-ness" describes me, post tenure-promotion. I have a calmer and more conscious where-with-all to know and recognize the communities of which I am a member, a more grounded understanding of my scholarly competencies, and a clearer sense of direction in pursuing the issues that most animate my academic concerns. There is no one event which led to this way of seeing or thinking; although I see a continuous thread from 1986, the year I started teaching. However, tenure-promotion signaled acceptance and recognition from the academy in ways that opened up horizons, and expanded ways of being, knowing and researching (searching again).

In this chapter I examine the impact of tenure-promotion with a focus on how it has affected my work and identity within a 27-year career in education. Concerns I had when I first started working in a faculty of education—the absence of a teacher's voice in scholarly circles—continue to ground my role and animate much of my work. However, the sense of settled-ness that has come with tenure-promotion has freed me to pursue the issue with greater confidence, clearer direction, and academic purpose.

The upcoming discussion is organized around the themes of competence, relatedness, and autonomy. It is in these three areas that my sense of settled-ness is most clearly revealed and evidently known.

Competence

Prior to my appointment in 2013, I had worked in the field of education for 27 years, primarily as a high school social studies teacher. But whilst teaching high school, I also worked as a national corporate consultant and educator, participated in provincial K–12 and university curricula development projects, and developed several study-abroad programs (high school and university). Many people considered me competent: I was respected, invited, and even fêted (in 2003 several colleagues nominated me for a national teaching award.). But I never felt entirely competent—often times I felt like a faker and an imposter, thinking that perhaps I was not really up to the task. Whether as a consequence or not, after a time, I was diagnosed with clinical depression. The depression has lurked ever since, on the fringes of consciousness, compelling me to more honestly live what I know to be true (i.e., live with integrity). When I applied for the tenure-track assistant professorship in a faculty of education in 2013, one of the few things I knew for certain about teaching was that *it takes a lifetime to learn to become a true teacher*, "not because it takes years to master poses and techniques" (Walck, 1997, p. 478), but because, as Walck says, it is an un-ending process of building a frame of mind: one of freedom and openness to all that can and will happen—and to move beyond the boundaries of the classroom to write the text of students' lives.

The new academic position, while marking a culmination of many years in the field of education, provided opportunities to continue my work in different directions and through different means. I now had time to think, write, create, and collaborate in ways unimagined before (indeed it was requisite for the position). My past work life informed and contextualized my new work. I was in a place that allowed for and encouraged the pursuit of lifelong academic interests, where I believed that previous work necessarily and meaningfully mattered. I felt fortunate and grateful.

However, almost immediately, I began getting messages from the academy that the work I did before July 2013, the date of my appointment, would not be considered scholarly for promotion purposes, most simply it seemed because it did not fit the criteria of service/teaching/research in post-Ph.D. and post-secondary contexts. University friends and colleagues alike warned of university Tenure and Promotion Committees (TPCs) who, appealing to academic tradition and precedent, would not recognize pre-appointment work.

The consequence of the forewarning unfolded in two ways. First, even though my 27 years in the field was characterized by intense bouts of self-doubt, I knew in my heart that I had learned from that experience, most principally, learning to be and continuing to become a teacher (Kornelsen, 2006). I had come to "know" this through the "heat and thick" of classroom teaching and I believed that knowledge (including doubts, questions, and understandings) derived from practice was crucial. It could advance research and teaching in faculties of education and was therefore worthy of scholarly recognition. To that end, from appointment to tenure-promotion application, I revisited past work experience, recalling seminal events and paradigm-shifting experiences, looking to understand how they might inform matters of scholarly concern.

Second, it exacerbated my self-doubt, and my sense of being an imposter and outsider: Did I really know enough to profess?

How could I make claims for scholarly recognition when I felt my university colleagues were much more conversant in their fields than I was in mine? I spent years managing classrooms, grading assignments, and attending parent-teacher nights. In those years my colleagues were reading scholarly literature, writing SSHRC grant applications, and defending research claims. How could I possibly think of myself as an equal, when in many ways I was not? These insecurities animated much of my reading and writing as I pursued language and epistemologies that could help bridge teaching experience with education research and philosophy. Thinking about how professional experience might inform academic concerns meant needing to better understand the perspectives and requirements of academe. It also entailed explaining one to the other, the field to the academy and the academy to the field, and serving as an interpreter for each. I felt responsible to school teachers and university professors (Kornelsen, 2017).

It was for this reason, believing that pre-appointment work was worthy of scholarly recognition that I applied for tenure-promotion two years following my initial appointment, four years before I was required to so do. My promotion-tenure application package which included the requisite body of peer-reviewed publications, conference presentations, and evidence of teaching success, rested on the notion that teaching and research insights that school teachers derive from experience is indispensable to research and teaching undertakings in faculties of education. My application material was organized as a seamless whole—school and university experience—with most of the supporting artifacts pre-dating my initial appointment.

Ten months later I received a letter from the president of the university granting me tenure-promotion. I felt an indescribable sense of relief and satisfaction when I read "Congratulations on this important recognition of your achievements, and best wishes for continued success as member of our Faculty." This recognition from the academy, from my scholarly peers, represented a vindication of my contribution to education academe. Whether or not the assessors of the application—the TPC, external university examiners, Dean of Education, Vice-President Academic, University President—took into consideration the argument that pre-appointment work merits scholarly consideration, I did not know. It does not matter. Since most of my work (publications, conference presentations, and teaching), post-appointment, was devoted to making the argument, at the very least, the assessors must have believed that engagement with the question was worthy of merit—therewith signaling confidence in my scholarly abilities.

In part, because of my peers' formal acceptance into the academy, tenure-promotion has led to a growing sense of self-assuredness: in the value of the questions I ask and the claims I stake. I feel less the outsider and more a member of a community, one with unique knowledge producing and propagating responsibilities. I still doubt my scholarly competence at times, but take solace in the tentative nature of the knowledge for which I seek. In the words of Bullough (2014), "Education ... is messy, and highly context sensitive, with outcomes uncertain and proof of accomplishment always indirect and usually long delayed" (p. 189). Since I now have the time and presence of mind to reflect on past experience and to consider various philosophical and theoretical interpretations of that experience, I am bringing greater clarity and richness to the pedagogical meaning of that experience. In short, I have become more conversant in my field.

Relatedness

I am less angry now, post-tenure. First, I have discovered that on the question of teacher voice and scholarship, I am not alone and the issue is not a new one. According to Loughran (2004) and Aulls and Shore (2008), messages from education academe that knowledge acquired through teaching experience as not being on par with the knowledge more typically produced in and by the academy is not surprising. Their studies in the early 2000s found that teaching practice is often given low status or little account in teacher education literature and scholarship. This disparateness, in what counts for knowledge production in education, has been noted in academic literature since the 1980s. At the time, numbers of young scholars in teacher education committed to teacher education improvement, often times themselves former school teachers, struggled to negotiate tenure and promotion (Bullough & Pinnegar, 2001). They saw the value of teacher self-study for teacher education and recognized the limits to knowledge and modes of research typically and traditionally rewarded by the academy. Teachers' professional knowledge, they argued, should be conceived as experiential knowledge (or as reflection-in-action as Donald Shon (1987) called it). It is knowledge derived from decisions made and actions taken in the "heat and thick of teaching" (Bullough & Pinnegar, 2001, p. 9), making it fully on par with university-produced knowledge. Since then, I have recognized that numerous others have taken up the cause, from critical theorists, to phenomenologists, to narrative inquirers (among others: Tetsuo Aoki, Jean Clandinin, Michael Connelly, Joe Kincheloe, and Max Van Manen), articulating the critical and singularly efficacious value of teacher insights and understandings. It has been reassuring and affirming to know that scholars from an array of philosophical perspectives have undertaken an issue critical to my professional identity and academic work.

Second, since the beginning of my appointment I have been working on teacher-led research with university colleagues and school teachers from across the province. As described previously (Kornelsen, 2017), a month after my appointment, a colleague and I were asked by the Manitoba Education Research Network (MERN) (with funding support from Manitoba School Improvement Program (MSIP) and Manitoba Education (ME)) to organize and facilitate a series of meetings with a select group of teachers who were teaching the new grade 12 social studies course. The objective was for teachers to share their impressions and observations on teaching the new course, with a view to writing papers on insights derived from their classroom experience and to make recommendations for curriculum implementation. In March of that year participants presented their papers at a MERN-sponsored forum at the University of Manitoba attended by school administrators, university professors, education students, curriculum consultants, and government policy-makers. Their papers were subsequently published in a special edition of the MERN journal, with one of the papers reprinted in the *Canadian Journal of Teacher Research*, and the project was lauded in a national education publication (*Education Canada*). According to responses from project participants, forum attendees, and representatives of supporting organizations (ME, University of Manitoba, University of Winnipeg, MSIP, MERN, Manitoba Teachers Society (MTS)), the Grade Twelve Inquiry Project (GTIP) could serve as a model for building a community of support, one that honours teachers and trusts their ability to produce and disseminate research (Kornelsen, 2016).

The GTIP research venture, with an expanded mandate to include any K–12 social studies course, has operated every year since 2013 (see Kornelsen, 2016). In the autumn of 2017 one of the participants was invited to speak about the GTIP program at the annual

International Conference on Education Research and Innovation (ICERI) conference in Spain. Since 2013, more teacher/faculty research groups, modelled after GTIP and under the direction of MERN, have been set up by others: Math Teachers Inquiry Project (MTIP), Science Teachers Inquiry Project (STIP), and Brandon Social Studies Teachers Inquiry Project (BTIP). These 'TIPS' represent classroom teachers getting together to talk about their most vexing challenges and distressing questions derived from living and working in classrooms, (re)searching ways of responding—thereby informing the sorts of questions we ask in faculties of education.

Because of the work and support of MERN (and its financial supporters from education institutions across the province), the gap between university researchers and school teachers is being bridged. It is affirming to see teachers' experiential knowledge being recognized and supported by the university research community. Through working with GTIP, I have heard of other teacher research collectives doing similar work in different parts of Canada. I feel less alone, as though I am part of a university-school community now and realize that I may have been mistaken about the nature of the anti-field resistance I felt from peers in 2013.

But now this:

Autonomy

A few weeks ago, on a Wednesday night, I was looking out over the lights of downtown Mexico City from the 28th floor of the hotel where I was attending an international conference on comparative international education. I marveled at what my life had become: a tenured associate professor, well paid, someone who is expected and trusted to attend an international conference to meet with colleagues from all over the world to discuss, review, and consider recent research findings. I felt at once elevated and relieved: elevated in having moved "beyond" and "above," relieved that I was no longer there—"there," as in being a high school teacher. Typically, on a Wednesday night in spring, I would be grading term projects and thinking about teaching the next morning, planning how I might, yet one more time, engage my 16-year-olds in discussions about their world. I thought of my friends who were high school teachers still, working that night, and in that moment, I felt like a fraud—a complicit participant in a pretentiousness called academic conferencing. Over 1000 participants were attending this conference on education—presenting papers, displaying posters, facilitating workshops, participating in roundtable discussions, and all the other usual conference activities. We expected our offerings would inform public policy, curriculum development, teaching practice, and education research and philosophy. Yet, at this meeting of educationists, I had not met one practicing K-12 teacher (not unlike other conferences on education I have attended), neither as presenter nor as audience member, persons with indispensable knowledge and critical insight into the issues about which we had gathered to talk, those persons who could temper, nuance, enrich, and challenge our findings. Where were those people; and why were they not here?

It was hard to believe that we, conference participants and organizers, valued or respected their voice. I felt much like I had the previous month when the Government of Manitoba eliminated funding for MERN. Presumably, the decision-makers had neither seen nor understood the value of teacher-generated research, since they did not provide a rationale for the cut, nor announce any replacement research program. I felt sad, angry, and guilty—sad that a perspective critical to our understanding of education was absented, angry at the willful silencing of unspoken voices, and guilty over my privilege and complicity (in this case, padding my annual activity report with peer-reviewed international conference presentations and having these activities paid from the same provincial education funds that had just eliminating a teacher-based research program).

In years past I would have reacted with hopeless and self-righteous indignation, railing against a culture that has little regard for the work and wisdom of school teachers. Not now. Now, I have a forum with which to propagate ideas, whether on campus or beyond. Furthermore, I have the freedom and resources to seek out enriching and dissenting perspectives (thanks to tenure-promotion) and a community of colleagues with whom to debate, commiserate, and organize more teacher research collectives. In short, I feel a sense of agency and responsibility—and a growing awareness of academic autonomy.

In the first few years following the appointment, I had myriad offers and requests from the university community related to administering, researching, teaching, and presenting. All of the choices and offerings were enticing, but I felt directionless; the options seemed equally weighted and important. I said yes to almost everything, not knowing whether I could say no without hurting academic prospects and not knowing exactly what was important for tenure-promotion. In retrospect, the tenure and promotion experience showed that there are many ways of being a scholar; there is freedom in pursuing academic ways of being and working. While I embraced my new-found freedom in the first several years, reveling in the time I had to think about those issues that had animated my work for years, I often felt a little lost and uncertain. Now, post tenure-promotion, I no longer feel obliged to say yes for fear of losing *academic face*, no longer feel pressure to publish solely for tenure-promotion's sake, or compelled to win research grants to quantify my scholarly value. I feel freer to pursue academic projects more aligned with my research interests, intellectual curiosities, and academic sensibilities, which I perceive as living and working with greater integrity. To wit, the past year I have returned to the question: Given my work and life pre-academy, what inimitabilities do I bring to scholarship and what responsibilities are owed the academy, including my peers who have signaled their trust through tenure-promotion? In 2013, a few months after appointment, I wrote this:

> In the past several years many of my social studies teaching friends and colleagues, master teachers, have begun to retire, taking with them rich insight into educating youth for democratic and global citizenship—insight and wisdom that comes from years of seeking to engage students in dialogue about themselves and their world. Hannah Arendt referred to it as "unveiling work" and Parker Palmer called it "teaching with presence." Teaching is hard work and emotionally exhausting. It seems a waste, teachers leaving in midlife—a lifetime of energy expended and inimitable understandings acquired—taking their educating acumen and teaching wisdom with them. My new academic position frees me to seek out social studies teachers and ask them about their teaching insights and understandings: investigate what their interpretations unveil, their reflections reveal, and their stories illumine, and examine how their offerings broaden our horizons of teaching practice and social studies education. (Kornelsen, 2014, p. 12)

In the past four years, I have been interpreting past teaching experience through education theory and philosophy, and seeing education theory and philosophy through a practitioner's eyes. With what I have learned, it is clear this undertaking—asking teachers for their teaching insights—is critical to questions we ask in faculties of education. Tenure-promotion has contributed to the confidence to know this and the academic and community support needed to actualize it. But most importantly, it has provided the autonomy to circle back to the beginning, to experience, to ask others of theirs and together make academic sense. This is what I bring; this is my academic responsibility. To that end, I am currently working with colleagues to help establish a teacher research collective based at the University of Winnipeg, as a partial replacement of MERN. I am also in discussions with a national publishing house about publishing an edited volume/book to be written by classroom teachers about global citizenship education.

Conclusion

I have worked in the field of education since 1986, most recently as a member in a faculty of education. Since being granted tenure-promotion, I have been experiencing a sense of settled-ness. It is an affecting feeling and cognitive bearing that is new, something not experienced since my appointment in 2013, nor for that matter, at any other time in my career. I have a more confident understanding of my scholarly competence, one grounded in years of teaching high school social studies and enriched and informed by exposure to education academe; a more conscious where-with-all to know and participate in the communities of which I am a member; and an emboldened sense of professional autonomy. Even though this bearing of settled-ness may have something to with the arc of my career—I am now at a time and in a place where reflection on past work matters—tenure-promotion has provided a sense of security and confidence in pursuing those signals these reflections reveal.

References

Aulls, M. W. & Shore B. M. (2008). The experienced teacher and action research. In M. W. Aulls, & B. M. Shore (Eds.), *Inquiry in education*. vol. 1, (pp. 69–81). New York, NY: Routledge.

Bullough, R.V. & Pinnegar, S. (2001). Guidelines for quality in autobiographical forms of self-study research. *Educational Researcher, 30*(3), 13–21.

Bullough, R. V. (2014). Toward reconstructing the narrative of teacher education: A rhetorical analysis of preparing teachers. *Journal of Teacher Education, 65*(3), 185–194.

Kornelsen, L. (2006). Teaching with presence. In P. Cranton (Ed.), *Authenticity in teaching*, (pp. 73–82). San Francisco, CA: Jossey-Bass.

Kornelsen, L. (2014). Global educators in the classroom. *Education Manitoba 12*(2), 9

Kornelsen, L. (2016). Researching practice: Findings from teacher inquiry into the implementation of the global issues course in Manitoba. *Manitoba Education Research Network Occasional Paper Series,* Teacher Research, Number 1, http://www.mern.ca/occ/ted-1.pdf

Kornelsen, L. (2017). For academy's sake: A former practitioner's search for scholarly relevance. In T. M. Sibbald & V. Handford (Eds.), *The academic gateway: Understanding the journey to tenure* (pp. 159–178). Ottawa, ON: University of Ottawa Press.

Loughran, J. J. (2004). A history and context of self-study of teaching and teacher education. In J. J. Loughran, M. L. Hamilton, V. K. Laboskey, & T. Russel (Eds.), *International handbook of self-study of teaching and teacher education practices*, vol. 1. (pp. 7–39.).

'settle' (2018). In *Oxford English dictionary.* Retrieved from http://www.oed.com

Schon, D. A. (1987). *Educating the reflective teacher.* San Francisco, CA: Jossey-Bass.

Walck, C. L. (1997). A teaching life. *Journal of Management Education, 21*(4), 473–482.

CHAPTER 8

Indigenous Scholarship: What Really Matters and to Whom?

Onowa McIvor and Trish Rosborough

Academic success is still measured at an institutional level in terms of how many peer-reviewed articles are available in the library for other academics who know how to access them and not in terms of developing relationships, building community knowledge, effecting positive changes in communities, or the policies that affect those communities. (Styres, Zinga, Bennett, & Bomberry, 2010, p. 640)

(*Image used with permission, from* www.tomgauld.com)

Through writing in personal narrative voice, two Indigenous professors reflect on the processes they experienced with tenure and promotion at a mainstream western Canadian university. They share their different but interconnected stories of maneuvering the tenure and promotion system. One moment being experienced in mainstream universities, it seems, is the acceptance of more broadly defined measures of scholarship and, yet, the implementation of these updated and more inclusive policies remains questionable. Are these changes an indication of the recognition of community-based and community-engaged research and scholarship as legitimate by senior colleagues, or are they a pleasant afterthought once the "real measurements" are met? Throughout this chapter, we share our tenure stories and reflect on the questions: What really matters, and to whom?

Indigenous scholars are growing in number, and allyship[1] is more prevalent as colleagues with social justice agendas gain traction via widespread reconciliation efforts. This is resulting in greater influence of Indigenous-grounded knowledge and ways-of-being are becoming embedded into the fabric of universities' policies and practices. Our chapter focuses on the ways in which Indigenous thought and ways of knowing have influenced policy at one mainstream western Canadian university, and highlight the further work that remains. Advocating for a balance between the various audiences and benefactors of Indigenous scholars' work is an important part of this chapter's contribution as we continue to fight for voice and space to matter in a system that historically did not value the aspirations and intellectual contributions of Indigenous peoples (inside or outside the academy). We explore tangible examples of the tension between the importance of accessibility of knowledge and the value system held by many tenure committee members. These tensions often exist in the debate between open-access journals (or book chapters) versus top-tier journals, as well as plain-language reporting targeted towards community members and the general public (also often not valued by tenure committees as it is deemed not peer reviewed). Further to this, the authors explore the importance of working with community research partners and hearing their expectations for meaningful (to them) scholarship and research contributions. Throughout this chapter, the authors reflect on the importance of living the "four R's" of Indigenous-engaged research—Respect, Relevance, Reciprocity, and Responsibility (Kirkness & Barnhardt, 1991) as foundational to this work of bridging the space between mainstream tenure and promotion expectations, and the incorporation of significant Indigenous contributions into academic policies and processes.

Inspiration of Method

This chapter follows the rich tradition of autoethnography largely credited to Carolyn Ellis (2009) who is often considered the grandmother of this method. However, storytelling in various forms is also an ancient Indigenous practice. Onowa merged these two worlds by applying autoethnography in her doctoral work, blending it with Indigenous methodologies, as explained in McIvor (2010, 2012). In her dissertation, Trish used a narrative inquiry approach that included the use of personal stories and journals (Rosborough, 2012).

Several other Indigenous scholars have also demonstrated the effective use of storytelling or narrative methods in their writing, helping to create new ways of sharing knowledge. While Absolon (2011), Archibald (2008), and Wilson (2008) are pioneering and foundational exemplars, subsequent Indigenous scholars also provided inspiring, influential and innovative examples of Indigenous storying scholarship toward the formation of this chapter. Angela Jaime (2008) interweaves the stories of two Indigenous professors describing their struggles and active resistance in the academy. Antone and Dawson (2014) discuss Antone's Indigenous worldview approach to the tenure and promotion process through the use of first personal dialogue and narratives. Anishnaabe-kwe activist and organiser Wanda Nanibush (2014) demonstrates, through an interview-style journal article with Rebecca Belmore, a Winnipeg-based Anishnaabe artist, about her journey to becoming both an artist and an *Idle No More* organizer, that Indigenous-style conversational interviewing can stand alone as enough. Kahnawà:ke scholar and political activist Taiaiake Alfred also demonstrates an Indigenous style of conversational interviewing in his two books, *Peace, Power and Righteousness* (1999) and *Wasáse* (2005). Most recently, Rosborough and Rorick (2017) "apply an Indigenous relational approach" (p. 12) to their work by introducing one another and by using a narrative approach to explore their research and explain their process of knowledge making. Our chapter was inspired by all of these examples and follows both the Indigenous storytelling tradition and scholarly exemplars provided by these authors.

Storying

In accordance with this interweaving story method, we begin with a rich discussion about our shared and different experiences of traversing the tenure and promotion process. As the chapter progresses, we discuss what changed for us once we were informed of our successful navigation through this process. We agreed on four themes, formed around sets of questions that we hoped to answer in order to focus our ideas. The first theme is the tenure process itself of going up and going through. We reflected on the process of preparing our tenure packages, the advice we received, our understanding of the process and access to information, and the challenges of aptly describing community-engaged work. The second theme is developed through a set of stories focuses on what changed for us (after success in the tenure process). It gave us the opportunity to reflect on the early days of being newly tenured, on what (if anything) changed for us post-tenure in how we did our work, and on what surprises awaited. The third theme focuses retrospectively on what we believe needs to change (about the tenure process). Specifically, what would foster greater success for future Indigenous academics coming through the tenure process? The last theme is developed as a set of stories focuses on the concept of reciprocity. As an important Indigenous value that was nearly impossible to include in our processes of building our tenure packages, we felt it was important to write about those who had helped us along the way. We reflect on the support we received from other Indigenous scholars and, in the sense written about by Kirkness and Barnhardt (1991), the responsibility we now carry to reciprocate by supporting other Indigenous scholars.

Our Stories

The Tenure Process

Trish
There are some life events, like planning a wedding or a memorial for a loved one, that require learning on the job. Since we go through these experiences rarely, or maybe even just once, we do not have much prior knowledge to depend on. Going through the tenure and promotion process reminds me of these other once-in-a-lifetime events. Much about the tenure-track process was a mystery to me. Certainly an important part of achieving tenure is about the work

one does: the research, publications, grants, service contributions, teaching, course experience surveys, and other role expectations. What was not so certain for me was how much would be enough, what would count, and how to articulate that work by building a tenure and promotion package. Getting information about the criteria, the process, and the preparation of my package was a much bigger job than I imagined. Like with other infrequent life events, in the months following the achievement of tenure and promotion to associate professor, I have reflections about what I know now that I wished I knew then.

If I were at the start of this journey now, I would turn my attention to learning about the tenure and promotion process much sooner than I did. I jumped into my appointment as assistant professor without much thought about what it meant to be on a tenure-track. My excitement and focus for my new role was the opportunity to work with communities in something I cared deeply about: Indigenous Language Revitalization (ILR). I learned quickly that teaching takes as much time as one will give it and that devoting time to engagement with our community partners is essential to building better outcomes in ILR. Of course, I was aware that 40 percent of my role was meant to be dedicated to research, and yet, the research and writing took a back seat in the first two years of my appointment. Despite the good advice I had been given to publish some articles from my dissertation while the content was current, I did not make the time to write. At that two-year mark, I recorded a dream in my journal: "I am with some scholars in an informal setting. Wanting to give me some feedback and support, they ask me to read something from my notebook. I flip back and forth through the pages but I can't find anything. I haven't written a thing." If I had been more thoughtful about the expectations for publications, I would have better paced my writing. Instead, in the third and fourth years of my appointment, I had to push hard with my writing and research agenda to fill the gaps.

Had I paid attention to tenure-track expectations earlier on, I would have also been more deliberate about documenting and collecting the evidence of my work. In the months before building my package, I reviewed the department, faculty, and collective agreement documents, and developed a table that brought together the processes and criteria for tenure and promotion. This exercise took some of the mystery out of the expectations. The table gave me confidence that I had met the criteria and helped me to be thoughtful about the evidence I needed to provide. It was also in these months before preparing my materials that Onowa, who had applied for tenure the previous year, shared her package with me and provided some guidance about the process. I have such gratitude for her generosity and mentorship. Through our discussions, it became clear that I would have to tell the story of my work to make it possible for the committee to understand the ways in which I had met the criteria.

Onowa

I am not like most of the jury of my peers, by whom I was ultimately to be judged, because the essence of who I am comes from a different time and place. My homeland (far away in Treaty 5 and 6—overlapping Northern Manitoba and Saskatchewan) runs thick in my veins and I find commonality and comfort in the similarities of worldview with the peoples whose land I visit, those of the SENĆOŦEN and Lkwungen speaking peoples on southern Vancouver Island. My first responsibility is to the community, both my own and those I serve, to listen to what they need and to use the privilege I have gained by being inside an institution we were not allowed into until the 1960s, to create spaces and programs that serve our people. Following this, the privilege of being a scholar is to participate in knowledge creation. Most of this also happens alongside and within Indigenous community, those who are also sophisticated research partners. I define partnership as "each contributing their talents, knowledge, and curiosities to the research agenda and process." The ultimate judgment, however, of your trajectory and worth as a scholar, is offered by a group of individuals who largely hold a different worldview, who make the rules of what counts and then unilaterally decide if you are worthy of staying in the academy. This creates a massive challenge for Indigenous scholars, in capturing, presenting, and promoting our work for what it is, as well as honouring our collective experiences within communities in a highly individualized process, while fearing that it will be either misunderstood or dismissed as unimportant—or both. Most Indigenous scholars hold a collective worldview, where their work comes from a place of service and responsibility to community and society. In addition, many of us have cultural teachings that are in direct conflict with the promotional nature of putting together a tenure and promotion package that is focused on the individual and our achievements. Oftentimes in community, this kind of accolade can actually only be offered by others and not by the person themselves. Also, in a traditional Indigenous education, there is much more emphasis on the journey itself and less on the outcome. The experiences of learning, absorbing, learning some more, integrating that learning, and then being held up by your community when they feel you are ready for a certain job, task, or duty is a high honour, but not one that you would normally self-nominate. Antone and Dawson (2014) explain that for Indigenous faculty members, "almost every aspect of the process may be alienating and contrary to [our] belief systems" (p. 287).

Antone and Dawson (2014) also describe the difficulty of including an understanding of who we are as Indigenous people, a cultural foundation foreign to that of our tenure packages. One of the stories and experiences Antone and Dawson share is about a smudge ceremony held at the institution (with great difficulty). For me, the early realization of not being able to smudge my office when I first moved in, an important spiritual practice for me whenever occupying new space, was the first clash I felt that I could not bring or be my whole self in to this place. (The reason it was not permitted is because of the smoke produced from the burning of traditional medicines, even with the door closed and windows open, and the few minutes that it lasts. What is an essential and sacred cleansing ritual for me is considered a health hazard for others.)[2]

Because I was concerned the committee may not be able to fully judge my portfolio due to lack of similarity in scholarly background, early in my tenure process I requested that an Indigenous scholar to be added to my committee. From some of the comments in the letter I received, I believe it helped the committee better understand me as a scholar. The committee's comments were often complimentary and fair; however, the cultural bias towards certain kinds of representation of scholarship remained apparent (despite the perhaps lone voice). One example of this was the committee members disapproving of the kinds of Indigenous-focused and open access journals I had chosen to publish in. They recommended a more direct aim towards leading journals at the next stage of my career. In addition, the committee commented in my letter on the quantity of co-authored publications I had (an important approach in relational knowledge building and mentorship work) but more troubling was that "the committee ha[d] some concerns about how [my] scholarship was presented." They had complimented how well put together my package was, leaving me to interpret the meaning of this statement. I was surprised at how strongly I reacted to this comment. While I was alone in my office, the atmosphere in which we receive most feedback, I felt my face flush at the reminders of the European-worldview privilege in our workplace and how difficult it is to stay true to who we are as Indigenous peoples, and to meet the expectations of our families, extended families, and communities, while also adhering to the rules and expectations of this other world.

What Has Changed?

Trish

Konelīne—beautiful place—is how the Tahltan describe their territory. It's true. This place in northern British Columbia, with its rivers, mountains, forests, and wildlife, is breathtaking. It is also a long ways from Victoria. When I teach in the Tahltan territory, it takes me two days to get there and two days to return to Victoria. I make arrangements for childcare, schedule other work to accommodate my time away, and pack my suitcase with textbooks, program materials, and teaching supplies. I fly from Victoria to Terrace, Smithers, or Whitehorse. From any of these airports, it is a seven to eight hour drive through the mountains into Dease Lake where the program in Indigenous language revitalization is being delivered in partnership with the Tahltan Central Government. If our schedules align, I make the drive into Dease Lake with another instructor or the program coordinator. Before heading out, we pick up groceries for the program and sometimes prescriptions or other items that students and Elders have requested.

Teaching in this community-based program is a privilege and a rich experience. The courses I teach are well supported by the community and fluent Elder speakers. The local college provides us with classroom space, the school with access to a kitchen for hands on language learning, and community members generously host us in their camps for on-the-land immersion. The students actively give back to community through course projects and their work in the immersion preschools and school classes. To teach and learn well in this setting requires that we engage with community and with this beautiful place beyond the course syllabus. Community engaged work is not unique to me or to our language program; it is an approach that is common, and is perhaps required for Indigenous scholars. In conversation with Tahltan academic Edōsdi/Judy Thompson, we spoke about how community work plays a vital role in who we are as Indigenous scholars. Speaking about the importance of language, Patricia Louie, one of the Tahltan students, has said, "I think our language and our culture is what makes us unique, it's what makes each nation strong. And if we don't have it, then we're just, we're just like everybody else" (Edōsdi/Thompson & Bourquin, 2016). Edōsdi and I recognized how this might parallel the importance of community-engaged work for Indigenous scholars, without it, we're just like everybody else.

When I think about achieving tenure and promotion and what it means for the communities I work with, I see an interesting dynamic. In the same way that community-engaged scholarship may be invisible to tenure and promotion committees, the tenure and promotion process is often invisible to the community members. The way in which my publications, research, service, and teaching are evaluated by the institution is mostly unknown to the communities. Indeed with my own community, when my university commitments keep me away from language and cultural activities, I worry that I might be viewed as too busy—not a characteristic I value.

I had expected that putting some things on hold, particularly learning and teaching my own language, Kwak'wala, was a temporary situation while I focused on meeting tenure and promotion criteria. Here I am, five months after the effective date of my tenure and promotion to associate professor, and I am still struggling to keep up with my workload. Because I applied a year early, I have yet to take a study leave since beginning my tenure-track position. Perhaps my upcoming study leave will be when I feel a break from the focused push to meet expectations, and I will be able to get back to Kwak'wala research, learning, and teaching.

While achievement of tenure might not be very visible to our community partners, it does bring stability to the work. Having tenured faculty strengthens the capacity of the unit to respond to community direction. I see this appointment not only as an acknowledgement of my work, but more importantly, as an acknowledgement and investment in the work of language revitalization. As a new and developing area of scholarship, each new tenured faculty member in language revitalization builds the profile of this field.

Onowa
As I was both late—having been in a faculty position for eight years when I put my package forward for consideration—and early—because only four of those years were in a tenure-track position, like

Trish—it has meant a one-year delay in waiting for my (post-tenure) study leave to begin. This made what was already a one-year long process (from the time you put in your package until your official transition to being officially tenured) into a two-year process of waiting for the reward of a one-year study leave. Sometimes people asked me, "How does it feel now to finally have tenure and promotion behind you?" When I could answer honestly, I would often say, "anti-climactic." Eight years is a long time in a position, and even one year is a long time for a promotion process (while the standard for our profession); then waiting an additional year for study leave to begin was harder still. I do not regret going up early (year four rather than year five), as I was ready to test the system and myself, but it would have been more celebratory to have been able to go on study leave at the end of the tenure process, as is normally intended. A (slight) caution about going up early.

A few surprises awaited me in the post-tenure year. One is that I falsely believed I would have more time for research, reading, and writing because that big focus and push for tenure was out of the way. Instead, you start doing all the others things you have been putting off—it is remarkable how quickly the rest of your life piles up and gets disordered when you neglect every other thing. I cleared out crammed closets in my home that would barely close, and reconnected with my children. I started to purge duplicated and volatile electronic filing systems that made no sense. I cleared out years of old paper files and dusted! I agreed to supervise more graduate students, as my tenure letter had suggested—a lot more. I agreed to a new leadership role in my department, as Graduate Advisor, plus more committees and service commitments. Why, I ask myself now? I was already doing a lot along the road to tenure! But suddenly you think, "well, now I can do more!" and it seems that everyone else has this expectation too. What I wasn't doing more of was reading, writing, and completing my research project(s). In fact, it seemed, I was doing less scholarly work than before I went up for tenure because during that time you are so driven. This seemed a ridiculous trend, and it is one I have not yet figured out how to fully reverse—even now on study leave.

I guess what people expect you to say when they ask you about tenure is that you are relieved to have job security, and of course that it true. But it is deeper than that, as it is also peer recognition that you *are* a real scholar and that your work is worthy of a lifelong investment and deeper exploration. That is an amazing feeling, and an honour that I will be forever grateful to have received. Perhaps more importantly though, as Trish has stated, it brings stability and greater strength to our field of study, as we recognize that there are still too few Indigenous scholars taking on the role of professor, particularly in the discipline of Indigenous language revitalization.

What Needs to Change?

Trish

I went through the tenure process when Indigenous education was a small unit within another department. Having recently become our own department, we are in an excellent position to develop policies and procedures that will serve Indigenous scholars well. However, all departments have the opportunity to consider how their appointment, tenure, and promotion policies and practices can be changed to advance the success of Indigenous scholars within the academy. Giving consideration to the ways of knowing and being that are important to Indigenous scholarship and to the needs of the communities we work with can build a stronger and more responsive academy.

Considering what counts for tenure decisions is a good place to begin. I agree that publications are an important part of my scholarship and are one way that I meet the responsibility to the field of ILR. I appreciated that the year I went up for tenure and promotion, the department had established a clear minimum number of expected publications. I thought I had gone beyond that threshold, but I was surprised to learn that some of the writing I judged to have the most impact was not counted toward this total. Two of these pieces were not counted because they were chapters in a book that was not considered to be peer-reviewed. However, the co-editors of this book are highly regarded senior Indigenous scholars in Canada and I believed that contributing to this text was meaningful in the field of Indigenous education. I had enough other publications, however, so there was not much of a consequence to having these chapters disallowed. What concerns me is that the way impact is perceived and measured by tenure and promotion committees may discourage and limit tenure-track scholars from publishing in the places that have the most impact in the intended community of practice.

I would also like to see some changes to how community-engaged scholarship is weighted for tenure and promotion decisions.

The department I was in has policy that describes community-engaged scholarship, which is a good start. This policy invited me to tell the story of my community-engaged work that might otherwise be invisible to the committee. However, it is not clear to me what has shifted in the other expectations to make up for the time that I dedicate to community-engagement activities. It would be helpful to tenure-track faculty and committees to have clear criteria about how community work is considered as part of a scholarly agenda. My hope is that as a new department, we will find ways to value community work by shifting, rather than adding to, expectations.

Onowa

Indigenous scholars are almost always the minority within larger departments or other configurations, and so both the policies and committee make-up then are based on a foreign worldview. Having more Indigenous-led and Indigenous-centred academic units, where we can be the majority and not the minority, and develop our own policies and standards from our own worldviews, is necessary for significant change. Further to this, we need considerably more Indigenous leadership within academic institutions at the decanal, vice-president, and presidential levels. Encouraging and promoting more Indigenous leadership in vital positions throughout the academy would do more than many of the current recruitment and retention processes we have today, encouraging and supporting Indigenous success in the academy at all levels, including moving through the professorial ranks.

Increasingly, academic units are adding community-based and Indigenous scholarship policies to their tenure and promotion processes. This was not in place when I went through, but it was the following year (when Trish went through). However, we both wondered how seriously it was taken up by the committee, since even in the policy, it was a fourth category. We got the sense it was taken as a nice-to-have and bonus material, but only if you fully met the standard criteria first in the three traditional sections (i.e. not genuinely integrated). It moved us to discuss our desire for future scholars to have a more meaningful experience with this policy and for committees to receive support for this shift to fully implement this kind of scholarship and its evidence as equal. We have since been so fortunate to be a part of creating our own Indigenous Education department and will have the opportunity to be a part of this kind of policy creation and implementation in a majority Indigenous environment.

Finally, in contemplating what needs to change, from what I learned in the process of going up for tenure and promotion and the reaction I had to my committee letter, I sincerely believe we have to let go of so much counting and find a way to view tenure portfolios more holistically (a view shared by Antone & Dawson, 2014). There are 36 numerical references in my five-page letter, not including grant dollar amounts or the years that I was involved in various initiatives. The 'counting' was about courses taught, number of sections, teaching scores, averages, anomalies, numbers of graduate students completed, defenses chaired, students withdrawn, summation of articles, book chapters and reports, presentations, keynotes, awards, number of grants, committees served, and reviews performed by category type. Summarized at the end of each section simply as "she has met the standard." Overall, I found this letter, which was essentially the committee's interpretation and summary of my life's work to this point, disheartening.

I often say to colleagues when discussing this, it seems to me that the tenure and promotion system has lost the plot. The questions I think we should be asking ourselves are: Is this person showing promise as a scholar? If a community-based scholar, are they engaging with community? Are they writing grants? Are they creating or co-creating knowledge and finding important ways to share that knowledge—to both broad audiences and academics? Is there a trajectory of creative, useful engagement, and does the future for this person look promising? Are they making a difference in the lives of students? Are they engaging in the life of the academy and community? If one can answer yes to most of these questions, then they are probably ready to be confirmed with tenure so they can keep doing their good work. I sincerely hope we can all find a way to regain focus and purpose with tenure and promotion processes and focus more holistically on each faculty member's contributions and trajectories in the future.

Reciprocity

Trish
I am grateful to the mentors and advocates who supported my tenure and promotion process. I am especially grateful for the fellowship of other Indigenous scholars. The institution can misunderstand my community work, the communities can be unaware of academic

requirements I have to meet, and while my family supports me in many ways, they have little knowledge of the complexities of the tenure-track professor role. It really is other Indigenous scholars who understand what it means to be an Indigenous scholar in the academy. My intention is to give back by offering support to others, both to individual scholars and to influence change from within the system. At this time, there are still too few Indigenous scholars to take up the roles in ILR in the academy. Supporting new scholars to pursue and be successful in tenure-track roles makes a contribution to the Indigenization of the academy, the strength of the ILR field, and expands my own circle of collaboration.

A very helpful gesture from others has been the invitation to collaborate in research and writing projects. I value collaborative approaches to scholarship and believe this aligns with Indigenous ways of knowing. Working together serves as a meaningful form of mentorship. Through collaborative relationships with experienced scholars I have learned much about research, writing, and publishing. Besides the opportunity to learn together, the commitment made to others when co-writing is a good motivator to get the work done. Since publications are an important criterion in the awarding of tenure, writing together can be especially supportive to new scholars.

I came into my academic journey aware of the importance of privileging the voices of Indigenous scholars in my writing, as well as acknowledging those who have influenced and made space for my scholarship. From my mentors, I have learned the value of including the work of new scholars in my writing. I am appreciative of others who reference my writing in their own publications and courses. We have the opportunity to hold each other up by how we access and share each other's work. Cherokee scholar Daniel Heath Justice advocates for ethical citation practices and reminds us of the importance of broadening the inclusion of diverse voices. Justice's hope for his own text is "meaningful, expansive, and transformative inclusivity" (2018, p. 242). Inclusion of Indigenous voice by referencing both established and new Indigenous scholars is an act of reciprocity that can make positive change for both individuals and the academy.

Onowa

This chapter would be incomplete without an acknowledgement of the many people who offered useful advice and encouragement throughout this tenure process, and really, over the eight years leading up to it. Some of these experiences were just one conversation, while others are multi-year enduring friendships and collegial partnerships, but all had a place in the journey. Besides some of the confusing administrative processes and contradictory advice I received early on in my career, the majority of colleagues were generous and kind. Many shared both their physical packages, stories of their journey, and meaningful encouragement. Without these people, this process would have been lonelier, more frustrating, and more uncomfortable. Together with my family and community, these people helped me to stand tall, and maintain the courage to represent myself the way I knew I needed to.

According to Kirkness and Barnhardt's (1991) principles of Indigenous scholarship the responsibility of reciprocity now falls to scholars like Trish and me to provide meaningful and beneficial mentorship to incoming and junior colleagues. I accept the responsibility to check in with people and offer myself to help in the ways I can—to decipher and interpret, advocate when necessary and appropriate, and be encouraging while people are finding their way. We all do this with our graduate students, but new and incoming faculty also need mentorship, supports, and guidance. I remember feeling the transition from doctoral completion to navigating the road to tenure as somewhat abrupt and without many indicators as to whether I was on the right path.

Styres et al. (2010) remind us that "currently, the representation of Aboriginal PhDs in academia is deficient" (p. 629). This is not only due to the barring of Indigenous people from universities until the 1960s and the substandard education received in residential and day schools, although these are important factors. There are contemporary factors for this modern-day phenomenon as well. As Indigenous authors in an edited volume by Mihesuah and Wilson (2004) have theorized, we must continue changing the academy. We cannot simply make room for Indigenous people anymore, but rather we must create leadership positions, autonomous and majority Indigenous spaces, genuine and true partnerships, and Indigenous-led and Indigenous-created policies to genuinely change the way academic business is done. Within universities, Indigenous people must see space to bring their worldview and cultural and spiritual lens with them into the buildings, classrooms, their research projects, their writing and other forms of their scholarship, as well as into leadership roles.

Conclusion

A senior administrator once told Onowa, after examining her curriculum vitae, which that person judged as being too service focused and therefore not scholarly enough, "I think you are ambivalent about being a scholar" (see McIvor, Rodríguez de France, & Rosborough, 2017). Yet, as Antone and Dawson affirm, "teaching, learning and research are often inseparable in community contexts" (2014, p. 299). Simply put, universities need to learn what is valued by Indigenous peoples and the communities they serve. Styres et al. (2010) remind us that the experience of "walking in two worlds" and "creating ethical space" for research

> is sacred, spiritual, engaging, ambiguous, and challenging. It will simultaneously bring us to our knees in humility and raise us up to new heights of understanding and awareness in creating collaborative knowledge systems no longer based on colonialist notions of domination, power, control, and usury, but rather on mutuality, egalitarianism, shared knowledge, and a new way of relating. (pp. 645–646)

While the experience Onowa had with a person in a power-over position unsettled her, it ultimately led her to rise up to new heights. Rather than change herself to better conform, it pushed her to articulate her Indigenous-led and focused scholarship in a way that she had to trust the committee would understand. While Trish did not share this experience, she learned from the experiences Onowa had—both by questioning if her contributions as well as her collaborative and community-focused efforts would be seen as scholarly (enough) and then used these warnings to form robust arguments for her scholarship to stand firmly on its own.

ekosi / he'am (that is It)

It is a tremendous privilege to be given the opportunity to tell our stories. It is our shared hope that our stories may be helpful to others going through this process, as well as for those supporting or leading processes like these. To that end, we have offered our advice on changes that could be made in departments and university policies to assist Indigenous scholars' further success in advancing through the academy. Some of these offerings are perhaps not necessarily specific to Indigenous scholars and may benefit others as well.

Antone and Dawson (2014, p. 307) encourage us to "live our responsibility"—the same responsibility we believe that Kirkness and Barnhardt (1991) promote. It is through writings, such as this chapter, that express Indigenous voices and methods of presenting as scholarly, along with (and of equal importance) the way we conduct ourselves each day with our students, with colleagues, and in community that we hope we have offered some new knowledge and encouragement to emerging Indigenous scholars—those to whom we are now responsible.

Endnotes

1   Defined as a "supportive association with another person or group, specifically, members of a marginalized of mistreated group to which one does not belong" (www.merriam-webster.com/dictionary/allyship). For further information, see http://www.guidetoallyship.com/
2   Years later, when the First People's House was built, they allowed for smudging in the building at any time, and we can now "notify" our Dean's office as well as Facilities Management and are allowed to smudge in our offices with 72 hours' notice.

References

Absolon, K. E. (2011). *Kaandossiwin: How we come to know*. Black Point, NS: Fernwood Publishing.

Alfred, T. (1999). *Peace, power and righteousness: An Indigenous manifesto*. Don Mills, ON: Oxford University Press.

Alfred, T. (2005). *Wasáse: Indigenous pathways of action and freedom*. Peterborough, ON: Broadview Press.

Antone, E., & Dawson, T. (2014). "But how do I put this dream catcher into my teaching dossier?" Learnings and teaching from one faculty member's tenure experience of documenting community-based teaching and learning. In C. Etmanski, B. L. Hall, & T. Dawson (Eds.), *Learning and teaching community-based research: Linking pedagogy to practice* (pp. 287–307). Toronto, ON: University of Toronto Press.

Archibald, J. A. (2008). *Indigenous storywork: Educating the heart, mind, body, and spirit*. Vancouver, BC: University of British Columbia Press.

Edōsdi/Thompson, J. C., Bourquin, M. (Producers), & Bourquin, M. (Director). (2016). *Dah Dẓāhge Nodeṣidē: We are speaking our language again*. [Motion picture]. Canada: Tahltan Central Government. Retrieved from https://vimeo.com/217095185

Ellis, C. (2009). *Revision: Autoethnographic reflections on life and work*. Walnut Creek, CA: Left Coast Press.

Jaime, A. (2008). Native women: Decolonization and transcendence of identity. *International Journal of Multicultural Education, 10*(2). https://doi.org/http://dx.doi.org/10.18251/ijme.v10i2.119

Justice, D. H. (2018). *Why Indigenous literatures matter*. Waterloo, ON: Wilfrid Laurier University Press.

Kirkness, V. & Barnhardt, R. (1991). First Nations and higher education: The four Rs- respect, relevance, reciprocity, responsibility. *Journal of American Indian Education, 30*(3), 1–15.

McIvor, O. (2010). I am my subject: Blending Indigenous research methodology and autoethnography through integrity-based, spirit-based research. *Canadian Journal of Native Education, 33*(1), 137–155. Retrieved from https://search-proquest-com.ezproxy.library.uvic.ca/docview/864885228?pq-origsite=summon&accountid=14846

McIvor, O. (2012). *îkakwiy nîhiyawiyân: I am learning [to be] Cree* (Doctoral dissertation, University of British Columbia, Vancouver, BC, Canada). Retrieved from https://open.library.ubc.ca/cIRcle/collections/ubctheses

McIvor, O., Rodríguez de France, M. D. C., & Rosborough, T. (2017). I think you are ambivalent: The realities of Indigenous scholarship in mainstream universities. In T. Sibbald & V. Handford (Eds.), *The academic gateway: Understanding the journey to tenure* (pp. 93–110). Ottawa, ON: University of Ottawa Press.

Mihesuah, D., & Wilson, A. C. (Eds.). (2004). *Indigenizing the academy: Transforming scholarship and empowering communities*. Lincoln, NE: University of Nebraska Press.

Nanibush, W. (2014). An interview with Rebecca Belmore. *Decolonization: Indigeneity, Education & Society, 3*(1), 213–217. Retrieved from https://jps.library.utoronto.ca/index.php/des/article/view/21311/17377

Rosborough, T. P. (2012). *Ḵangex̱tola sewn-on-top: Kwak'wala revitalization and being Indigenous* (Doctoral dissertation, University of British Columbia, Vancouver, BC, Canada). Retrieved from https://open.library.ubc.ca/cIRcle/collections/ubctheses

Rosborough, T. P., & Rorick, čuucqa L. (2017). Following in the footsteps of the wolf: Connecting scholarly minds to ancestors in Indigenous language revitalization. *AlterNative: An International Journal of Indigenous Peoples, 13*(1), 11–17. https://doi.org/10.1177/1177180116689031

Styres, S., Zinga, D., Bennett, S., & Bomberry, M. (2010). Walking in two worlds: Engaging the space between Indigenous community and academia. *Canadian Journal of Education, 33*(3), 617–648. https://doi.org/10.2307/canajeducrevucan.33.3.617

Wilson, S. (2008). *Research is ceremony: Indigenous research methods*. Black Point, NS: Fernwood Publishing.

CHAPTER 9

Establishing Balance to Define a New Normal

Timothy M. Sibbald

As I write the first draft of this chapter it is early fall. Back in the spring I heard I would receive tenure and a promotion as of July 1. That night my wife and I went out for a celebratory dinner and the next day I began thinking in earnest about life after the tenure decision. However, it was in the months ahead of that—between submitting the Academic Gateway (Sibbald & Handford, 2017a) and its being published—that Victoria and I developed a theoretical model of tenure-track experiences. The interpretation of my own experience through the lens of the model is the focus of this chapter. Specifically, I contrast the tenure-track years to the period after being granted tenure and promotion with the intention of understanding the transition associated with earning tenure.

The theoretical model draws on a grief model and self-determination theory. In my initial interpretation, which has been subject to change as this book develops (and I am writing this as a chapter author with few opportunities for revision, as opposed to exercising privilege as an editor with more frequent revisions), I envision the grief aspect as addressing losses associated with changing institutions, living conditions, and work-life balance. It is not grief in the sense of death, but does highlight diminished connection to one's circumstances prior to joining the academy. It is anticipated that this aspect will vary in relevancy according to circumstances. In some cases authors remained in the same city where the losses might be much less than those who moved long distances or uprooted after a long period of being established in one place. The other component is self-determination theory, which, for me, highlights the self-directed nature of programs of research and being in a rarefied situation with very few colleagues being positioned to impose on the choices I make. It is a theory I find powerful because autonomy and intrinsic motivation are primary attributes I have lived within the academy.

Theoretically this chapter considers the model of tenure-track (Sibbald & Handford, 2017b) and examines its veracity through the tenure-track years and the transition to tenured associate professor. The model uses self-determination theory (Deci, 1980; Deci & Ryan, 2000; Broeck, Ferris, Chang & Rosen, 2016; Ryan & Deci, 2000) augmented with a grief model (Sibbald & Handford, Submitted). The word "grief" is somewhat ill-suited and is better thought of as a model to address losses associated with moving to a higher education environment. Rather than focus on the semantics, in this chapter I focus on various components of the theoretical model and connect them to my own experiences.

Each major component of the theoretical model is identified as a heading and spoken about directly. Effort, agency, and commitment are addressed first as they are precursors to self-determination. Following this the components of self-determination are considered. Connections between the components are not explicitly addressed but are evident. The totality of action arising is evidence of self-determination and the connections arise because the outcome is achieved by having all of the components working in a coherent coordinated manner. Toward the end of the chapter I also consider whether the model achieves saturation—that is, are there relevant experiences that do not fit the model?

Demonstrated Effort

When I completed my Bachelor of Education and qualified to be a teacher there were very few teaching jobs available. The situation led to my being employed as an applied mathematician in a research company focused on remote sensing. The work entailed considerable computer programming but the times were quite fluid as new computer capabilities emerged every few years and different computer languages vied for market share. Over the decade I was in the private sector I worked with eight computer languages and three operating systems. This required ongoing learning and exploration of languages that, at the time, was a vibrant area of study and piqued my curiosity. The experience established a work ethic that continued for years after.

When the research diminished it was natural to migrate into teaching. The work ethic served me well for developing course materials and instructional approaches in the early years of my teaching career. As my teaching career developed, the school board provided opportunities for further training and I naturally took advantage. That approach led to attaining further teacher qualifications that were specific to instruction in the classroom.

When I began feeling comfortable with my expertise as a teacher, I began casting about for new ways to keep the learning going. I exhausted the obvious options and then decided to enroll in graduate studies. I have likened this to having a second job that allowed telework (Sibbald, 2017a). It was during that time that the fusion of roles became important. This was essentially *relatedness* as defined in SDT—the connection between different roles (teacher, graduate student, parent) informed one another. It was empowering to have theoretical discussions in graduate courses that could be acted on in my high school classroom during the day. It also corresponded to my own children aging and becoming more independent, so I had time to engage intellectually with the academy and colleagues.

What emerges when I look at the history of my own efforts is an ongoing pursuit of curiosity with a strong work ethic. The work ethic has been present as long as I can remember, but curiosity combined with relatedness has also been a significant form of intrinsic motivation. The combination was foundational to my move to higher education where "... professors may put effort in their teaching both because they enjoy it (i.e., intrinsic motivation) and because they see it as needed for tenure [(i.e. work ethic)]" (Broek et al., 2016, pp. 1197–1198).

Agency

The background of personal efforts demonstrates a historical tendency to pursue opportunities. The agency that came from those opportunities was because they were selected for relevance. Within the field of education, courses I have taught have been relevant to my role in one way or another. What I have found is that there is an element of attitude that informs the agency component. When I took leadership courses, it was not because I would become an administrator, but because of a fundamental belief that the education obtained from the courses would be useful in one way or another. I chose to perceive the teacher as an instructional leader of students. (This approach is not dissimilar to an interest in the teacher as researcher notion that came later in my graduate studies.)

It seems likely that my perception of education can be interpreted as agentic. I pursued courses believing I would find them relevant, as opposed to pursuing education because of some generalized aspiration for change. Though the education did facilitate changes, particular moving to higher education, it was not the reason for pursuing these opportunities. In a proverbial sense there is a difference between opening a door because you wish to go through it, and opening a door simply to learn how to open the door. The options on the other side of that door become clear, not that I was doing this to pursue them.

It is noteworthy that this view is consistent with Ivengar and Lepper (2002) suggesting agency could be culturally-based and that I might be an "American individualist" (p. 76). The view that one can pursue education because there will be some form of agency discovered by the student, whether that was the intended purpose of the course or otherwise, aligns with my experience.

An aspect of agency was not revealed during my tenure-track years relates to the observation that "faculty at many tenure-granting campuses also maintain much power and agency in determining expectations for performance" (Gardner & Veliz, 2014, p. 129). While I was willing to be agentic, and sought meaningful ways to engage learning from professional development, the same was not true of the tenure and promotion process. By virtue of it being a process I did not feel it was ethically appropriate to inquire about that process beyond asking general questions through appropriate channels. I spoke to colleagues in a general way and asked my dean, on occasion, for specific advice. In effect, I drew a line between pandering to the process and doing what I maintained was professionally responsible and appropriate.

Commitment

In Ontario teaching is a profession in the sense that it is self-regulated by teachers and has standards of practice and ethics. At the intersection of those standards and personal work ethic, I had a strong sense of professionalism within my teaching career. This includes being committed to developing pedagogically appropriate instructional practices and working with the curriculum to further the level of understanding of my students. This is what effective teachers do—they use their learning to help their students. I went further and committed to sharing my classroom learning. A presentation record developed along with a publication record. While this is not unique, very few K–12 teachers do both. This record over a decade in a high school includes 11 workshops and 13 practitioner publications including two that included students as coauthors.

The level of commitment continued into the higher education role. When I was hired as a tenure-track assistant professor for August 1st, I showed up at the university on August 1st ready to work, because that is what the contract said was my start date. I did not appreciate the flexibility that the role offered and simply assumed that I would be engaged in working full time on a daily basis from that day forward. This is an example of commitment through lack of awareness, but to this day I feel it is the sort of keel that one's work needs to stay on track.

Since arriving, I have come to appreciate the need to exercise the flexibility in work schedule to achieve desired results. In my first five years I routinely had out of town meetings on Saturdays. This was when committed teachers were available to meet without incurring undue expense or use of supply teachers. As a professor, the meetings were of value and I began considering how to work within the flexibility of my university hours.

Effort, agency, and commitment are precursors for self-determination, and they were demonstrated routinely through my professional practice, graduate studies, and other extra-professional activities such as running workshops and publishing. These features covered research and service and, along with part-time teaching in a faculty of education, account for how I earned a role in higher education contributing to the training of the next generation of teachers. As I entered the role in higher education it was with the same approach that had provided prior success. That approach made assumptions about routine working hours as a starting point and modified that practice slowly as the institutional norms became clarified. However, it was not simply a case of following institutional norms and entailed much more of a consideration of how I wished to balance my professionalism within the institutional norms.

In self-determination theory, three key components are competence, relatedness, and autonomy. Within the Sibbald and Handford (2017b; Submitted) framework, relatedness has additional features but I will address the features in this order because it reflects the order in which I gained control of them.

Competence

I recall riding on a large Ferris wheel at a fair and having cyclic feelings of admiring the view when I was at the top of the wheel, watching the crowd as I descended, debating the risks of injury if one potentially attempted to jump off as it moved through the lowest point, and then the exhilaration of climbing with an increased scope of sight. The tenure-track years had a similar feel. In the early days I made plans (admiring the view), learned to navigate new institutional norms (watching the crowd), recognized some of the challenges such as selection of journals and weighing up wait time with risk of rejection (risks of injury), and the exhilaration as tasks got completed and I considered the options for adding a new task (increasing scope of sight). But, just as the analogy suggests, this was cyclic within the academy.

As the tenure-track years unfolded I found more structure to the initial Ferris wheel model. In Sibbald (2017b) I spoke of distinguishing personal, professional, and technical roles. This was an early attempt to reconcile that the cyclic timing had begun to separate according to details within the role. The early years had a degree of coherence disrupted by strong emotional ups and downs but, when I wrote about three roles, there was already a separation of the overall role into aspects that had different timing profiles. This fits the tripartite model of tenure where teaching and service tend to dominate the fall and winter semesters, while research tends to dominate the summer and lower workload points of the fall and winter. Since I am primarily in a teacher preparation program, my students leave the faculty for several blocks of time when they are in K–12 schools; this affords an opportunity to focus on scholarship and research.

Competence is derived from many prior experiences. Work ethic is key, but also professional attitude, a strong knowledge of mathematics education, which is my primary area of focus, and ability to engage students and colleagues, all comprise competence. Broeck et al. (2016) consider that motivation can be *identified* or *intrinsic* and both were clearly evident in my case. The primary motivator was to regain the career stability that I gave up when I left a permanent K–12 teaching position. This was a simple case of not wanting to have to back-track on a choice and not wanting to have to begin seeking financial security again after more than twenty-five working years. It was this form of motivation that dominated the early tenure-track years. I was worried when things did not go well because of the potential long-term ramifications of having to leave academia if I was not successful; and things sometimes did not go well. After all, there is a lot to learn! However, as the tenure-track years moved along the successes slowly outweighed the challenges and the identified motivation gave way to increased intrinsic motivation.

The intrinsic motivation emerged slowly and was not evident in the early tenure-track years. It began to be evident in the third year and more so in the fourth. The self-perception was found in periods of academic work that I could afford to tackle regardless of extrinsic value—I could simply do some tasks because I wanted to and without concern for whether it added to a portfolio that would argue for tenure and promotion. In some cases, these tasks were adding to marginal evidence that would be in the portfolio because it helps clarify the individual in the same way that the background in a painting can contribute to the focal features in the foreground.

The portfolio and making my case was always in the back of my mind. But there was a tipping point where I began to recognize that I was on track to earn tenure. As that gained clarity there was more intrinsic motivation and a sense of concern began to emerge that if my case were not clear enough from the mounting evidence then the process itself would have to be flawed. Yet, there are stories, always shared with a scarcity of details that suggest things can and do go wrong.

Intrinsic motivation was boosted during the tenure application year each time feedback about the tenure and promotion dossier came forward. The external reviews, the faculty committee, and the university committee all led to increased confidence that my case would be successful. Yet, the stories implying things can go sideways always left some worry. The day I received the letter stating I had tenure and promotion was the day intrinsic motivation began to dominate for me. It was at that point that I took a week to consider the overall picture of the projects that I had engaged with and gave a long hard look at where I wanted to go, as opposed to how I could build evidence. The two have significant overlap, but the domination of intrinsic motivation was evident when I started to wind down a project I was not overly interested in but had succeeded with.

Relatedness

As a high school teacher who spent a decade in one school there was a cultural familiarity with the school and the community it served. I was routinely familiar with the geography of the streets, local shops, and could place student references within the area. Relationships with other teachers were professional and routine. There was a certain degree of collegial banter—it was as enjoyable as any other workplace I have worked in.

The move to higher education began with a move of 500 kilometres. It was not unusual for me and my spouse to travel that sort of distance and that did not concern us. However, our youngest daughter was entering her final year of high school and so my spouse stayed behind with our daughter. It was a semester of living on my own for the first time in over twenty years. In principle there was nothing concerning about the change of cities. It was smaller with 50,000 people instead of 350,000, but we had lived in a town of this size before and, in fact, had lived in much smaller towns. There was, however, a cognitive load associated with carrying out routine tasks because of the unfamiliarity of the new surroundings. Every day, for the first year, seemed to require some new learning associated with the town. Initially there were questions of navigation around the town and where to find certain merchandise. In time those questions transformed to specific details of the region and neighbouring towns.

The lack of local knowledge permeated all aspects of day-to-day activities. Within the workplace it was a lack of organizational knowledge. Having arrived at the beginning of August the university had staff working and, to the best of my knowledge, few professors. I have subsequently been on campus working in the summer and recognized that there are some academics with workplace routines that continue through the summer but, at the time, I had no familiarity with them. So the initial connection was with staff members, which was useful and valuable as they provide important services for academics. It was only in time that the different working groups within the university became apparent. Different clusters of people that loosely align with the different unions were not something that had been significant in the high school environment.

It was in the early years of tenure-track where the loss of high-school culture and knowing the locale caused the most grief. It was directly associated with time and tiredness. As the years went by it diminished but the grief aspect took approximately three full years to run its course. It is considered in terms of the Kubler-Ross phases because they fit the experience.

Denial
In the earliest period I recall feelings of frustration. It was a lonely place with few sources for local knowledge. When I did acquire local knowledge facilitating routine tasks the tasks still took much longer because of unfamiliar details. With only so many hours available in the day the pressure to achieve personal goals was very slow or stymied. In large part this was because of increases in the cognitive load due to having far less routinized knowledge to achieve the end results. In simple terms I denied that anything had changed and went about expecting to achieve daily results. The denial was not without recognition of the situation, but it was with an expectation that each day should see a marked improvement. That expectation was denial in its own right about the time required for local and institutional learning.

Anger
The denial of being held down by the situation slowly evolved to frustration. Tasks I had managed to do a few times would be stymied by some new element that had not arisen before. Since it is a smaller town, the local library is open for fewer hours than libraries in the larger city. While I had attended this library a few times I once arrived to find it closed and learned that I needed to learn a new profile of operating hours; frustration built because the task required a second trip.

Frustration circulated around the personal demands I set on myself but also on my new role. The institution supplied me a computer and I thought switching from Windows to Mac would be simple given that I have considerable experience with computers. It was exceedingly irritating and I measure the loss of productivity in hundreds of hours. A large majority of those hours were in the first year when I could least afford them and I resented tasks taking much longer because of a computer I was obliged to come to terms with. Matters improved with the second year being notably better than the first and by the third year it was much less frequently an issue.

In my first year I had two sections of a course that were marginal to my expertise, but had been set in the schedule before I accepted the role. While I was new and struggling with so many items, the teaching portion of my role was also a struggle in these sections. The frustration from a wide range of phenomena led to anger that I had moved in the first place. I lived in a dichotomy of continuing to do what I had set out to do but feeling defeated at every corner of the new circumstance. It would have been easier to have never moved, and it angered me that I had made the choice to enter such an irritating new existence.

Bargaining

Having my spouse move provided considerable support. It meant getting back to teamwork on daily tasks, and she provided some venting and objectivity. She was a sounding board for constructive advice. At the same time, the personal degree of effort required for regular tasks was decreasing as my local and institutional knowledge improved. I recall recognizing how much local knowledge I had gained through witnessing my spouse struggling to reorient herself.

Slowly opportunities that provided tangible new steps toward earning tenure provided a sense of direction. While I periodically pined for the old days, this gave way to interest in new opportunities. I began to see growth and the earliest stages of a sense of accomplishment. It was small and frequently overwhelmed by other aspects of the role that continued to provide issues. A particular detail of the new role was that it has much more multi-tasking. As a high school teacher I taught approximately the same number of courses, but in academia the number of meetings was much higher and the entire research aspect added to the number of tasks.

It was during this phase that I wrote a chapter (Sibbald, 2017b) that was essentially an attempt at sense-making. Reconciliation of a theoretical model with what was happening with daily events was pursued as a way to maintain a sense of direction in the face of ups and downs. It was an overt attempt at bargaining with myself between what I believed I was experiencing and how I could direct my actions to make things go more smoothly. When I look back upon the distinction of technical, professional, and personal roles I see a view of myself trying to come to terms with these roles growing apart and the ups and downs becoming independent between them. A concern, at the time, was that they could coalesce and essentially everything could be down simultaneously (such as a denial of tenure decision). In fact the technical role was leveling out to be a steady routine as I gained institutional and local knowledge. The professional role continued to oscillate though I felt I understood the experience better because of the chapter I had written and had a sense of catharsis that the ups and downs were largely beyond my control—I simply needed to keep applying myself.

The personal side of life was in flux at that time because my spouse had moved up. It was good to return to that normal, but it underscored that I needed a better balance between home and work. This was a unique challenge. A large part of the daily schedule was self-directed; having no children at home meant my spouse and I were negotiating an entirely new approach to daily scheduling. Routines we had lived by for many years no longer applied and we were obliged to exercise choice rather than have scheduling imposed by work, children, and routine activities. The exercising of choice may sound wonderful, and in the end it has been, but it was an oddly disruptive process to live through.

Depression
The number of active tasks was a new management problem I had to learn. While I prioritized and stayed on top of the task list, there were facets of the role that slowed because they were less urgent. An example was the time demands of teaching scheduled classes and writing up research; teaching had priority but accomplishing the writing was important for tenure. When I was not achieving both, usually because of a need to grade assessments, feelings of not accomplishing what I set out to do would arise. Further insult came from student evaluations, which have been described as a popularity contest. Few people talk about course evaluations and it was very late in the process of applying for tenure that a colleague finally confessed that they do not talk about them much because they do not put any stock in them. While that likely overstates the situation, it takes time to establish a realistic way to interpret and respond to an evaluative tool that is not very good at what it does but is difficult to replace.

Acceptance

The Kubler-Ross model was developed to describe grieving experienced when some close to us dies. In those terms 'acceptance' is neither jovial nor a moving-past. Instead it is a coming to terms with a new 'normal' state of being. That describes the final stages of my tenure-track years. I could work within the norms of the new institution, had a sense of the ebbs and flows of the tripartite roles, and could anticipate events that affect workload. It led to a much more even keel in terms of the ups and downs of daily, weekly, and monthly goals and accomplishments. The same was true of the larger community where navigation became routine and local knowledge was restored to equivalence with the city my spouse and I had moved from. There began to be some recognition of significant advantages from the change, particularly around lifestyle, and the flexibility that the schedule offered.

Through the tenure-track years, the familiarity of both local knowledge and institutional knowledge improved. As time passed, growth in this area slowed; with local knowledge growth slowed because of time pressure constraining learning about local items that are further afield or rarely needed. For example, whereas I recall searching for a beer store in the early months, toward the end of my tenure-track years that kind of searching was specific to where to find rarely needed items such as hardwood lumber. With institutional knowledge, locating my classes transformed to learning who books rooms for events. Growth of institutional knowledge was hampered by not having tenure. For example, there were discussion points I was reluctant to raise when I did not have permanence; the concern was not for dire consequences, but a sense of keeping the peace and avoiding creating friction that could develop into dire consequences. Avoiding the concern implied the importance of maintaining good relations because tenure ultimately entails peer review. It is not blind peer review, nor is it disconnected peer review, and the potential for interconnections to impact the tenure and promotion review led to diplomatic consideration around exercising my voice within the institution. This may have been a more sensitive issue in my case than other institutions as there was animosity within the institution that increased to the point of a strike in my third year of the tenure-track.

Autonomy

Personally, autonomy is the pivotal descriptor of the model of tenure-track (Sibbald & Handford, 2017b). I associate it with the research aspect of the role where choices had the fewest constraints, and this will be addressed momentarily. However, it also applied to teaching within some constraints imposed by institutional norms. The content and organization of classes was based on personal decisions with little direction other than course descriptions and understanding the placement of courses within the program. During my tenure-track years, within Ontario, pre-service teacher education was reformed from a one-year program to a two-year program. The discussions around the transition were a significant help in understanding the structure of the program.

The service component lacked autonomy except where one could choose whether to engage or not. However, I likely fit in the category of doing too much service—because I believe that is largely an oxymoron. Engaging in service is relatively simple and preparation does not involve a rigid schedule. Living in an empty nest it was easy to find time in the day to read through documents ahead of meetings. It is a demand on time, but I felt it was more important to make sure that I was seen to be doing something. The autonomous aspect, which was only applicable to the preparatory aspect of meetings, did not provide as much autonomy as it did for teaching or research. After several years the autonomy increased when my service roles migrated to increased responsibility. For example, as chair of a committee I ran the process to establish the schedule for meetings and that facilitated choice of what times were offered as options.

With research, autonomy was the key component and the lack of guidance in research was a mixed blessing. On one hand, it allows choice of projects and personal organization of tasks. However, my interest for engaging in research was likely driven by a large and multifaceted curiosity. When the panorama of opportunities became available within academia an unfamiliar challenge of having to confine that curiosity emerged. It was a simple case of having too much choice (Ivengar & Lepper, 2002).

Research also posed an issue because feedback was significantly removed from the major aspect of the work. Consider, for example, that in my first year of higher education I collected interviews. They were transcribed through the use of a graduate student in the second year. Academic publishing accounts for years three to five. The feedback from that publishing process provides virtually no tangible connection to the actual research process as it unfolds. Over time experience with the norms of publishing do create an ethos of expectation that an astute researcher addresses. However, there is little to no guidance to alleviate the stumbling blocks of the process. In my case, as this was taking place, I learned of Memorial University's Education Writing Group (2017), which demonstrates that there is a relatively straightforward way to address the need. That contributed to feelings of irritation within the relatedness aspect because there clearly was something that could be done to help with academic writing. That led to my wrestling with the notion of whether I should attempt to start such a group at my institution—but I was a lowly tenure-track newbie and I believed it would seem presumptuous that I could start such a group.

While autonomy was pervasive in all elements of the tripartite role, it was most obvious in research, has the most rapid consequence in teaching, and grew slowly within the service component. Beyond the academic role, it also had an impact on life outside the academy. In the early years I recall questioning why I would go shopping on a Saturday when Wednesday had no commitments and stores were far less busy. Similarly, working after dark facilitated more opportunity to take advantage of daylight hours. A renegotiation of work-life scheduling took place. This was recognized almost from day one, but the consequence was that work-life balance was thrown off by the pursuit of tenure. The use of flexible hours, combined with the pressure of needing to earn tenure, blurred the assessment of time expended on the career task. As progress unfolded, and especially in the six months after earning tenure, the regaining work-life balance is an ongoing work-in-progress. It will continue to receive attention because it has highly tangible benefits and, for me, is proving to be the source of justification for the level of effort expended in the transition.

Summary

My experience is consistent with the use of self-determination theory. I find it a clarifying model allowing a reconciliation of what has transpired. It passes the simple test of providing a way of making sense of what is otherwise a murky situation and collection of experiences.

As I gain experience within higher education I find the theory to be too broad for predictive validity. While it allows a dissection of the past and current situations, it is not indicative of what is to come. Some elements are indicative, but others, particularly the aspects contained in the grief model, are behind me. What I could not predict, with respect to relatedness, was the emergence of colleagues willing to engage in purposeful conversation. This has arisen much more after the tenure decision, as if there was an effort to avoid getting to know someone whose career might well go off the rails. The reassurance of earning tenure was much more of a collegial rite of passage than self-determination theory allows one to predict.

The alteration of scheduling to take advantage of flexibility afforded by academia while pursuing my vision of work-life balance is again something that self-determination theory explains but in a manner that cannot predict the future. It is likely that any prediction based on current trends would be subject to any whim of directional change or project adoption/alteration afforded through the autonomy of research. However, to the extent ideas emerge over time I can likely predict the primary potential sources of influence and that suggests a probabilistic model of the future—perhaps analogous to weather forecasting.

The Future Within the Role

What was striking during the period between receiving the tenure decision and the actual receipt of tenure and promotion was the opportunity to self-assess my situation. It was an opportunity to ask what I now wanted to do, as opposed to what I needed to be doing. This is a small but important distinction because some projects I had been working on were not self-sustaining or I was not overly interested in them, but had felt obliged to see them through as they offered tangible evidence to support a positive tenure decision.

The aftermath illustrated what the long term would look like. Talking to colleagues, I pointed out that achieving tenure and promotion allowed me to forecast my financial future through to retirement. In fact, my pension is a defined benefit plan and allows forecasting for the rest of my life (a different kind of relatedness factor that points toward using time wisely). Such planning contrasts with the deep concern I had in the first place about relinquishing the stability of being a permanent high school teacher to joining the academy. Beyond the family-oriented financial permanence, there was a subtle consideration of how I wanted to tailor my academic efforts. For example, which research projects would I keep and which would I curtail in the interests of having more time to focus on what I really wanted to do? How would I negotiate the requirements for becoming a full professor or should I plan to remain an associate professor?

These were weighty considerations, but as the tenure and promotion process progressed toward its ultimate end these were considerations I toyed with. None of the answers were simple except for one: seeking funding was purposefully put on hold in the tenure year as a pragmatic matter of wanting tenure decided before having the commitment to an action plan based on funding. In simple terms, if I had not received tenure, the plan was to return to the school system and having funded research would not help that endeavour.

The consideration of looking for promotion to full professor in the future is not clear. Some seem to think it is inevitable that I will. I have also heard remarks about financial benefits because I am in a defined benefit plan; it has a substantial salary increase which then impacts pension earnings forever after. Yet I am not sure because one has to submit an annual report and the expectations are more challenging for full professors than associate professors. In particular, there is an emphasis on international components that I have found challenging in education because, in Canada, it is provincially based. Yet I have colleagues who seem to think I am destined for full professorship.

The conviction of colleagues has not convinced me of a course of action. In what strikes me as a curious twist, they have led me to wonder if I am doing far more than necessary—perhaps I am overworking within the role I hold. That has struck me as the sinister side of tenure, the simple fact that tenure decisions are made by a committee and the minimum amount of work one has to do is not clearly defined. In that environment, how does one know what is an appropriate workload? I wrestle with that and suspect the suggestion that I am eventually headed to a full professorship is simply a reflection of my overworking. This speaks to a confusion that has been described: "Winning tenure and promotion is a major transition for faculty members. As thrilling as it is to reach a goal you've worked hard to achieve, once the dust settles, many faculty members feel confused, unsure how to adjust, and/or overwhelmed by newly escalated expectations for service" (National Center for Faculty Development & Diversity, 2017).

Within that confusion I question whether to break out in new directions. For example, should I start a writing group? There is a clear benefit to having such a structure. But then I was recently reminded that after five and a half years, I am the most recent permanent faculty member hired within my faculty. More promising is research that is oriented to perennial questions that cannot be resolved from within the school system. I have two such projects and find them remarkable because the questions they ask are much more fundamental to math education than I ever imagined being able to consider.

Looking forward I am headed toward a sabbatical. That may be the ultimate in autonomy. It is something of a prize, a sense of earned freedom, and yet with many goals and objectives that are self-imposed. Others have told me sabbaticals can be a shock as you learn how replaceable you are. However, I am looking forward to it as a way to engage in a focused period of research.

Finally, it is my observation that the model of tenure-track seemed to achieve saturation. In considering experiences that defy the model I am at a loss to come up with any. I remain concerned the model may be too general for predictive power, but I do not think this issue is due to the model. It is more likely due to the challenge of appreciating the complexity of self-determination.

Coda

The theory that is discussed here arose from consideration of the entirety of Sibbald and Handford (2017a). The preparation of this chapter preceded hearing from any other authors for this book. That was to maintain validity of my own thinking and to avoid bias as other chapters entered the editorial process. As I review this chapter some of the other chapters have entered the editorial process and, along with Tory, I have been reviewing them and providing feedback. I have found myself in the quandary questioning how much influence the theoretical model may have had. It suits me, but perhaps that is the qualitative flaw that I am my own lens of interpretation. Simultaneously I perceive a fundamental theory that resonates with a principled vision of what higher education should be. However, that has made me wonder if tenure-track positions lend themselves to idealistic leanings, while tenured positions tend toward the pragmatic realities that lead to a divisive process that overlays other visions and creates heterogeneity from the singular academic gateway of tenure.

References

Broeck, A. V., Ferris, D. L., Chang, C. H., & Rosen, C. C. (2016). A review of self-determination theory's basic psychological needs at work. *Journal of Management, 42*(5), 1195–1229.

Deci, E. L. (1980). *The psychology of self-determination*. Lexington, MA: Lexington Books D.C. Heath and Company.

Deci, E. L., & Ryan, R. M. (2000). The 'what' and 'why' of goal pursuits: Human needs and the self-determination of behavior. *Psychological Inquiry, 11*(4), 227–268.

Gardner, S. K., & Veliz, D. (2014). Evincing the ratchet: A thematic analysis of the promotion and tenure guidelines at a striving university. *The Review of Higher Education, 38*(1), 105–132.

Iyengar, S. S., & Lepper, M. R. (2002). Choice and its consequences: On the costs and benefits of self-determination. In A. Tesser, D. A. Stapel, & J. V. Wood. eds., *Self and motivation: Emerging psychological perspectives* (pp. 73–98). Washington, DC: American Psychological Association.

Memorial's Education Writing Group (2017). Women reflect on becoming an academic: Challenges and supports. In T. M. Sibbald & V. Handford (Eds.), *The academic gateway: Understanding the journey to tenure* (pp. 79–92). Ottawa, ON: University of Ottawa Press.

National Center for Faculty Development & Diversity (2017). What is the post-tenure Pathfinders program? Retrieved from www.facultydiversity.org/pathfinders

Ryan, R. M., & Deci, E. L. (2000). Self-determination theory and the facilitation of intrinsic motivation, social development, and well-being. *American Psychologist, 55*(1), 68–78.

Sibbald, T. M. (2017a). Engaging academia as the nest empties. In C. DeRoche and E. Berger (Eds.), *The parent-track: Timing, balance and choice within academia* (pp. 213–221). Waterloo, ON: Wilfred Laurier University Press.

Sibbald, T. M. (2017b). Practitioner to academic: A composition of transitions. In T. M. Sibbald & V. Handford (Eds.), *The academic gateway: Understanding the journey to tenure* (pp. 133–144). Ottawa, ON: University of Ottawa Press.

Sibbald, T. M. & Handford, V. (2017a). *The academic gateway: Understanding the journey to tenure*. Ottawa, ON: University of Ottawa Press.

Sibbald, T. M., & Handford, V. (May, 2017b). *A Substantive Model of the Tenure-Track Experience*. Presentation at the Canadian Association of Action Research in Education (CAARE) portion of Canadian Society for the Study of Education (CSSE) 2017 conference, Toronto, ON.

Sibbald, T. M., & Handford, V. (Submitted). A substantive model of Canadian tenure-track experiences.

CHAPTER 10

The Mid-Career Indigenous Scholar: Navigating the Institutional Confluence of Indigeneity and Academia in Post-Tenure-Track

Frank Deer

The experience of a university professor of Indigenous descent can involve negotiating how one's ancestral identity may affect the way his/her professional role is perceived by others. In the case of Indigenous faculty, whose lives may be situated in numerous cultural contexts, the ascent to the role of university professor may be one that is not only associated with an academic discipline, but also with the values and cultural perspectives that may be reflective of their ancestral background. Because many universities are actively recruiting Indigenous academics with a view of improving those academic and non-academic areas for which Indigenous studies are relevant, such recruitment has often been carried out with a stated desire to achieve Indigenous cultural representation as well as suitable scholarly knowledge. Universities, Indigenous students and communities, and portions of the general public have a desire to see Indigenous faculty with discernible Indigenous identities; it is believed such Indigenous faculty would be in a position to shape institutional change with respect to Indigeneity in academic and non-academic realms.

In this chapter, I explore how being an Indigenous professor may be in tension with the goals held by universities as they relate to Indigenous achievement.[1] In order to explore these issues, this chapter will look principally at how the career trajectories of Indigenous faculty may be affected by the frequently unstated yet palpable expectations to represent specific cultural aspects of an Indigenous identity. This chapter will focus upon my ancestral background (that of an Kanienkeha'ka/Mohawk person in Canada) and that of my research and teaching interests. These professional contexts are important because the demands upon Indigenous faculty at many Canadian universities are considerable and the nature of those demands may be unique.

Background

When asked to describe what I do for a living, I sometimes respond that I am a public intellectual. I didn't come up with this on my own; on the day that I was interviewed for a tenure-track professorship at my university, I was told by the dean that if I were the successful candidate, this would be my role—one reflecting the fundamental responsibility of the position as well as those to whom I would be accountable. Although the various formal titles that I have carried since I joined my university in 2009 have changed—from assistant professor to associate professor to acting associate dean—my real job, directly aligned with the acquisition and dissemination of knowledge, has been in service to the Canadian public.

With tenure secured, I was nominated-for (and awarded) a Canada Research Chair (CRC) which commenced in 2017. Similar to my previous roles, the CRC has a focus upon Indigenous topics, for which an Indigenous candidate was required. This essential quality—being Indigenous—has been desired overtly or tacitly with every role I've occupied in the academy, as well as elsewhere. This is not something for which anyone in a similar academic role, especially those who are Indigenous, should be apologetic; the lack of Indigenous representation in many social and institutional spaces which affect Indigenous peoples and communities is a problem that many in government, public service, and the private sector have been working to correct (Luffman & Sussman, 2007). However, in ascending to a professorship in the academy, the constituent elements of one's Indigeneity, as well as knowledge of that background (beyond just ancestry), may be of interest to those who are responsible for hiring and supporting scholars who work in areas relevant to Indigenous peoples. These elements of identity, which may or may not have any relevance to academic disciplines affiliated with an Indigenous scholar, are frequently those that minister to the needs of the academy in the area of Indigenous achievement. For example, Indigenous cultural and/or spiritual knowledge, familiarity with Indigenous cultural protocols, and even partial fluency in an Indigenous language are elements that are clearly valued by the academy.

It is now clear to me, after almost a decade of employment at a U-15 university in Canada, for which Indigenous achievement has been identified as an institutional priority, that some in the academy privilege characteristics of Indigenous identity beyond simple declared identity. Cultural knowledge, language, and other phenotypes do appear to have a currency in contemporary Canadian universities—especially when exploring such topics as well-being, academic achievement, and student recruitment. Authenticity, as perceived by students, communities, and university faculty and administrators has become an important consideration, whether that authenticity is overtly or tacitly understood.

At the time of writing this chapter, I'm reminded of two instances involving faculty and students that have shown how episodes of Indigeneity beyond declared identity are viewed as important.

Episode I
In 2016 and 2017, I occupied a role in higher administration at my university for which I held the portfolio of *Indigenous achievement*—a role that managed the development and improvement of an Indigenous climate on campus that would support improved access, recruitment, retention, and success for Indigenous learners. During that time, my university hosted an annual event titled *Indigenous Awareness Week*—a week of celebration and learning that focused on Indigenous peoples, experiences and topics that took place during the winter of 2017. During this event, I invited a relatively well-known and well-published scholar of Métis (i.e., people of mixed ancestry who descend from First Nations and European settlers; Kulchyski, 2007) background to deliver a lecture on the Canadian Métis experience. This lecture, attended by university faculty, students, and community members, was a survey of principally western-Canadian history along with how Métis peoples negotiated a co-existence with others and the grounds upon which Métis nationhood may be asserted.

The nature of this lecture represented, for some in university communities at least, a relatively new avenue of historical inquiry. Although the existence of the Métis peoples has been acknowledged in Indigenous and academic communities for some time, their assent into the broad public consciousness as an Indigenous group is a relatively recent development (Fiola, 2015); the Indigeneity of the Métis peoples is sometimes viewed as contentious in comparison to the triumvirate of Indigenous populations in Canada (Burnett & Read, 2012). At a time when the completed work of the Truth and Reconciliation Commission of Canada has facilitated discussion on such things as the history of Indian residential schools, thus providing large focus upon the First Nations and Métis experience, it may be that Métis peoples are regarded with a less appreciative view in discussions on Indigenous Peoples in Canada (Métis National Council, 2012; Dumont, 2012).

At the completion of this lecture, the customary question and answer period yielded numerous learned questions of the sort that one would normally expect from such an event. However, near the end of the question period, one query was quite different from those previously posed. An older gentleman, who declared himself to be an Elder from a local First Nations community, posed a question for which a palpable sense of discomfort emerged. The question, asked after the Elder affirmed his own First Nations background, was more or less like this: *How is one supposed to recognize and affirm what you've said? I look at you and you don't appear native to me.*

This is not an isolated incident; I have borne witness to similar questions being posed in like forums and situations in the past. This particular scholar, whose declared Indigenous ancestry is commensurate with the communities for which he claimed affiliation, was being queried for his appearance—not in relation to the content of his work. As tired and tenuous as this notion of racial appearance is, there are some for whom such appearance is an important dimension of authenticity. Although one should not dismiss the importance for students and community members to perceive Indigeneity in universities at a time when Indigenous achievement is regarded as important, the inclusion of physical appearance as a criterion for adjudicating the authenticity of one's scholarship is a barrier to the vitality of free intelligence and should be resisted.

Episode II
In teaching undergraduate courses, my principal focus has been upon the journey toward integrating Indigenous perspectives into primary and secondary school curricula. For the record, I am a professor

of Kanienkeha'ka/Mohawk ancestry teaching in Manitoba where localized Indigenous perspectives are more aligned with those of the Anishinaabe, Cree, and Metis peoples.[2] In Manitoba, as is the case elsewhere, the spiritual dimensions of the Indigenous Peoples' experience has become a frequent consideration for Indigenous and non-Indigenous educators. In primary school settings, an area for which I claim some competence, as I am an elementary school teacher by trade, a particularly ubiquitous topic relevant to Indigenous perspectives is that of the Seven Teachings[3]—a set of teachings that offer insight into how we should interface with one another. In Manitoba, the Seven Teachings are frequently affiliated with the Aniishinaabe and Cree peoples, but are also cited in the contexts of other Indigenous groups as well.

In my experience, religious beliefs, and the nature of how such beliefs are developed, are not normally explored topics in the areas of initial teacher education or in the on-going professional development of in-service teachers with any extensive focus. If classroom teaching and learning occurs with a principal focus upon the content knowledge that is reflected in outcomes-based curricula, especially if the content of that knowledge is predetermined and delineated, then it may be no surprise that the religious beliefs of teachers or students is not a predominant consideration. It also may be of no surprise given the nature of most of the content and the respective teachers for whom the causing of learning is responsible—early elementary teachers tend to believe in the value of literacy in the learning development of children just as physics teachers believe in the value of physics as a means of understanding the world. Teachers tend to recognize and affirm the importance of the content knowledge with which they work (Kronowitz, 2004).

This may not be the case when exploring topics relevant to Indigenous religious observances. This became a potent possibility during a student presentation in an undergraduate course that focused upon Indigenous perspectives and the curriculum. During this presentation, an Indigenous student was describing how the seven teachings might be employed in elementary school contexts. The presentation and subsequent discussion that was led by the student was one that explored the benefits of using such teachings toward understanding Indigenous worldviews as well as how symbolism played a part in the use of these teachings (each of these teachings are represented by particular animals). One series of questions/comments from the presenter's fellow students led to the topic of a deity's (frequently referred to as the "creator") influence on the moral imperatives that are reflected in the seven teachings. When the student presenter responded in such a way that revealed that he was not an adherent to a belief system that includes a creator, the palpable feeling of disapproval and comments related to the authenticity of the lesson that was being presented created a sort of discord in the class. In a brief and arguably trivial concession of non-belief, a student's (and future educator's) ability to cover a topic that is relevant to Indigenous Peoples was called into question. My concern with regard to this is that such a dismissive reaction to the presenting student's efforts may affect his willingness to explore such areas in the future. I've approached my career in initial teacher education and in frequent in-service professional development with a view that teachers ought to be enabled to explore Indigenous perspectives that are relevant to school programming. It is instances such as this that may create a barrier toward teachers' journeys toward integration of Indigenous perspectives.

Mapping the Identity Debate onto My Career

Indigeneity has and continues to be reflected in the two main dimensions of my career: that of my identity as an Indigenous Canadian (Kanienkeha'ka) and that of a scholar (one who is involved with Indigenous education studies). In considering how the institutional climate and culture of Indigenous achievement has affected my work, it seems fitting to explore these two dimensions followed with how they may be commensurate with Self-Determination Theory (Ryan & Deci, 2000).

As an Indigenous Canadian
In a recent exercise of internal program development to which I was one of a few major contributors at my university, I offered the following description of myself—an offering which, as alluded to earlier, has become customary when working on initiatives relevant to Indigenous Peoples or issues:

> She:kon! Aronhio:tas tanon Frank ion'tiats. Kanienkeha'ka ni'i. I am Kanienkeha'ka (Mohawk) from the community of Kahnawake, which lies in Kanienkeha'ka territory within the

Haudenosaunee Confederacy. Kahnawake lies to the South of Tiotiake (Montreal) in the Province of Quebec. Both of my parents, Dennis and Mary, are Kanienkeha'ka. I am a status Indian through the Mohawk Council of Kahnawake. I attended school in my community where, for a lengthy period of time, I was taught only in my ancestral language.

Rather than dispense an unnecessarily long story of myself, I feel this passage is sufficient not only because it captures the basic elements of who I am as an Indigenous person but it also appears to represent, in the currency of Indigenous achievement at Canadian universities and other public spaces, some of the important features of a declaration of Indigeneity. I've verbally stated or written this declaration, or parts thereof, frequently over that last decade in a manner that resembles territorial acknowledgements that are offered at universities in Canada and abroad. I'm unsure if there's been an event or gathering at which I was speaking where I didn't recite this at least in part.

As I've mentioned earlier, the declaration of genuine Indigeneity of Indigenous academics in Canada who may be in a position to affect the climate, culture, and academic direction of their universities is important and should not be dismissed. This sort of declaration should also not be seen as unique to Indigenous Peoples; most people would describe or affirm their respective identities with similar sorts of referents as I have above. Whether we are making such declarations verbally, by way of cover letter in a job application, or by checking the requisite box on a census form, we frequently take advantage of opportunities, however grand or minor, to affirm who we are, where we are, where we are from, and who our ancestors are.

In some ways, what I've mentioned about myself is as far as my Indigenous identity goes in terms of utility for my current professional role. I'm not currently living and working in my home territory, nor is there a surfeit of fellow Kanienkeha'ka with whom to confer on shared interests. Thus, my admittedly limited knowledge of my own cultural background may be of little use in the traditionally territories on which I currently live and work.

As a Scholar

My scholarship is Indigenous insofar as it focuses upon how Indigenous perspectives may be reflected in primary and secondary school programming. In an era in which a multiplicity of denotative and designative definitions may be advanced or adduced for what Indigenous means in this context, this declaration of my scholarship merits explanation. I study topics that are relevant to, or associated with, the Canadian Indigenous experience. Specifically, I study education and language as it relates to Indigenous Peoples in Canada. In my work, this entails collaborative work with Indigenous Peoples and communities. It entails studying non-academic works and resources that reflect the Canadian Indigenous experience with academic theoretical perspectives. It also entails consideration of how my work may be of benefit for all people in this era of reconciliation.

My area of scholarship is relatively new compared to that of other disciplines for which their presence in the academy is long standing and respected. Not only is Indigenous studies in education relatively new to the academy, but its contributions to society and the labour market are also relatively new: Indigenous content knowledge as a necessity or asset for teachers in primary and secondary education has only become, generally speaking, a consideration of public school administrators in the last decade. Thus, what constitutes Indigenous perspectives and what is viewed as appropriate approaches with which to employ such perspectives is a developing discussion. In initiating explorations of the Canadian Indigenous experience, educators have invoked numerous topics and issues that are viewed as informative points of entry, some of which are topics of cultural knowledge and faith.

Indigenous achievement in the academy, as well as in primary and secondary schools, is currently developing with the support of a cadre of academics who have demonstrated commitment to institutional change. One of the less understood challenges of such desired institutional changes is the diversity amongst Indigenous Peoples and communities reflected in the territories upon which that institution is situated. Indigenous faculty of an institution that is associated with a multiplicity of national, linguistic, and cultural groups might not be from one of these local populations and are not necessarily learned in the cultural or religious practices of these local groups. There is a currency of sorts associated with being Indigenous and involved in Indigenous studies in education, the expectations that someone like myself will be representative of an Indigenous cultural identity, including those belief systems that may be associated with such identity, are palpable. In my time as an professor of

Kanienkeha'ka background, I've been asked to, for instance, offer a prayer, lead a smudge (an Indigenous ceremony where flora such as sage and cedar are burned; the smoke that emanates is believed to cleanse people and places), and offer insights into community processes and protocols of a ceremonial nature. Although I have piecemeal familiarity with such activities, none of these are apropos my scholarly area and I don't believe I occupy a sufficiently appropriate role to lead such activities. I am confident in my belief that others assume I would be proficient in such areas. Although I once initially felt compelled to fulfill such responsibilities, I've come to offer regrets to such requests; I confess a lack of knowledge. I've come to believe the view other Indigenous academics and community members have of me has been affected by my lack of proficiency in these areas. A positive development in some universities in Canada is consultation with local Indigenous people, sometimes from outside the university community, who may offer appropriate advice on matters relevant to Indigenous cultural and spiritual knowledge.

In considering the journey of establishing a career in the area of Indigenous education, I'm reminded of the work of self-determination theory that is related to how one's professional growth may be affected by internal forces such as motivation and external ones such as the work environment. According to Ryan and Deci (2000), self-determination theory is concerned with

> the investigation of people's inherent growth tendencies and innate psychological needs that are the basis for their self-motivation and personality integration, as well as for the conditions that foster those positive processes. . . . SDT also examines environmental factors that hinder or undermine self-motivation, social functioning, and personal well-being. (pp. 68–69)

It may appear too straightforward and triflingly familiar to assert that my personal motivation—as well as my Ryan/Deci-esque needs of competence, relatedness, and autonomy—have been important and enabling factors in my own professional growth; however, it's worth a mention. Being a faculty member who is engaged in areas of inquiry that are of importance and interest to me has been enabling, yet this proclamation of enablement and satisfaction may, at times, only be adduced tentatively; environmental factors such as those cited in this chapter, as divorced as I would like to consider them from my academic pursuits, may have an undesirable impact upon career—especially in terms of how I'm viewed by some colleagues. In considering those "environmental factors that hinder or undermine ... social functioning" (Ryan & Deci, 2000, p. 69), it appears that an Indigenous faculty member's lack of Indigenous cultural and religious knowledge may lead some in the academy to view that individual as deficient in their skills and/or background.

This potential liability can have repercussions in the career of a scholar. For instance, one of the key responsibilities of a professor who conducts research and other scholarly work is dissemination. As a public intellectual, making one's findings and points of view available to others such as scholars, students, government officials, and the public is a crucial endeavour and frequently a requirement of agencies that fund research. It is in the dissemination of knowledge, including research findings and views of such things as social phenomena and government activities, that I've personally felt vulnerable. A presentation, community discussion, podcast episode or even a minor sound bite from a media interview may offer evidence of disbelief; others have perceived this of me in the past. The older I become, the more sensitive I am to the notion that one shouldn't be reticent under such pressure. After all, continued conversation on difficult topics is necessary in order to realize improvement in our world.

Endnotes

1. In this chapter, the phrase "Indigenous achievement" is used to refer to the developing efforts by universities and affiliated fields toward utilizing Indigenous perspectives in the academic, student services, and community relations aspects of their institutions.
2. Relevant to this discussion is the recently emerged custom in Canadian academia to state who you are (individually, communally, and nationally) and on what (if any) traditional territories you are situated. This need, seemingly in response to the desire to acknowledge where you are and what social, governmental or environmental impacts may have been experienced by the people of those territories, has led to a need be acutely aware of where you are but also of your experience either as an Indigenous person or a non-Indigenous person. Offshoot developments from this emerging exercise is the frequent declaration by non-Indigenous peoples as "settlers" as well as the acknowledgement of the places from which key resources such as water are acquired.
3. The teachings may be articulated as Baskin, McPherson and Strike's (2012):

- *Respect*: showing honour to someone or something; considering the well-being of everything; and treating everything with deference or courtesy.
- *Wisdom*: the practice of balance in all things.
- *Love*: treating people with special care and kindness.
- *Honesty*: being sincere, open, and trustworthy.
- *Humility*: place the needs of others first, and avoid criticizing others.
- *Courage*: Personal bravery in the face of fear; doing what needs to be done even when it is difficult or frightening.
- *Truth*: coming to know, and trying to understand the previous six teachings. Truth also focuses on the overarching picture as we try to understand both the past and the present.

References

Baskin, C., McPherson, B., & Strike, C. (2012). Using the seven sacred teachings to improve services for Aboriginal mothers experiencing drug and alcohol misuse problems and involvement with child welfare. In D. Newhouse, K. Fitzmaurice, T. McGuire-Adams & D. Jette (Eds.), *Well-being in the urban Aboriginal community: Fostering biimaadiziwin, a national research conference on urban Aboriginal Peoples* (pp. 182–194). Toronto, ON: Thompson Educational Publishing.

Burnett, K., & Read, G. (2012). Locating Métis identity. In K. Burnett & G. Read (Eds.), *Aboriginal history: A reader* (pp. 132–133). Don Mills, ON: Oxford University Press.

Dumont, Y. (2012). Métis nationalism: Then and now. In K. Burnett & G. Read (Eds.), *Aboriginal history: A reader* (pp. 141–151). Don Mills, ON: Oxford University Press.

Fiola, C. (2015). *Rekindling the sacred fire: Métis ancestry and Anishinaabe spirituality*. Winnipeg, MB: University of Manitoba Press.

Kronowitz, E. L. (2004). *Your first year of teaching and beyond* (4th ed.). Boston: Pearson.

Kulchyski, P. (2007). *The red Indians: An episodic, informal collection of tales from the history of Aboriginal people's struggles in Canada*. Winnipeg, MB: Arbeiter Ring.

Métis National Council. (2012). Métis nation a long way from reconciliation. Retrieved from www.metisnation.ca/wp-content/uploads/2012/02/Métis-Nation-a-long-way-from-reconciliation-Efforts-continue-for-recognition-and-compensation-for-Métis-residential-and-day-school-survivors-Feb.-27-2012.pdf

Ryan, R. M., & Deci, E. L. (2000). Self-determination theory and the facilitation of intrinsic motivation, social development, and well-being. *American Psychologist, 55*(1), 68–78.

CHAPTER 11

An Incredible Journey: Passing Through the Gateway

Victoria (Tory) Handford

The act of beginning, I have learned, is possibly the most difficult part of writing, teaching a course, marriage, motherhood, or of becoming a scholar—to name a few beginnings that have applied to me. There is the belief that the path you choose, and advancing on that path, matters. This implies that the act of choosing and beginning may be highly important. Less obviously, any beginning also entails giving up. In order to add a new dimension to ourselves, we nearly always lose some aspect of another dimension; after all, there is only so much time in a day. This chapter, much like moving to academia, is no different. I choose to write and it is challenging to begin. But . . . *on y va*! (Let's go!)

It has been an incredible journey. I had not realized when the title for the first book I edited (along with Tim) emerged—*The Academic Gateway: Understanding the Journey to Tenure*—how poignant the word "journey" would become for me. Two parts of my life's narrative come together with that word. As a child I saw the Disney movie, *The Incredible Journey*, which was based on Sheila Burnford's book of the same name. The movie featured three animals, a Siamese cat, a Bull terrier and a Labrador retriever, all house pets, lost on a family vacation. The trio journey together through the wilderness and, after many adventures (some of which are very dangerous), find their way home. Along the way they learned to care for and support each other; it takes the individual and collective strengths of the three to complete the journey. Perhaps memories of this movie smoldered in my subconscious, influencing our title. Quite separate from this, I also have spent many years considering the words of Robert Frost's poem, *The Road Not Taken*. It is becoming ever clearer to me that the road may not be the point, but I will leave this until later.

This chapter addresses my journey through the gateway of tenure and promotion, including the application, the process following submitting the application, and my experiences of academia following receiving my news. In theory, the journey is part of the accomplishment of the entire department or faculty. We work collegially; therefore, our successes are part of the collegial endeavour. This is not always the case, although I love the idea that we see our successes in the success of others. I have written this narrative as I've travelled, thus it is derived from a longitudinal record of short diary entries. The goal of adopting this approach was to track, in some manner, my own sense of accomplishment, failure, frustration, doubt, and occasional enlightenment, chronicling the issues encountered as I passed through the gateway. I begin with a summary and then expand on details afterward.

My Short History of Tenure and Promotion

July (4th Year in Tenure-Track)
I attended a workshop about tenure and promotion. This provided a one-hour walk-through of the process. A few questions were asked and answered. Time ran out. People left the session thinking things through.

I was not a person with concerns; I was a person who wanted certainty and exact answers to issues that, ultimately, are quantifiable (at least in theory). I really did not care how I or anyone else felt—I wanted to know exactly what was required to get the proverbial checkmark in the box. Of course, answering questions directly is something people in leadership frequently try to avoid; ambiguity always exists, leaders know this. It is not exclusively a characteristic of leaders, however, senior leaders are often more comfortable presenting trends and options, as are university professors. When asked by a student how many words an assigned essay must be, many of us give a range (e.g., 8,000 to 10,000 words). The generalizing of what is detailed and agreed upon feels more comfortable and less authoritative. People trying to work within a system, however, need clarity. I listened, knowing definitive answers would be elusive, and found participant questions interesting.

September 1
I submitted my application for tenure and promotion. I created most of the dossier in July and August by establishing categories and making a line-by-line table that identified the terms for tenure and promotion in the collective agreement and quantitative data identifying 'totals of materials required' in each category. This design eliminated uncertainty about what was in the submission, and reiterated, in case there was a lack of clarity among tenure and promotion committee members, the exact expectations by category as identified in the collective agreement. I provided more documentation than required, just to be certain there was strong and comprehensive evidence for consideration. While I knew that reviewing tenure and promotion applications was serious work, and this over-submission would be annoying for some, I was not leaving any room for doubt. It was all there.

It was something of a relief to get the process to this point—my portion completed. I could stop agonizing over tables of content, the order of documents, details of descriptions, and the many, many component considerations of a tenure and promotion application. The dossier was done and submitted. I felt it was well done. Now I needed to trust the process, something much easier said than done.

December
I received a letter that identified my application (i.e. me) as "outstanding" in all three areas (teaching, research, and service). My application was moving on to the next committee with full support. This was great news.

February
I received a letter stating the second committee fully supported my application. It was moving on to the final stage for consideration. I received a private acknowledgement from a person in the know indicating pride in the accomplishment and, while not yet finalized, also indicating that a small celebration would occur when the process was officially completed and tenure and promotion was granted.

March 22
Today I was in my office reflecting on the next step. Tomorrow is another review of my tenure and promotion package. Unless something goes seriously wrong, the letter granting me tenure and promotion will arrive before long.

I recognize the committee members who have reviewed my application feel optimism and satisfaction; there is happiness for the other. For some there is a feeling of personal validation when colleagues achieve. Faculty members need to celebrate; they are under siege on so many fronts; moments of accomplishment should be shared. The experience of success, whether individual or collective, breeds the energy and efficacy it takes to keep the institution healthy and engaged.

I, however, do not feel validated, nor do I feel a sense of joy. It is more a feeling of tiredness, indicative of discouragement. There is no joy in Mudville, not for Casey, nor this batter. There is a tale to this lack of pride and satisfaction. I feel badly about this discouragement; I should be rejoicing; I should be allowing others to celebrate my success. The institution, and likely all higher education institutions, which I aspired to be part of for so long, is struggling, or so it seems as a lowly faculty member, on every front. A retreat into self seems the most viable option.

March 23
My application is on the agenda for a review at a meeting today.

This morning I received about 50 emails which included an article from a colleague I am working with, a request from a student for a discussion about her Master's thesis, a request from a research assistant to review our survey findings thus far, several issues in relation to scholarship/award applications, and multiple student admission applications for review. It is amazing how the work we do influences our view of the institution. This sort of work is purpose-driven and creates energy for me. Despite my dwindling optimism, it may be that the future is optimistic on some fronts! This is what I need to remember as personal direction: the institution, the governance structures, and the daily messiness—this is not the place to put my time. The granting of tenure puts to rest the ambivalence about being enough, which should create space in my days. I can focus on tasks of meaning rather than tasks of quantitative point scoring. I am enough.

No news will come to me today. My name will be on the agenda at the meeting. This has never been far from my mind.

March 26
The letter arrived today—tenure and promotion granted, effective July 1. A leader came by and hugged me. Others congratulated me. Sixty-five of my Facebook friends wrote congratulatory comments. My family was very pleased.

I am pleased and—proud. It is a significant achievement. I shared the news with some colleagues. There is lingering doubt about the process, about what the process means, and the credibility of the achievement itself. While I did not celebrate earlier, today I did, just a little.

The Outcome
That, in a nutshell, is my perspective on what happened. I followed the process, it did what it was supposed to do, and because I met the criteria, I achieved tenure and promotion. However, it is also clear there was some disenfranchisement, something fractious, or perhaps simple tiredness, that is not fully evident in the description of my perception. The devil, as the saying goes, is in the details.

My Longer History of Tenure and Promotion

I actually submitted my first tenure and promotion application a year earlier. The process of organizing a coherent submission required significant reflection, as well as locating various documents. This parallels the experience of most faculty—where is my "stuff," what does my "stuff" mean, and how do I summarize it succinctly. I had reviewed my current accomplishments with an informed person, talked with another trusted colleague or two, and realized there was no reason for me to wait another year. There was ample evidence in the required categories. So, I got cracking and created the application. This took the better part of the summer, on and off, but I found the process an interesting one.

As things were being tallied, it confirmed the beginnings of a research agenda that was aligning into three main themes. I had not stopped and reflected on how my publications and research were looking, nor had I considered there to have been any progress. There was a moment of enlightenment—a path was emerging. I considered how my teaching had changed over the first three years and realized that, while improvement was forever possible, I had definitely understood the needs and expectations of my students better as time went on. It revealed that there was no need for more service. I was proud of my application, and submitted it by the deadline.

Then came the bad news: I was being asked for more teaching evaluations. I had put in exactly the number required by the existing collective agreement, I believed, but more were requested. It was a bit complicated, as the collective agreement changed by virtue of a Letter of Understanding becoming active on September 1, the day my application was due, and issues of interpretation existed. I believed I had been doing exactly what was required, the Faculty Tenure and Promotion Committee acknowledged this, but did not change the request. I had multiple additional samples of documentation; I had simply not included them to avoid cluttering up the dossier. After a process of verification, I was informed that I was not allowed to add to my package after the fact. Two options were presented to me: I could state my case, when an oversight committee convened, or I could withdraw and resubmit the following academic year.

I decided to withdraw. I just could not worry about this process for six months, waiting to find out if I was going to need to do a presentation; worrying would consume far too much energy. The simplest thing to do, from my point of view, was reapply the following year. It really did not matter. Of course, letting go is different from saying you would like to let go. I still carry lingering resentment that the change in expectations had not been clearly presented in the summer training session.

I created a second tenure and promotion package the next summer. I imagined I would simply add in some elements, including a surplus of teaching evaluations. This is not what happened. Instead, I completely rewrote the application. I had more publications, more presentations, more course evaluations, more completed thesis supervisions, including one student who had won a significant award. I was proud of her, and proud of all my thesis students. I had done more service—I had actually changed quite a bit in a calendar year! In many ways, far from simply adding in a couple of course evaluations, it was a more refined and robust image of my research agenda, among other things. It was deeper and stronger in every single category, and I wrote much more confidently. Overall, it was a good thing to create an updated dossier. I did realize some additional nuances about my priorities and achievements by redoing it. I was annoyed, but I was pleased with the product.

In early October an email arrived requesting that I please provide them with two or three more names of potential external reviewers, and if possible, female reviewers. To quote mindfulness curriculum, I flipped my lid. I had provided nine names of potential external reviewers in my application, when only six were required. All individuals were established and recognized national contributors to my field and each was clearly at arm's length. I identified individuals from across Canada. I had provided this list before the submission date, as I knew securing individuals to do the review is sometimes problematic. There were both males and females on my list, although there were seven males and two females. I am in a male-dominated field, particularly among those with similar and relatable field experiences.

The gender inequity is not surprising—not to anyone who knows the field of educational leadership research in Canada. Yet there was a request for more, along with the additional request that they be female. In what part of the collective agreement was it required (or even suggested) that the list include specific members of identified groups? Nowhere. What the collective agreement states is that "the committee may also suggest names of potential external reviewers." Asking me to identify names, and only female (or any other identifiable group) names, is not described. It may have been that the females on the list were unavailable. But then, why not say they had been approached and were unavailable, and this was the reason for the request? Why does it matter what gender they are as long as they are appropriate reviewers for my application? Why add hidden interpretive elements to extend the terms of the collective agreement?

The anger I felt on receiving that email built on the pre-existing condition from the previous year's requirement for more, and continues to this day. It also came hot on the heels of several issues related to collegiality that had been swirling in the faculty for several months. I was awash with annoyance: What is the point of a collective agreement if it is not to ensure adherence to the exact process? What is the definition of a colleague? Is it someone who continually asks for more than the required documentation during something as significant as the tenure and promotion process? I felt it was an attack on several fronts—on me, on men, and possibly on my field. I responded, trying to first calm my own insecurity and anger with the process, before I wrote anything. But I did challenge the request by suggesting a read of the collective agreement. I provided three more names, all male, who could serve as reviewers.

The entire experience from the earliest stage of the tenure consideration through to today has reinforced that collegial is a word that universities and faculty use, but it may not always be operationalized, even in tasks with great individual consequences. I have identified three possible reasons for sending an email that requests something beyond the collective agreement. The first is that of the people enacting the process at this stage may not have read or understood the collective agreement. According to the collective agreement, it is an option for them to select individuals should they want to add to the list of external reviewers. There are clear guidelines in the collective agreement. The majority of reviewers must continue to be from the applicant's provided list. Having been told the year before that I could not submit something late under any circumstances, and then being asked to submit something late the next year was distressing. Why did this not apply this year? The second reason is darker: Was it an effort to unsettle me? Perhaps intended to create some sort of evidence as to how I deal with animosity? This is also not an item in the collective agreement. It seems hard to believe this could have been the intent, yet why the decision? The process might have been better-served by overruling the request and following the collective agreement in a precise manner. The third reason, for me, darker still: the process felt a certain moral authority/superiority by identifying a minority group and calling for greater representation of said group, and wanted to advance a social agenda in doing this. A great many other factors could be included in a description of representativeness, beyond sexual identity. Really? Is this possible? It seems unlikely. But doubt creeps in, nothing is certain. This all occurred early in the process. It was very unsettling.

Other issues of policy implementation, as opposed to policy itself, exist. The process as practiced involves individuals serving as reviewers with tenure who have been promoted to a minimum rank of Associate Professor/ Senior Lecturer and includes both bipartite (teaching and service) and tripartite (teaching, research, and service). This may be because those who have been promoted and who have tripartite positions are fewer. Tripartite faculty members are more expensive for the university, and although tripartite is essential to the university mission to add research to our world, fewer and fewer tripartite positions are being created. The inclusion of bipartite faculty may be a concern, since 40 percent of a tripartite position is the production of knowledge, typically through research, although other productions of knowledge (art installations, to name one) are seen as very important evidence of knowledge production. Why would a bipartite (teaching/service) person be involved in the process of review for someone who is tripartite (teaching/research/service, 40%+40%+20%)? They are not likely engaged in the production of research, as their teaching requirements are considerable (80%+20%). By the time they are tenured as bipartite they are at considerable distance from their doctoral research. I believe this question should be explored.

Finally, Educational Leadership academics primarily oriented to my area, a K–12 perspective, and who have been leadership practitioners at some point in their careers, are predominantly male. This is changing, but it has not yet changed. The imposition of some very limited version of equity that has not been officially described or investigated as to what equity might mean in different contexts, challenges me to constantly consider what we are really talking about in this sphere. If we are going to institute some form of equity qualification this most definitely needs to be done with a number of issues in mind. When the time comes to determine equity or representativeness there is a great deal more to consider than gender.

April
In the last month, I have started sleeping deeply and restfully. I did not know this tenure and promotion tension was having such a physiological effect on me. It was; thankfully it is over.

I am currently spending the first hour every morning writing and/or reading. I love this. It does not make me anxious, nor is it a luxury. This is exactly what I am supposed to be doing, and recovery from the physiological response to the tension enables this. I close my door and turn inward, enjoying the journey. On good days, I may get another hour later. Now, several months later, this routine is sustainable because I look forward to it. My sense of accomplishment and being on top of my interests is flourishing.

I continue to work weekends. My pattern has been to work two hours on Saturday and two hours on Sunday most weekends. That work is now mostly enjoyable. I am reading research, writing article summaries, and writing. It is something I look forward to rather than something I am squeezing in. Some weekends I handle email, marking, travel arrangements, complete peer reviews, and work on a few of the thousand other items that are constantly on the to-do lists. Those are less satisfying, but sometimes it clears space later in the week.

June

Almost two months have passed. My term as a program coordinator continues. This service task seems to have so little reward that others are not eager to engage in this work; we take turns stepping up. Since it has to be done, and it is my turn, here I am, scheduling away, doing it. I have to take a turn. Is this an example of collegiality? Yes.

I am back from the annual conference of the Canadian Society for the Study of Education (CSSE), which is the largest conference in Canada pertaining to education research. It's an event I now realize is about seeing colleagues from across the country, connecting with them, recognizing the group I belong in, and expanding the group so it takes on new and different forms. My colleagues, including a former thesis student who taught me how to use a Delphi Process, and I conducted one as part of a research presentation. This process, developed by Dalkey and Helmer (1963) is identified as "a widely used and accepted method for gathering data from respondents within their domain of expertise. The technique is designed as a group communication process, which aims to achieve a convergence of opinion on a specific real-world issue" (Hsu & Sandford, 2007, 1). Colleagues at the session thought it was a daring change to conference work—from presentation to inquiry—and was an excellent use of conference time.

I did not realize this was groundbreaking, but apparently it was! People seemed to like the idea that we used the time to research together; they saw a research methodology in practice.

Another ah ha moment was that serving on a national committee creates a certain understanding of the group you are serving. This, in turn, leads to at least some recognition of oneself as a researcher and academic. While I did not explicitly aspire to it, I became involved and have a major commitment to about 120 members. Many people do understand that program planning and many other details are quite involved. Others have served and they know the work involved. There are opportunities that arise when we are conferring within a specialized network. One colleague invited me to participate in his research. I had never spoken to this individual before. Another colleague invited me to a meeting at his university, and invited me as an equal, not as an after-thought. I invited two colleagues into a research project and both were eager to accept. Am I now a legitimate academic? Is this a different side of collegiality? The tenure and promotion process implies caution: We will see.

I have reviewed the list of students I am supervising in the Master of Education program for six credit projects or nine credit theses. There are nine of them. I am trapped in this service mindset; we are not given workload release for supervision. I've put a list on my whiteboard that includes my own writing on top, and the students beneath that, so I can be reminded, by simply raising my head, exactly who these students are, and why I need to tell the next few coming to my door, "No." Despite the time devoted to these students, they are the highlight of my weeks. It is such engaging work. I am trapped, not by service, but by my desire for relationship and co-learning.

June 29
>   It matters not how strait the gate,
>   How charged with punishments the scroll.
>   I am the master of my fate:
>   I am the captain of my soul. (Henley, Invictus, 1888)

Today, the penultimate day before tenure and promotion, I reviewed the details for taking a sabbatical. While I have thought about this in the past, today I contextualized details I had not previously considered, including the challenges/opportunities my taking a sabbatical would create in our Department. It dawned on me that I really do not owe much, beyond my solid contribution of say 60 hours a week. I need to do what is right for me, within the confines of the constraints (or interpreted constraints) of applicable policies, such as the collective agreement. "Once bitten, twice shy," as the saying goes; be sure to know what I need to know. Then read the rules again. Defining what is right for me, within this rule-driven environment, is really a matter of mapping the next five or six years, something that mirrors the five-year perspective of creating a tenure and promotion application. I am the captain of this ship, and the expectation is that I exercise autonomy. Wow. Lightbulb! I am applying for sabbatical!

The Finest Hour: July 1

Tenure? Done. Promotion? Done. Autonomy? Clearer. Journey? Ongoing.

What about this incredible journey did I actually know before I began? Actually, very little. My years in university as a student, full-time and part-time (while I worked full time, commuted to work, commuted to the university, and raised three children) totaled more than 17, resulting in five earned degrees and several additional professional qualification, but it did not teach me much about the university from a faculty member's perspective (i.e., the academy).

Did fussing about how to begin this tenure and promotion journey really matter? No. I did not know what road I was on, I did not know it was an incredible journey, I did not realize the costs of the journey to me personally, and I did not know what I would learn on the journey, and I definitely still do not know how the journey will end. The journey is the story.

I have been thinking most of my life about the Robert Frost poem *The Road Not Taken*:

> Two roads diverged in a yellow wood,
> And sorry I could not travel both
> And be one traveler, long I stood
> And looked down one as far as I could
> To where it bent in the undergrowth;
>
> Then took the other, as just as fair,
> And having perhaps the better claim,
> Because it was grassy and wanted wear;
> Though as for that the passing there
> Had worn them really about the same,
>
> And both that morning equally lay
> In leaves no step had trodden black.
> Oh, I kept the first for another day!
> Yet knowing how way leads on to way,
> I doubted if I should ever come back.
>
> I shall be telling this with a sigh
> Somewhere ages and ages hence:

> Two roads diverged in a wood, and I—
> I took the one less traveled by,
> And that has made all the difference.

Robert Frost was actually poking fun at a friend who was agonizing over the details of his future. Frost thought the perseveration about which path to take was unnecessary, that vacillation was a wasted use of energy; in the end we all end up in the same place. I look back and think about what would have happened if I had stayed in my school district, stayed at a provincial organization, or had not moved between provinces. Events would have been different, I would be a different person, but none of it may really matter—I will ultimately retire with roughly the same pension, roughly the same feeling of contribution, roughly the same feeling of satisfaction. I will have learned things. The details of the learning within that journey are not necessarily that important. It is a path, just follow it.

As a co-editor, I had lengthy discussions after *The Academic Gateway* (Sibbald & Handford, 2017) about possible theoretical frameworks for describing the tenure-track journey experience along with a transformation when one is granted tenure. A component that may apply is self-determination theory and I have considered its applicability. What generated feelings of competence, of relatedness and/or of autonomy, the backbone of self-determination theory, for me? A university tripartite faculty position is surely the very embodiment of expectations that lead someone to become autonomous, competent, and positioned in relation to others—relatedness.

In true positivist fashion, I have totted it up, and considered what mattered along my way.

Competence, Relatedness, and Autonomy

Competence generators helped me with

- Teaching: revising course outlines, revising assignments, revising lectures, teaching new courses, all the tasks of teaching: they all created a sense of competence.
- Program development: I had the opportunity to develop a non-credit program. I found working with the professionals who contributed to this program rewarding, validating, and

confirming of my skills. These individuals were primarily practitioners, although all had significant educational attainments, including terminal degrees. I was the research voice and I could see that I was the research voice!
- Publishing: I have managed to publish, learn from the writing process, and feel some pride in results. Rejections and revisions are part of the process. I have benefitted from peer reviewers' comments.
- Graduate Students: I have supervised a great many theses and projects for graduate students. While helping them generate a thesis or project is significant work, the pride I feel when they finish is tangible. Graduate students have generated considerable reflective thinking for me.
- Reading: I was listening to myself working with a thesis student this morning. The number of articles I directed that student towards was astonishing! I knew, without looking, author, year, and the basics of the title. This is competence.
- Presentations: I am aware that I present with increasing confidence, and with fewer references to experts from afar than I once did. Increasingly, I bring expertise to the table.

Autonomy generators helped me with

- Research: Working in a comparatively young graduate program (the MEd at my university began around 2010, the university itself began in 2005) that has grown exponentially, with little increase in hiring in the last three years, has meant autonomy has been required. Learning to accept the autonomy is a bigger challenge. I am a leadership research group of one. I am, indeed, autonomous, but working on research, publishing and receiving rejections are things that increase my autonomy. I go deeper, have a wide base of knowledge from which to contextualize what I read, and often dive into research, surfacing hours later, wondering where the time went. This is autonomy.
- Working weekends: Solitude and quiet dominate in my university office on weekends; it is a very productive space. Our faculty has worked hard to change our email culture,

so the computer is not pinging away with internal tasks on the weekend. I generally tackle tasks that are meaningful to me, as opposed to meaningful to the university.

Describing the relatedness generators that helped me constitutes a longer section. Relatedness, or conversely, the isolation that comes with a faculty position, is significant. The role is predominantly characterized by working alone. As the years go on, solitariness starts feeling normal. No one really knows what you are doing until you either publish, participate in a meeting, conduct a class, or engage in something else observable by others. In between, it is isolated. For some of us this can mean small irritants, such as the requirement of yet another revision to an article, can blossom into a tidal wave of discontent. There are few opportunities to share your experiences and the isolation is sometimes quite profound. Why does this happen? I will propose a couple of reasons.

There is competitiveness in the academy, in spite of espousing collegiality, and the juxtaposition of rhetoric and reality is different from other roles I have had. Most faculties are collectives of unlikes. A university has been described as "a multitude of microclimates, some of which resemble feudal fiefdoms" (Gunsalus, 2006, p. 46). While true of the university, it is also true within departments. We work beside each other but much of our actual work is quite different. We all seek funding; we are all drinking from the same diminishing water hole. Taking care to see beyond the competitive and to the relational is an important part of positive productivity. As colleagues we share many things that are of value personally and institutionally. The positive relational experiences need to be fed.

The exact opposite of isolation happens, but it is on a computer screen. The amount of email in a university is staggering. One possible reason for this is people are in front of screens and alone most of the day, which creates the opportunity to send email. This suggests some disconnectedness or personal identification that their isolated work is undervalued. Email at a university may be a mystery to me, but there is a lot of email. It is not unusual, for me, to face over 100 emails in a day.

Research is not public work. Faculty members engage in research that few in the world are interested in, and because of diverse needs in the institution, few within the same institution find interesting. This is true even in large, research-intensive universities, albeit the larger size may reduce the isolation. We learn to live in the worlds of advanced searches, keyboard time, drafting documents, and submitting items. Other activities start to feel like an interruption to this research-intensive meditative state.

The steady feeling of being of no value to funding agencies such as SSHRC/NSERC/CIHR and others further diminishes willingness to connect. The university itself promotes those who are able to generate funding, without acknowledging that there are niche research areas that for whatever reason are currently valued. Additionally, researchers with funding frequently sit on the very review panels that determine funding ... and a corresponding myopic view of research foci can develop. The university is a club where membership is highly coveted, and most applicants are rejected. Pet projects or strategic priorities generally have the same root as headlines, they seem to change with the political climate and are unpredictable—more isolation. The increased use of contract faculty, with no research requirements, significantly restricts hiring of faculty into tripartite positions. The pond keeps shrinking, even as management and teaching/service roles increase.

Despite all of this, and I will limit the lack of relatedness to those few paragraphs, there are things that help me feel a sense of relatedness and connection. Some of these include

- Writing with colleagues: I enjoy this. When the opportunity presents itself, I rarely say no.
- Serving a national committee: Much as there is little reward in serving on committees, the engagement does create a sense of relatedness for me. I know what colleagues from across the country are studying; I interact with multiple colleagues in the process of completing the peer reviews of submissions. There are endless emails about banquets, book launches, Annual General Meetings, awards, and other details, all of which create a sense that, at least in my field in Canada—we are related. It makes Canada smaller, and creates subject relatedness across the country, even as there is no subject-specific relatedness at my institution.
- Attending School of Education meetings: We are all educators, first. I enjoy this group.
- I continue to engage in an active professional relationship with my former doctoral supervisor, now co-researcher.

He encourages me to focus and to keep putting one foot in front of the other. He is the most constant part of my entire academic journey. Some do criticize this as evidence of a lack of autonomy. I think they are sorely mistaken. It is evidence of relatedness.

And How This Relates to Grief

In addition to self-determination theory, discussion of theoretical underpinnings of the tenure-track journey includes a component of grief. The journey, no matter what path we take in life, is about loss. We gain only to discover that something important to us is lost as we travel. We reflect on our path and perhaps see we took the (grassier, rockier, more scenic) route, but it led to the same destination.

My grieving related to moving to a university is mostly finished. I have come to terms with the concept that all futures have gifts and gaps—including the academy. In order to experience some of the gifts, I have left life-long relationships behind. The longer I stay here the more I realize the veracity of this. My closest friends are still my closest friends, wherever we are. My family is my family—we are well connected. What is lost is any sense of currency in personal relationships beyond these ancient connections. I am an important contributor—I do not see myself living in this community for the rest of my life, so I do not settle and establish roots. I may be done with feeling that I have lost valued things, or that I need to replace those life-long and distant individuals with local individuals.

My children have learned a great deal watching my doctoral/professoriate journey. All have completed graduate degrees, two are in doctoral programs, and all are publishing. In fact, one son was asked to read an article last week at his summer job where my other son was a contributing author! They have journeyed with me. They are young and optimistic. They do not know what they do not know. This is a good thing. I can see this journey of mine has been walked with each of them. Each now travels their own path. There will be moments, perhaps years from now, when they will remember some element of my journey, and it may bring a smile to their faces. Some of the path will be similar, much of it will be different. But, they will choose and they will journey. I rejoice. The last stage of my grief—acceptance.

References

Dalkey, N. C., & Helmer, O. (1963). An experimental application of the Delphi method to the use of experts. *Management Science, 9*(3), 458–467.

Gunsalus, C. K. (2006). *A College administrator's survival guide*. Boston, Mass: Harvard University Press.

Hsu, C. C., & Sandford, B. A. (2007). The Delphi technique: Making sense of consensus. *Practical Assessment, Research & Evaluation, 12*(10), 1–8. https://pareonline.net/getvn.asp?v=12&n=10

CHAPTER 12

Potholes and Possibilities: Pursuing Academic Interests in the Era of the Corporate University

Greg Ogilvie

When I wrote the chapter in *The Academic Gateway: Understanding the Journey to Tenure* (Ogilvie, 2017), I was still working on my doctoral dissertation and had just finished my first year working in the Faculty of Education at i the University of Lethbridge. Although I had applied for the tenure-track position in my field, I was offered a term position because I do not speak French and my predecessor in the position had established the norm of teaching all courses in Canada's other official language—a practice that became embedded in the psyche of my hiring committee and in the university calendar. In essence, the term position acted as a three-year audition for the tenure-track position for which I had originally applied. As I write this chapter, I am completing my fifth year at the University of Lethbridge and have secured a tenure-track position, with the intention of applying for tenure in the next year or two.

The four-plus years I spent working in the Faculty of Education have been very rewarding, but also very busy and exhausting. I have consistently taught five or six courses each year, including supervising student teachers in schools across southern Alberta. I have tried to support the faculty as much as possible by participating on numerous internal committees, and I have sought out opportunities to make contributions to the broader community, for example by becoming a board member for Alberta Teachers of English as a Second Language (ATESL) as the chair/co-chair for the organization in the southern region of the province. In addition, I have engaged in numerous writing and research projects, resulting in conference presentations and publications, but also improvements in my teaching practice. The life I have led as a young academic is not particularly different from what I had imagined it would be—challenging, yet fulfilling. Nonetheless, as I progress toward applying for tenure, I find myself confronting numerous dilemmas in my work as an academic, emanating from tensions between my professional identity and institutional discourses surrounding the work of academics; discourses largely embedded in a pragmatic, corporate rationale.

In the following sections, I will briefly outline how business principles have influenced the field of education and altered the ethos of universities. I will then outline how the corporate university has influenced my experiences as a novice academic as I pursue tenure, creating tensions between institutional expectations and my professional identity. I will then conclude by using Self-Determination Theory to explain how institutional pressures within the corporate university have created professional dilemmas, reducing autonomy and workplace satisfaction.

Neoliberalism and the Corporate University

The university is commonly referred to as an ivory tower in contemporary society. The irony of this description is that the institution, as the location for intellectual pursuits unencumbered by practical concerns, has not existed for quite some time. As outlined by Readings (1996), this conceptualization of the university has been laid in ruins, replaced by an institution with a definitive corporate ethos. The influence of business principles in education is not a new phenomenon, but the degree of influence of corporate thinking has never been greater, as it has become embedded within the fabric of higher education in recent years.

The increased influence of industry in education can be traced back to the turn of the twentieth century. At that time, Frederick Taylor's ideas about scientific management began to take root in the business community (Schachter, 2010). Taylor's ideas about management, which later became known as Taylorism, were grounded in the assumption that there existed a best way to do everything; therefore, the task of an industrial manager was to gather pertinent information about desired work, systematically analyze the task according to scientific methods, figure out the most efficient way to complete the task, and relay this information to workers to guide production (Au, 2011). According to Schachter (2010), over 200 businesses applied Taylor's principles of scientific management in the design of their production by 1915, resulting in increased earnings and more objective decision-making.

The success of Taylorism in the business world appealed to educators, such as John Franklin Bobbitt, who sought to apply the same ideas to the realm of teaching. What this meant was reconceptualizing schools as factory assembly lines by identifying the means to achieve predetermined outcomes in the most efficient manner possible. The Taylorist approach "allowed the curriculum to be broken down into minute units of work that could be standardized, determined in advance, taught in a linear manner, and easily assessed" (Au, 2011, p. 28). Objectives and educational standards dictated the educational process, with administrators outlining the methods to be used in achieving the goals and supervising teachers to ensure proper implementation. As the determination of methods to achieve goals was deemed too advanced for teachers, the role of the teacher was minimized to that of a technician. The influence of scientific management in education has been apparent in subsequent curriculum theories, such as the Tyler Rationale, and approaches adopted for the supervision of teachers (Sullivan & Glanz, 2009).

Although business principles have influenced the field of education for quite some time, the corporate infiltration of universities has been slower, relying more on the entrenchment of neoliberal policies in the government sphere. Broadly speaking neoliberalism is an "agenda of economic and social transformation under the sign of the free market" (Connell, 2013, p. 100). Neoliberalism first gained political power in Chile under the dictatorship of General Augusto Pinochet in the 1970s and ascended to global prominence during the tenures of Margaret Thatcher in England and Ronald Reagan in the United States during the 1980s. A central tenet of neoliberalism is the expansion of the free market; thus, government policies have sought to enlarge existing markets and create new markets through deregulation and privatization. This has resulted in the commodification of services that were previously deemed a public good (Connell, 2013) and increased pressure on public institutions to be competitive in the marketplace. Invariably this has led to the rebranding of institutions as "entrepreneurial universities" or the marketization or corporatization of higher education institutes to create a competitive edge (Wright & Greenwood, 2017). The competitive mandate has shifted the focus of higher education institutes, creating a greater emphasis on programs that are responsive to market demands. Hence, fields of study that are less aligned with marketable skills are either eliminated or in peril (Donoghue, 2018). The emphasis on free market principles has also resulted in declining tax revenues and corresponding decreases in funding for public institutions (Stromquist & Monkman, 2014). The financial challenges created by decreased government funding and the imperative to be responsive to market demands has contributed to increased collaboration with the corporate world. Although these collaborations have minimized the financial burden experienced by universities, they also raise questions about the viability of the university as a sight for unbiased knowledge generation and its general function in society. Regardless, the partnerships with corporate entities and financial challenges that have been experienced have made universities more amenable to importing organizational structures from the business world. This includes prioritizing services that have market value, promoting efficiency in the production of goods and services, and developing mechanisms to promote accountability. The impact of these emphases in the corporate university will be explored further in relation to my experiences as an academic in the sections below.

Star Stickers for Scholars
During the last academic year, I was approached by a colleague and asked to observe a class and provide feedback on her performance. I was happy to have received this request, as I enjoy supporting the professional growth of educators and gain a lot of insight by observing how different classrooms are organized and the instructional practices undertaken. Moreover, I believe supporting my peers in this way creates collegial bonds that will only help to improve communication and the functioning of the faculty in the future. I observed my colleague teach for over two hours, documented feedback about strengths and potential improvements in the lesson in a formal letter, and met with her to discuss the lesson and her teaching. We had an excellent discussion about teaching and I left feeling very positive about the experience.

Approximately two weeks later I found a certificate in my mailbox from this colleague verifying my participation in the activities and thanking me for my support. At first I was very confused by the certificate. Why did my colleague feel the need to create this certificate? Couldn't her time have been better used in other ways? What significance did the certificate have for me? My initial feeling was that the certificate diminished the experience in some way, as if the only justification for possibly engaging in such an activity were receiving some recognition, like a Scout receiving a badge to sew onto his or her shirt. As I reflected further on the experience I realized that my negative reaction to the certificate was based on the fact that the document was emblematic of a stifling, competitive professional system that does not cohere with my values as an educator.

Performance in an academic setting has always been measured; however, the quantification of performance has intensified in the era of the corporate university. Market forces require the quantification of production both at an internal and external level. Internally, the mechanism serves to identify those individuals who are contributing most to the institution so that merit-based incentives (whether in the form of increased salary, recognition, or status) may be awarded. Externally, the mechanism serves to track the performance of institutions in relation to each other, providing information to facilitate consumers making an informed choice and acting as an incentive for improved performance. While institutions establish the criteria for internal review, accountability mechanisms for the performance of institutions are often external. In Canada, for example, *Maclean's* magazine publishes a ranking of post-secondary institutions to provide information to potential attendees (consumers). The criteria utilized to establish the rankings influence how universities are perceived, so it will inevitably influence the priorities of institutions, reinforcing Greenwood's (2012) contention that external ranking organizations are seizing control of academic life away from campuses.

A ranking system based on the quantification of performance inevitably ascribes value to particular activities and not others. As tangible forms of production are much easier to measure, they are often given greater importance than other aspects of performance. As a result, assessment of performance is often limited to "how many research grants per faculty member, how much research money per faculty member and unit, how many publications in which journals, how highly ranked are the journals, how many citations to these publications, etc." (Greenwood, 2012, p. 118). The attribution of merit based on narrow quantitative measures doesn't act as just a tracking system, but also influences the work of academics in several important ways.

First and foremost, a quantitative system of evaluation dictates the type of work in which academics engage. Prevalent business terminology such as accountability and efficiency have become normalized and are no longer questioned as the guide for production. In the realm of industrial manufacturing, accountability provides the motivation to ensure optimal production through efficiency. When applied to the academic realm, however, the terms are highly problematic. Unlike factory lines that encourage limited, repetitive tasks to produce the final product, scholarly work is intense, multi-faceted and creative. Therefore, promoting efficiency through accountability does not lead to increased production in academic work so much as altered production.

To illustrate, pressure for immediate and sustained production would lead to more cost-benefit analysis being applied to academic work. This would result in privileging short-term research projects with the potential for a quick turnaround over long-term investigations (blue sky research) that would not yield immediate results. It would also lead to conducting research that is easier to publish. Although the landscape of publishing opportunities has evolved over the years, providing increased venues for alternative forms of research, there are still vastly more journals that prescribe to traditional forms of research. The quantification of performance would thus motivate the use of methodologies consistent with those accepted by the majority of journals (i.e., traditional). Similarly, market-driven forms of assessment would influence the topics of investigation. Academia is famous for bandwagon jumpers, having many researchers simultaneously pursue a particular research approach. At any given time, particular topics are in vogue leading to increased opportunities for funding and dissemination. For example, executive functioning has become a vogue concept that is the focus of a plethora of research articles.

Another manner in which the type of research conducted is influenced by the system of merit is the emphasis placed on funding. With cutbacks becoming a regular occurrence in higher education, opportunities for internal funding are in decline. This has led to increased competition for internal funds and greater prestige given to the procurement of external sources of funding. It has also resulted in funding becoming a sign of achievement within the merit system.

Funding is not only used to quantify the work of a scholar, but it is also used, rightly or wrongly, to justify the value of the work completed (work that is funded is assumed to have greater value than work that is not funded). By ascribing direct value to funds procured, universities are giving the power to direct research initiatives to funding agencies, thus diminishing the autonomy of academics to determine the research agendas to be pursued. Furthermore, the importance of funding to one's standing as an academic researcher results in increased time dedicated to completing funding applications, rather than the actual work of scholarship.

Second, the quantification of performance creates an imperative to engage in activities that have direct output. Scholarly activities such as reading, engaging in discussions with colleagues, and contemplative reflection are more difficult to justify when they are not directly linked to a form of production. Menzies and Newson (2007) conducted a survey of academics about the changing environment in higher education and found that "they are not reading as deeply and reflectively as they used to or as they want to. Nor are they reading as broadly and inter-disciplinarily as they used to or as they'd like to" (p. 90). As such, the frenetic pace of academic life promoted by corporate notions of productivity is leading to a more narrow, specialized knowledge base. As Berg and Seeber (2016) noted, it can also limit the forms of knowledge produced through research:

> Corporate time speeds up and instrumentalizes research . . ..
> The culture of speed (and its associated values of efficiency, productivity, applicability, transferability) is at odds with an understanding of the ethical dimension of time because it forecloses potential ways of being and knowing. (p. 58)

Hence, the imperative for production creates a pace of academic life that has repercussions for the manner in which work is undertaken.

The importance of output within the system of merit also encourages self-promoting, individualistic decision-making. Just as star stickers are used to motivate children to engage in particular behaviours, the quantification of productivity is intended to promote increased scholarly activity. As any teacher knows, though, star stickers are just a temporary measure and if the behaviour becomes directly linked with them, it can have an adverse influence on the learning process going forward. Similarly, when professional decision-making is directly linked to self-promotion, it can have an adverse influence on the program.

In the world of academia, name recognition has significant value. It is highly desirable to be a known commodity in a field, as this is evidence of scholarly achievement. However, when name recognition (or perhaps more appropriately name advancement) becomes the primary motivator for actions it can create a counterproductive working environment. To elucidate this point, I will recall an interaction I had with a colleague last year. The colleague had asked to meet with me to discuss ideas she had for a research project. She had not conducted research of this manner previously and wanted to consult with me about the process. What was noteworthy about the interaction was that she started it by stating that she would include me in the research. This struck me because the obvious assumption was that dedicating the time to help her could only be justified if there were a quantifiable outcome of the time spent with her. If such a pragmatic, instrumentalist attitude to work life were adopted more whole scale, it would lead to a dysfunctional work environment where collegiality and collaboration would be undermined by self-interest. Moreover, instrumental decision-making could also result in actions that benefit the individual but undermine the integrity and quality of the program. For example, in my context faculty engage in supervision of students in field experiences across southern Alberta. Traveling to distant rural schools and engaging in ongoing observations and conferences with students is a very time consuming process and there is minimal accountability related to the quality of supervision provided. As such, a faculty member focused on self-promotion could easily dedicate minimal time to supporting students in the field in favour of conducting research and engaging in other activities that would have more tangible benefit to career advancement. In this way, pragmatism based on the system of merit would undermine the professional development experienced by pre-service teachers.

The emphasis on self-promotion and tangible productivity within higher education has created significant tensions in my work as an academic. Most significantly, an institutional norm has been created that does not cohere with my identity as a teacher educator. First and foremost I identify as an educator; I entered into the teaching profession because I wanted to make a difference in the lives of young people, and I transitioned to teacher education because I perceived that I could have a more far-reaching influence if I worked with future teachers. The desire to make a difference is grounded in an understanding of teaching as a caring profession. According to Noddings (2013), care is not just a disposition that teachers adopt, but rather a relational quality that is based on reciprocity. As such, care cannot be enacted by projecting one's thoughts and desires onto the cared-for; on the contrary, caring interactions involve attentiveness and receptiveness to the expressed needs and desires of the individuals with whom caregivers work (Noddings, 2012). Therefore, academic work grounded in care is based on selflessness and humility.

The work of a teacher educator foundationally based on an ethics of care contradicts the merit-based system of career advancement at universities. The former is based on relationship building and sacrifice. It is about investing in students and communities in a manner that promotes dialogic engagement leading to novel and unpredictable outcomes. It is also about supporting students and communities in ways that do not always result in tangible academic benefits (Ogilvie & Fuller, 2016). In contrast, systems of merit within higher education institutes are based on individual interest and self-promotion. Within this system, relationships are viewed in instrumental terms and actions are often undertaken with the distinct motive of career advancement. Although benefit may be accrued by all individuals involved, when the foundation for decision-making is grounded in self-interest, it can significantly influence how academic work is undertaken and who benefits most from it (as demonstrated by the example above). This type of relationship mirrors what Buber (1958) called the "I/It" relationship—a relationship predicated on positioning the other as an object for personal benefit. It contrasts an authentic caring relationship characterized by openheartedness, honesty, mutuality, and spontaneity, labeled by Buber (1958) as an "I/Thou" relationship. As my goal in entering academia was grounded in a caring rationale, navigating a system of merit based on self-interest has been challenging, creating a constant tension between being true to myself and my students, and gaining recognition for achievements from external sources.

The merit-based system has not only challenged my identity as a teacher educator, but also created dilemmas in the work I undertake. As a young scholar who has yet to apply for tenure, the need for quantifiable production is paramount. Nonetheless, my desire to make a real impact on teachers and teaching, rather than following an academic agenda simply to promote career advancement, has also influenced how I engage in scholarship. Over the past few years, I have engaged in research with a colleague about the dynamics between the supervision triad (student teacher, mentor teacher, and university supervisor) and their influence on the professional development experiences of students. Although supervision is not a major topic within the education literature, we have been able to secure numerous sources of funding for the project and have had many outputs associated with the research. This research project has allowed me to pursue my interests while also satisfying the criteria for production set out by the university.

My scholarly interests have also revolved around collaborative communities of practice to support innovation in teaching. This academic year, six teacher educators have established a group to explore ways of indigenizing our practices. Although there was an expressed focus for the group, the exploration has proceeded in a very organic manner, leading to intellectually stimulating but not directly related discussions. In keeping with the tone of the meetings, the group has decided to engage in *métissage* related to our journey in centering reconciliation in our teaching practices. According to Blood et al. (2012), *métissage* "relies on collaboration and collective authorship as a strategy for exemplifying, as research practice and text, the transcultural, interdisciplinary, and shared nature of experience and memory" (p. 48). The approach fits perfectly not only with the structure of the group, but also the content of investigation. Moreover, it has contributed to significant insights that have influenced the work of members in the group. Nonetheless, engaging in work of this nature is very risky as the potential for publication is reduced by the unique, non-traditional structure of the approach. Therefore, a dilemma emerges between pursuing academic interests in a genuine fashion and adopting scholarly practices that will gain recognition in the corporate university.

To Teach or Not to Teach, That Is the Question

George Bernard Shaw's famous maxim "those who can, do; those who cannot, teach" permeates discussion about teaching across North America. For years governments have attempted to capitalize on the sentiment expressed in the saying by scapegoating teachers for perceived declining performance. Portraying teachers as lazy, incompetent, and overpaid has served a political purpose in combatting the power of teachers' unions and pushing forward educational reforms that are often grounded in limiting teacher influence through standardized testing and teacher-proof curricula (Compton & Weiner, 2008; Au, 2011). The political attack on the profession has also served to perpetuate the negative perception of teaching embodied in the maxim articulated by George Bernard Shaw many years ago.

The negative perception of the teaching profession has also influenced the way faculties of education are perceived. Recently, a colleague of mine in the Faculty of Education participated in a university-wide meeting to adjudicate research proposals for a funding grant. Much to her bewilderment, a number of academics from other faculties expressed surprise to hear that scholars in the Faculty of Education conduct research. This sentiment may have been the result of the fact that statistically the Faculty of Education at the University of Lethbridge does proportionately contribute less to the research agenda of the institution than other faculties and departments; however, what is not factored into this assessment is the fact that we have greater non-research related responsibilities, including teaching more classes and supervising students in schools spread across the southern portion of the province. Irrespective of the origins of the sentiment, the misinformed statement about the Faculty of Education as a site of knowledge production and dissemination is clearly a sign of the generally low perception of the field of education.

The low perception of education is also reflected in the importance ascribed to teaching at the university. The well-known publish or perish dictum is a fact of life in academia, emphasizing the importance of research in the advancement of one's career. A similar sentiment about teaching is rarely, if ever expressed, highlighting the clear hierarchy of value within higher education. A recent university-wide meeting to explore the process of career advancement within the institution clearly demonstrated this hierarchy. While the majority of the meeting was dedicated to highlighting ways research could be used to advocate for career advancement, mere minutes were provided to discuss the importance of teaching in the process. What is even more troubling is that the only comments made to verify the quality of teaching related to following university endorsed grade distributions and making ongoing changes to course outlines to demonstrate that teaching was being refined. No mention was given to fair assessment practices, innovative instruction, or pedagogy that challenges students to stretch their thinking in new ways. In essence, the only standard ascribed to teaching was in demonstrating self-reflective practice related to the need for improvement and maintaining institutional standards. The presentation of teaching in such limited terms clearly demonstrates not only a lack of knowledge about the complexity of pedagogy, but also a total disregard for its value to professional achievement and the institution more broadly.

The value of teaching (or absence thereof) can also be seen in the neoliberal response to shrinking institutional budgets. As government funding for higher education continues to erode, the natural response is to reduce costs or to tap into new revenue sources. The latter approach has contributed to the growing internationalization of universities (Sidhu, 2006). Whereas local populations provide a finite number of students for institutions, access to international markets provides opportunities for exponential growth. When the sheer number of students is combined with the increased fees asked of out of country students, it is clear why university administrators have sought to promote the internationalization of their institutions.

The alternative, and often complementary approach to dealing with declining budgets, is to reduce costs. A reduction in research budgets or incentives to lure prestigious scholars can result in the diminishment of the reputation of a higher education institution, so the natural response is to cut funding for that which is deemed to have less value to the institution, namely teaching. The general trend in the neoliberal era is to create corporate flexibility by reducing the number of full-time employees and replacing them with increased numbers of temporary workers. This approach has been applied to universities by reducing the number of tenured faculty, placing greater emphasis on the research production of the smaller number of tenured faculty, and increasingly hiring adjunct professors or graduate students to teach courses on limited contracts (Washburn, 2005; Donoghue, 2018). Although there are numerous adverse repercussions associated with the trend towards a precarious and more mobile teaching faculty (Washburn, 2005), one of the significant effects is the continued diminishment of the perceived value of teaching excellence.

All of this is important because it has created significant tension for me in my work as a teacher educator. I entered the teaching profession two decades ago because I wanted to make a difference in the lives of young people and through that process influence society more broadly. After working in Ethiopia for two years as an instructor at the Gondar College of Teacher Education and as a facilitator for the Gondar English Methodology Project and the World Bank sponsored Higher Diploma Program, I decided that I could make an even bigger difference by working in pre-service and in-service teacher education. This motivated my pursuit of graduate studies at the University of Alberta and continued work in teacher education during the completion of my master's and doctoral degrees by teaching courses in the Faculty of Education and the Faculty of Extension (which housed language instruction for international students) and by supervising student teachers during the completion of practicums in the field. It also contributed to joining the University of Lethbridge, as the program is well known for teaching excellence and provides unique opportunities for faculty to work with teachers in the field.

I enjoy conducting research and believe that disseminating research findings through conference presentations and publications can be impactful; nonetheless, I believe the relationships I establish with teachers and the work I do with student teachers is far more impactful in influencing what takes place in classrooms. As a result, I have consistently taught six courses per year on overload (a standard course load in our faculty is five courses per year) and have dedicated a substantial amount of time to my coursework, both in terms of exploring ways to improve teaching practice and providing extensive support for students. The passion and excitement I have for teaching comes in stark contrast to the general discourse surrounding teaching at the university, even in a Faculty of Education. It is commonplace to hear colleagues talk with excited anticipation about going on study leave or procuring funding that would facilitate a reduced teaching load. This discourse portrays teaching as a nuisance or a necessary evil that facilitates attending to the real work of academia. I do not believe that these are isolated expressions of individuals disenchanted with teaching, but rather a sign of the value attributed to teaching in career advancement in the contemporary university. This raises the question: How can I maintain fidelity to my commitment to teaching in an environment that devalues those contributions?

The Customer Is Always Right

The free market system requires mechanisms be in place to facilitate informed decision-making on the part of consumers about particular products or services and to promote efficiency and accountability on the part of producers. The theory is that free access to information and competition between producers will lead to the most efficient system possible in which the consumer has an optimal experience (both in terms of the cost and the product or service received). As more abstract measures of performance are difficult to track, the mechanism utilized to surveil achievement inevitably involves a form of quantification, often in the form of customer ratings, awards received, comparative cost and quality, etc.

The motto "the customer is always right" is prevalent in North American society. It highlights the importance of providing high quality products and services to promote customer satisfaction. It is a given within a capitalist system that questionable performance on the part of a business will result in its eventual demise, as consumers will inevitably take their business elsewhere. Hence, if food at a restaurant is undercooked, dissatisfaction on the part of the customer will result in improvements in the product or reduced patronage, as failure to rectify the situation will result in the customer not returning to the restaurant. Similarly, dissatisfaction with the quality of electronics will result in improvements to the product or reductions in sales, as demonstrated by the recent history of cell phone consumption. Hence, consumer satisfaction serves to act as a safeguard for improved performance.

In the era of the corporate university, market logic has been applied to higher education institutions. Hence, students are now positioned as customers, while university faculty and staff are viewed as service providers. Within this arrangement, the satisfaction of consumers in relation to the quality of the service provided is of utmost importance. As a result, program surveys and course evaluations are viewed as important mechanisms for customer reviews to be provided, giving feedback on the quality of the program and making programs accountable for continued improvement. Although student evaluations are proven to be biased and unrelated to actual teaching performance (Canadian Association of University Teachers, 2018a; Mitchell, 2018; Ontario Confederation of University Faculty Associations, 2018), they are often utilized as evidence of the quality of teaching provided. On numerous occasions I have heard administrators praise the teaching of a faculty member based on the numerical scores received from student evaluations. Moreover, course evaluations are used as one of the primary sources of evidence about teaching ability on professional activity reports and applications for career advancement. According to market logic, these course evaluations should hold instructors accountable to provide and maintain high quality instruction. The logic applies to restaurant meals and consumer electronics, but does it apply to education within a professional faculty?

To address this question, I would like to recall an interaction with a very influential professor from my past. This professor taught during my undergraduate studies in the Faculty of Education at the University of Saskatchewan. She taught an education foundations course that encouraged exploration about privilege and means of promoting social justice. Although the course helped to elucidate how social and cultural capital had influenced my experiences and worldview, I recall significant levels of resistance being demonstrated, as students grappled with the implications of confronting their own privilege. Several years later while completing doctoral studies, I met this influential scholar again at a conference. I knew she had experienced significant frustration while instructing the course many years before, so I wanted to convey my appreciation for what I had learned. In our discussion she articulated the challenges she had experienced teaching controversial courses, but also the important understandings developed when students were pushed out of their comfort zones and forced to examine their deeply held beliefs. She emphasized that her purpose as an instructor was to create a challenging environment that would push learners towards substantive learning. In emphasizing this point, she made the comment: "If I get good course evaluations, I know I am *not* doing a good job." This comment still resonates with me and points to some of the issues associated with applying the market logic of customer satisfaction to a professional faculty.

First, the concept of customer satisfaction assumes that there is only one relationship of accountability—the one between the customer and the service provider. In many business contexts, this is true; however, in teacher education there are numerous stakeholders who have an interest in the outcome of teacher education programs. As a result, teacher educators are not only accountable to the students who come through faculties of education to prepare them for the rigours of the profession, but also to the profession itself, school divisions in which graduates work, and society more broadly to ensure teachers are prepared to promote quality education in schools. Furthermore, teacher education programs are required to ensure qualifying teachers meet the professional standards outlined by provincial governments. In such a context of multiple and potentially competing interests, focusing on the satisfaction of the consumer in the business relationship (i.e., the student attending a higher education institution) could be problematic, as it could contradict or undermine the broader goals and responsibilities of the program.

Second, the notion of customer satisfaction is premised on the consumer knowing what constitutes a quality product or experience. In typical transactions in a capitalist society the determination of the quality of the product or service provided is based on the experience of the consumer. For example, if an individual has a good experience at a hotel and enjoys the amenities offered, she will likely provide a positive review about the hotel and return to stay there in the future. In the context of teacher education though, individuals with limited knowledge about the teaching profession, let alone an understanding about the complexities of the teacher education process, are being asked to comment on the quality of the service provided. Research in the field of education has demonstrated that socialization into the teaching profession begins during the thousands of hours individuals spend as students in a classroom, what Lortie (1975) called the "apprenticeship of observation." During this time, teacher candidates develop an understanding about the work of teachers that frames how they interpret what takes place within a teacher education program. The problem is that the apprenticeship of observation provides a narrow, limited view of teaching and the work of teachers from the perspective of a student. It also sets as a standard of practice, pedagogical approaches that may not align well with contemporary understandings of the teaching-learning process. Therefore, the process of socialization into the teaching profession may result in the adoption of a lens that cannot account for the complexities of the teaching profession or the process of becoming an effective teacher. This undermines the value of the concept of customer satisfaction as a mechanism to hold service providers accountable for a quality product in a professional faculty.

Despite the aforementioned issues associated with customer satisfaction as a guiding principle in a professional faculty, discourses surrounding market imperatives continue to influence faculties of education. Market demand influences dialogue about the future structure of programs; rather than exclusively focusing on how to create programs to optimize professional learning, programmatic decisions are now also ensconced with strategies to promote competitiveness within the global market. This has resulted in altering the structure of programs to attract students (e.g., altering the length of programs or the mode of delivery for programs). Responsiveness to market demands is not limited to programmatic decision-making, as it also influences how individual courses are structured. Although some administrators overtly espouse the limitations of student evaluations and the opportunity to demonstrate teaching effectiveness using alternative means, student evaluations have been established as a baseline norm for ascertaining teaching quality. This is evident based on the fact that strong course evaluations (in particular, in terms of numerical scoring) are used as justification for excellence in performance without having to attend to the quality of instruction itself, whereas lesser evaluations require extensive justification to rationalize why higher scores were not obtained. This means that customer satisfaction within the corporate university has a direct impact on the articulation of teacher educators' work.

The emphasis on customer satisfaction within the structure of higher education institutions has had a significant impact on my work as a teacher educator. I feel an obligation as a teacher of future generations of teachers to provide a supportive yet challenging atmosphere to promote professional growth. I believe in providing experiences to challenge students' pre-determined notions of education and to encourage stretching their practices in new directions. Nonetheless, I have encountered resistance to this approach, in particular when students have deemed it to involve significant amounts of work. During the fifteen years I have taught at higher education institutions in Canada, I have noticed a correlation between numerical scores on course evaluations and the way I make students feel; the more accommodating and enjoyable the course is, the better the evaluations. Conversely, common criticisms of my teaching have focused on the number of readings and level of difficulty of the readings I assign and the rigour associated with assignments. As a result, I have experienced a continual tension between maintaining the rigour of the courses I teach and achieving high scores on student evaluations.

In addition to pressure related to workload, I have also experienced pressure from students related to the content of courses. Most students view education in very pragmatic terms and deem the primary purpose of coursework to prepare them for the real work of teaching during field experiences in schools. As a result, there is a tangible desire on the part of students to have classes focus on tips and tricks that can be applied in the classroom. Deviations to explore curriculum theory or the political character of education are often welcomed with scorn. Similarly, investigations about privilege and the maintenance of inequity, or the influence of the ideologies of meritocracy and individualism on teaching practices in schools are met with resistance, as they are deemed irrelevant to their work as teachers. In such a context, I am faced with the dilemma of educating teachers to navigate the complex, political terrain of teaching or succumbing to the desires of student teachers to be told how to teach. While I do not believe this is a new dilemma for teacher educators, the emergence of a corporate ethos in higher education has heightened the pressure to cater to customer satisfaction.

Conclusion

The journey to tenure in an academic position is an arduous one, characterized by numerous years of schooling and a rigorous process to prove one's ability to contribute to an institution on an ongoing basis in the areas of teaching, research, and service. Attainment of an academic position can be very rewarding, as it affords the individual the opportunity to pursue academic interests that can lead to a very satisfying career. The freedom and flexibility of work in academia is also accompanied by performance pressure that can enhance academic anxiety (Canadian Association of University Teachers, 2018b). This pressure to perform has been increased in recent years by the adoption of corporate principles in institutions of higher education.

Accountability measures are a normal aspect of professional and academic work, but in the context of contemporary faculties of education, the application of business principles in determining the value of academic performance has negatively impacted scholars and indirectly the programs in which they work. Educational research has demonstrated that measures of accountability undermine autonomy and adversely affect the creative energy dedicated to tasks (Ryan & Deci, 2000; Niemiec & Ryan, 2009). Research has also demonstrated that in situations where pressure to maintain standards results in controlling behaviours, attainment of the desired goals is actually undermined (Deci & Ryan, 1985). This research mirrors my experiences in that accountability measures that emphasize the quantification of production, privilege non-teaching related activities, and exacerbate the importance of student evaluations create an ongoing professional dilemma between acting in a manner that I perceive most benefits the field of education and pursuing personal interests related to career advancement. In addition to creating internal tensions, the infusion of a corporate ethos in higher education can encourage behaviours that are counterproductive to the goal of the program, namely the development of quality teachers and the advancement of the field of education. Hence, the market principles of efficiency and accountability can undermine job satisfaction and promote questionable professional practices. Nonetheless, while corporate imperatives create potholes in the form of tensions for academics to overcome, possibilities always exist for academics to exert their prerogative to challenge and resist the encroachment of business principles on their work.

References

Au, W. (2011). Teaching under the new Taylorism: high-stakes testing and the standardization of the 21st century curriculum. *Journal of Curriculum Studies, 43*, 25–45.

Berg, M., & Seeber, B. K. (2016). *The slow professor: Challenging the culture of speed in the academy*. Toronto, ON: University of Toronto Press.

Blood, N., Chambers, C., Donald, D., Hasebe-Ludt, E., & Big Head, R. (2012). Aoksisowaato'op: Place and story as organic curriculum. In N. Ng-A-Fook & J. Rottmann (Eds.), *Reconsidering Canadian curriculum studies: Provoking historical, present, and future perspectives* (pp. 47–82). New York, NY: Palgrave MacMillan.

Buber, M. (1958). *I and Thou* (2nd Ed.). New York, NY: Charles Scribner's Sons.

Canadian Association of University Teachers. (2018a). The end of student questionnaires? *Canadian Association of University Teachers Bulletin, 65*(8), 13–16.

Canadian Association of University Teachers. (2018b). Academic anxiety. *Canadian Association of University Teachers Bulletin, 65*(5), 14–19.

Compton, M., & Weiner, L. (2008). *The global assault on teaching, teachers, and their unions: stories for resistance*. New York, NY: Palgrave Macmillan.

Connell, R. (2013). The neoliberal cascade and education: An essay on the market agenda and its consequences. *Critical Studies in Education, 54*(2), 99–112.

Deci, E. L., & Ryan, R. M. (1985). Education. In E. Aronson (Ed.), *Intrinsic motivation and self-determination in human behavior* (pp. 245–271). Boston, MA: Springer.

Donoghue, F. (2018). *The last professors: The corporate university and the fate of the humanities*. New York, NY: Fordham University Press.

Greenwood, D. J. (2012). "Doing and learning action research in the neoliberal world of contemporary higher education." *Action Research, 10*(2), 115–132.

Lortie, D. (1975). *Schoolteacher: A sociological study*. Chicago, IL: University of Chicago Press.

Menzies, H., & Newson, J. (2007). No time to think: Academics' life in the globally wired university. *Time & Society, 16*, 83–98.

Mitchell, K. (2018). Student evaluations can't be used to assess professors: Our research shows they're biased against women. That means using them is illegal. https://slate.com/human-interest/2018/03/student-evaluations-are-discriminatory-against-female-professors.html

Niemiec, C. P., & Ryan, R. M. (2009). Autonomy, competence, and relatedness in the classroom: Applying self-determination theory to educational practice. *Theory and Research in Education, 7*, 133–144.

Noddings, N. (2012). The language of care ethics. *Knowledge Quest, 40*(5), 52–56.

Noddings, N. (2013). *Caring: A relational approach to ethics and moral education* (2nd Ed.). Berkeley, CA: University of California Press.

Ogilvie, G. (2017). The 'ten-year road' to tenure: A personal narrative of the beginning phases of the journey. In T. M. Sibbald, & V. Handford (Eds.), *The academic gateway: Understanding the journey to tenure* (pp. 217–232). Ottawa, ON: University of Ottawa Press.

Ogilvie, G., & Fuller, D. (2016). Restorative justice pedagogy in the ESL classroom: Creating a caring environment to support refugee students. *TESL Canada Journal, 33*(10), 86–96.

Ontario Confederation of University Faculty Associations. (2018). Significant arbitration decision on use of student questionnaires for teaching evaluation. https://ocufa.on.ca/blog-posts/significant-arbitration-decision-on-use-of-student-questionnaires-for-teaching-evaluation/

Readings, B. (1996). *The university in ruins*. Cambridge, MA: Harvard University Press.

Ryan, R. M., & Deci, E. L. (2000). Intrinsic and extrinsic motivations: Classic definitions and new directions. *Contemporary Educational Psychology, 25*, 54–67.

Schachter, H.L. (2010). The role played by Frederick Taylor in the rise of academic management fields. *Journal of Management History, 16,* 437–448.
Sidhu, R. K. (2006). *Universities and globalization: To market, to market.* Mahwah, NJ: Lawrence Erlbaum.
Stromquist, N. P., & Monkman, K. (2014). Defining globalization and assessing its implications for knowledge and education, revisited. In N. P. Stromquist & K. Monkman (Eds.), *Globalization and education: Integration and contestation across cultures* (pp. 1–19). Lanham, MD: Rowman & Littlefield.
Sullivan, S., & Glanz, J. (2009). *Supervision that improves teaching and learning: Strategies and techniques* (3rd Ed.). Thousand Oaks, CA: Corwin.
Washburn, J. (2005). *University inc. sold: The corporate corruption of higher education.* New York, NY: Basic Books.
Wright, S., & Greenwood, D. J. (2017). Universities run for, by, and with the faculty, students and staff: Alternatives to the neoliberal destruction of higher education. *Learning and Teaching, 10,* 42–65.

SECTION 4

Reflecting on the Tenure Journey: The Personal and Individual

The authors included in this section discuss how personal and individual experiences have informed change for them. Most of them include some systemic and/or institutional considerations but, overall, they emphasize personal experiences as they make their ways in the academic world.

    The emphasis on the personal may simply be a reflection of a choice made by each author. However, we assume such a choice would be informed by the author's self-assessment of what was of primary importance to them. Within this section we find instances where the journey through the tenure-track has led to self-discovery. While the personal seems to be emphasized, there is no doubt that these authors have negotiated their way within the institutional setting, and it is interesting to read these chapters while considering how the institution fits in. Is this exercising academic freedom or a form of diplomacy?

    We begin this section of the book with **Lyle Hamm**'s chapter, titled "Finding energy from 'productive anguish': Avoiding descents into tenure-track darkness." Lyle had the title of his chapter, from the first book (Hamm, 2016) tattooed on his forearm. "Just today and just tomorrow" has been inked in more than a book! Tattoos are a commitment, and Lyle was certain his story about the tenure-track was a significant life event. In this new chapter, Lyle offers some personal advice about life in higher education a little further along in the journey. He focuses on a quotation: "Live the life you are living, not the one you are searching for."

Lee Anne Block's chapter is titled "Relationships, Associations, and Authority." Lee Anne has carefully considered teacher identity and the perspectives and relationships involved in being a teacher educator and those of being a teacher candidate. She considers important theorists such as Foucault and Freire as well as Indigenous understandings and worldview. These perspectives inform the collaborative relationships with students that are necessary for educators in the 21st century.

Kathy Snow speaks to challenges within the assessment process arising from a culture where criticism is the normative behaviour. She expresses frustration and diminished trust because many processes, including the tenure process, are contrary to the purpose of higher education and established principles of learning organizations.

Joan Chambers has provided a brief statement. She aimed to provide a full chapter but found herself unable to meet the timeline for the book. In light of this, and our desire to maintain a connection between this book and all of the authors in *The Academic Gateway*, we asked her if she would be able to provide a brief statement about the challenges she has experienced.

Greg Rickwood's chapter emphasizes the Kubler-Ross aspect of the model of tenure-track. However, it shows that the grief aspect can persist even when one is successful in obtaining tenure and promotion.

Cam Cobb's chapter, "Who am I? Professional identity on the path to tenure," is our final chapter in this section. Cam describes his sense of who he is, as he has evolved from interviewing for his tenure-track position to becoming a tenured associate professor. He discusses issues such as imposter syndrome and change over time, and he draws from an interview with the local Canadian Broadcasting Corporation (CBC) radio station, which led him to reflect more deeply about who he is as a tenured associate professor. Cam's path is one in which the personal and individual are very much the focus.

CHAPTER 13

Finding Energy From "Productive Anguish": Avoiding Descents Into Tenure-Track Darkness

Lyle Hamm

I begin this project on July 2, 2018, two months before I submit my application for tenure. I have successfully completed two full academic reviews since being hired in 2013—one review for promotion to associate professor in 2015–2016, and a probationary review in 2016–2017. In the past five years, I have worked diligently to find sustainable energizing light, hope, and meaning in this post-secondary position. At the same time, I have tried to identify and respond appropriately to potential downfalls and descents into personal and professional darkness that have shrouded my academic doubts and role-related uncertainties. There is not a day that goes by where reflection on what I wrote in my previous chapter in this series (and that was to focus on "just today and just tomorrow") does not occur (Hamm, 2017a). It has been challenging, sometimes, to keep that focus. There are many complexities associated with my job; limiting worry to only the immediate tasks takes energy and discipline. However, the five-word phrase has served me well as a personal symbol. I come back to it every time I perceive my attention and commitment wavering. In fact, I even had the phrase tattooed on my right forearm as a constant reminder to help me remain steadfast in my pursuit for success and tenure in my faculty, among my many trusted colleagues and friends (See Figure 13.1). In short, I love it here at the University of New Brunswick (UNB) and I do not want to lose my job and start over again.

Figure 13.1. *Just today and just tomorrow.*

Like many scholars who cognitively toil to understand their academic journey from graduate school to the tenure-track and, hopefully, beyond (Coke, Bensen & Hayes, 2015; Tilley-Lubbs, 2014), I admit that I, too, have often felt trapped in the scholarly web of constant disruption of doubt mixed with temporary states of elation and success. For instance, there have been times the past few years where several projects were reviewed, accepted, and published in a short span of time in national and international journals. Some of my work has been found on the Internet by scholars who have asked if they can publish it in their country (Hamm, 2014; 2016). As well, another Canadian scholar invited me into a large project after he discovered an article of mine aligned with his ideas (Hamm, Doğurga & Scott, 2016). These instances were highly energizing for me and motivated me to stretch my work further.

And then, all of a sudden, I experienced academic silence for several months: The cycle of uncertainty returned, and remains; darkness, again, has become my companion. This perpetual reality has only intensified the mystery of the tenure-track process for me and for my wife, who also works in the Faculty of Education at

UNB. Together, we fully realize that, as hard as we try, we will never completely understand the dynamic forces at work that impact the life and ways of being for an emerging scholar. So each day we try to live our lives as intentionally as we can and enjoy the journey. After five years at UNB, we simply do not know what we are searching for anymore. Is it tenure? Is it a different life experience than what we had in western Canada? We have become more at ease with this uncertain reality.

But because I have chosen this pathway, with the support of my wife and most of our family members, I find that I am constantly examining how I am feeling as I try to explain my often bizarre psychological responses about racing against my tenure clock. It is quickly running out. I tell my wife, "Lauren, I feel anguish; that's for sure. It's a constant anguish. But it is like a productive anguish and it keeps my blood flowing and my energy levels high." Perhaps if I am granted tenure next year, my educational and academic purpose may be further illuminated for me in the years to come. If not, so be it. I do not feel I am even close to retirement, though I have been an educator for 27 years (as of today—22 years in K–12 and five at this university). For now, I will continue to control how hard I work, knowing that I do not control the decisions made at the Faculty and Inter-faculty levels of assessment next year when those committees will review my tenure file. Having spent considerable time contributing to both of those committees this past year, I know how my file will be assessed and I feel ready for that process.

So, What Have You Learned, Lyle?
It was always my intention to write this chapter at exactly this time in my short university teaching and research career. I feel there is no better time to reflect on five years of my intense, often paradoxical behaviours that have been cloaked in some personal suffering and some educational achievement, than now (I was the co-recipient of the Allan Stuart Excellence in Teaching Award in 2015 at UNB along with my Physics colleague, Dr. Ben Newling). Am I exaggerating all of this? I don't know, but in the next several pages, I am going to try and capture, in a systematic framework, some of the most significant learning and experiences I have had on the tenure-track at this wonderful university in this wonderful faculty situated in beautiful Atlantic Canada, where I am surrounded by incredible teachers, researchers, and mentors. It is my hope that my contribution to

this important book may provide a few modest signposts for new scholars who enter the same game as I did in 2013—and make no mistake readers, this process *is a game* and knowing what to expect and when it may happen will be very helpful for you, as it has been for me, when you are navigating the thorny and narrow pathways of your own tenure trek. Certainly, as I will expand upon in my narrative, I have often felt like a walking conundrum amidst many of my colleagues who, for many of them, project abundant confidence, are highly productive in their scholarship, and appear in my mind to be quite stable performing the multiple roles related to their positions. And at other times, I have felt securely in charge of my academic journey while contributing to the educational preparation of hundreds of educational leadership graduate students across the world in such a short period of time. For these reasons, I agree with Joshua Gleich (2016) who writes about the transition from graduate school to assistant professor stating, "I do not want to add yet another lament or rationalization for the current state of academia. This is a fraught climate that nonetheless shapes rising scholars and continues to generate remarkable new work and precocious new thinkers" (p. 134). My view is firm: Every new academic needs to face adversity to become more effective and productive in order for them to contribute their ideas and educational service in the larger social arenas of our world. Indeed, had I not experienced and overcome some of the challenges I have had these first five years, I may have given up and returned to western Canada.

Constant reflection has allowed me to identify that bad moments here were rare and often simply the result of my own misguided perceptions and prolonged over-analysis. These fixed states of mind (Dweck, 2006) eroded my energy and spirit and caused me some psychological agony. As I got better, I learned how to control my thinking more effectively when the darker moments of my academic journey were at hand. Unlike the K–12 school environments I was a part of for so long (22 years) where there was very little time for thinking and reflection, I am now in an educational environment where I have plenty of time to think and reflect and most of that time is well spent. However, when things have gone awry, I have sometimes thought my way into conflicts that simply did not exist. Taking time to walk and think before I write, and talk to people about the struggles I confront with my work, has been beneficial. Moreover, it is healthy to do this. Perhaps because we are such a small faculty

I have never felt isolated, and being alone to work has always been a choice. For me, it has been a choice that has led to more writing production and better course planning that has increased my academic agency and leadership capacities.

Hmmm . . . I see I have written myself to that reflective moment in this project where I can clearly and confidently admit I have no regrets about taking this job in 2013; no regrets about leaving a secure teaching and administration position and drove 4,400 kilometres to the other side of the country and started my career over again (or extended it) in New Brunswick; no regrets about the struggles and barriers—both real and perceived—I have encountered here and for which I will now elaborate on and try to gain additional understanding. Perhaps I should keep these thoughts for the conclusion in my chapter, but they will stay here for now. So, in short, I will share what I will reference as my critical growth experiences at the University of New Brunswick that have helped me increasingly understand this crazy process called "getting tenure." I do not fully understand this process and possibly never will. That is why this project has been so important for me as a new scholar. As an academic work in progress, I know I have a ways to go, still.

My Cabin, My Sanctuary
Since the time when I wrote my first chapter in this series (Hamm, 2017a), I submitted my professional portfolio a year early (in 2015) to support promotion to associate professor. I was fortunate to publish several articles in my first two years, I was presented with a university teaching award, and I believed I had a positive record of teaching, professional service and conference presentations. I felt confident, on that basis, that I would earn a promotion. I was wrong: The assessment process was very slow and required me to clarify two claims I had made in my cover letter. To this day I don't know why; this progressive step, one I thought I was ready to take, became a dark period where I falsely perceived myself to be in some type of trouble and it caused me personal, professional, and psychological struggles for several months.

This tension might have been related to the letter in my mailbox in January of 2016 that had "CONFIDENTIAL" written across the bottom in a large font. It might have been because the letter was constructed with legal jargon that was referencing our collective agreement and I didn't understand it. I was never one who carefully read collective agreements, either as a classroom teacher or as a school administrator. I figured if I served my students and employer diligently with commitment and passion, I could avoid the in-depth understanding of our binding contract. Perhaps my stress was because I thought I was being called a fraud by our inter-faculty assessment committee; a liar, in fact. After all, I had placed the documents that were requested in my portfolio and that provided evidence for the claims I was making in the letter; the assessment committee members couldn't have missed them. I had even highlighted sentences in the documents that I wanted them to notice. One document was an email from a publisher inviting me to write a book with his publishing company. Was this a joke?

I quickly gathered the evidence and I walked it down the hill to the office of the member who had signed the letter on behalf of the committee. Then I waited two long months to learn the outcome. My thoughts were out of control. Do I sell my house? Do I start looking for a new job? What does this mean? What do I tell my family and friends? CONFIDENTIAL. CONFIDENTIAL. CONFIDENTIAL.

When I received my final letter, I had been promoted by a slim, but favourable, vote of 3–2. In my view, the letter was glowing and reflected all the things I thought I was doing well. There was just one sentence at the bottom of the letter that stated:

> Some members concluded that Dr. Hamm had not demonstrated the degree of academic competence and activity appropriate for promotion to the rank of associate professor at this time and that this was not a case that would justify an exception to the practice referred to in Article 25D.07.

That was it. I needed to write more and I needed to get my research program off the ground. I needed to apply for more research grants. I was on it already, but in my mind, the committee was saying, "faster, faster!"

I have reflected that my perception of the process was flawed, which led me to seriously doubt myself as a teacher/scholar, and to briefly question if I wanted to remain in academia. I spent dark moments and days at my cabin in the woods speculating on my perception of the assessment protocol and process. With no one present and only the fireplace to warm me, I verbalized my feelings and perceptions aloud to listen to and analyze the thoughts

I was having about the review process. And then I was better, but only briefly.

Soon after I received my letter for promotion to associate professor, I received another letter stating that I would have to undergo my probationary review (after Year Three). One assessment coming on the heels of another stoked the ember of assessment despair and gave rebirth to the struggles that had just begun to subside from the process to become an associate professor. The torturous cycle began again: I experienced excessive fear, frustration, and anger in the assessment process (Coke et al., 2015). I distanced myself from the faculty building and from my friends, which was not healthy. In time, I realized that, in spite of the challenges, I was in a fairly good educational and life space. In fact, when the assessment letter arrived several months later, I learned that I was on track in my tenure process and had recorded 5–0 votes, a favourable outcome, at both the faculty level and interfaculty levels of assessment.

I have now reached a point (near the end of Year Five) where I no longer concern myself about my future success on the tenure-track—though, at this moment in my life, it is still very much an elusive and, yet, a primary goal of mine to achieve. I will accept the assessment committee's decisions next year. In the meantime, I will simply enjoy my work and strive for wellness.

Thank You Magdalen
I will frame this chapter around several suggestions that were provided to me and 20+ other new scholar/teachers at the University of New Brunswick in 2013. The suggestions arrived via our excellent Orientation Day leader, Magdalen, near the conclusion of our full day workshop. At the time, I didn't realize how important my scribbled notes would be for me during the past five years. I have included a picture of these notes (see Figure 13.2) that I placed above my work desk in my office the day after the orientation session.

It was my hope that the coaching suggestions posted above my computer would keep me on track in a process that, far from my understanding then, was ultimately going to define my academic identity at UNB. I have expressed my gratitude to Magdalen several times for facilitating the orientation that day and for providing the wisdom to the listeners. The first five suggestions I owe directly to Magdalen; the next three I wrote down at later stages based on my expanding experiences in the Faculty of Education, my time as a

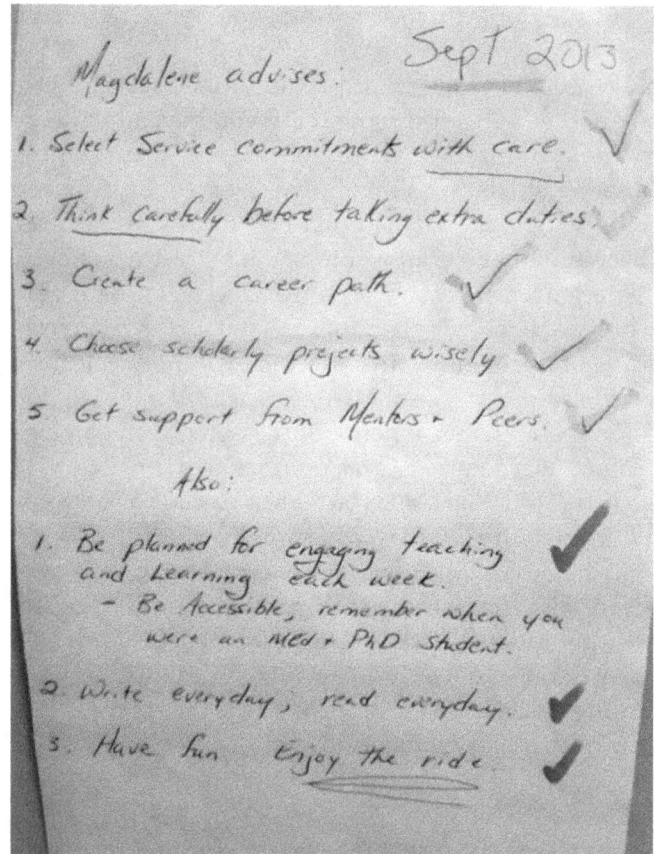

Figure 13.2. Magdalen's notes, which I wrote down in September 2013.

graduate student in Alberta, and from my own experiences teaching, leading, and mentoring in K–12 schools.

Looking back, the first couple of years I was on the tenure-track were a sensational blur. I clearly didn't know what to do, and what to expect, and every one of my colleagues I spoke to about their experiences seemed to have their own plan in place that they were following. My colleagues shared their knowledge and ideas willingly, but what works for one, may not work for someone else, and that was the case for me. What I did learn was that there would be no absolute clear way to a successful tenure application—an important message for new scholars! You need a tenure-track plan that is constructed with flexibility, adaptability and sustainability in mind. Somewhere

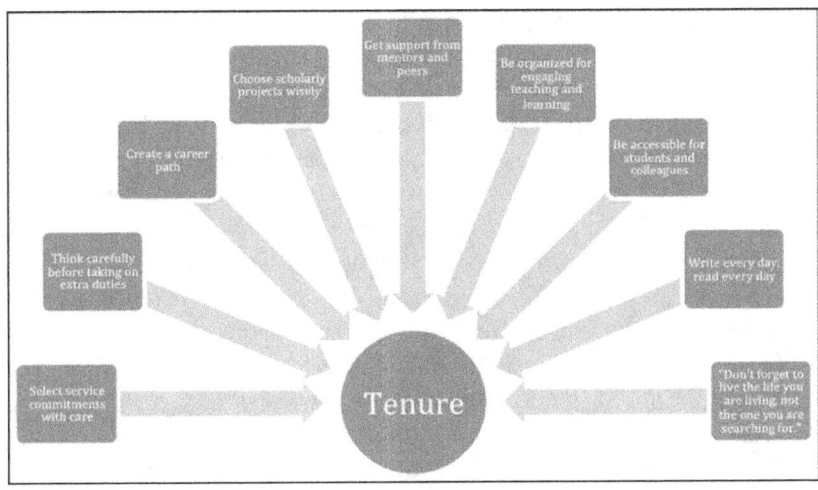

Figure 13.3. *Pathway to tenure model* © M. Normandeau, L. Hamm, and L. A. Hamm.

long ago, in a classroom I taught in, I taped a laminated poster on my wall to guide my young learners in their writing projects. It stated, "If you don't know where you are going, you'll end up somewhere else" (Yogi Berra). I have learned there is no greater truth while on my tenure pathway. I have planned, re-planned, and then planned some more while all the time taking action in my teaching and while I am in the field on project. My plan is constantly revised to hold me in place at the helm of my tenure-charted course. I have leaned on Paulo Freire (1970) who might call these pedagogical behaviours "praxis." Thus, the nine suggestions I have represented in the diagram above (see Figure 13.3), has served as the lighted pathway on my journey. I sincerely believe I will challenge effectively for my long-term position next month (August, 2018) and, as they have done before, the assessment committee's decision will not be rendered for a few months. No worries yet. I do not even have my letter and tenure package prepared. That will be next month's project.

1. Select service commitments with care.

As a new scholar teacher, I wanted to contribute to leadership within my faculty in roles that were challenging, but where I would not feel too far outside my comfort zone. Messing up on a committee, or worse, not being able to contribute my share of the work, might make me appear incompetent which would only fuel my despair. I joined two other members from my faculty on the Research Ethics committee my first year. Both colleagues coached me as I got accustomed to our collective responsibilities. I took on additional duties on another committee in my third year. In my fifth year I took on additional roles on two more committees. This work required substantially more time and greater commitment. By performing these service responsibilities in incremental phases of development, I was able to keep up with my teaching, develop my research program, and build my capacity in performing faculty service work. Colleagues have identified they took on too much committee duty early in their academic careers, and it negatively affected their teaching and research and caused them stress and burnout. By asking colleagues questions about committees and the general workload commitments they required, I was able to gain experience on several committees in my five years and plan meeting times around my teaching and field work in my research program.

2. Think carefully before taking on extra duties.
Now, this suggestion might sound similar to the argument I am making above (I thought that), but it is anything but and it took me some time to figure out. Just as in any K–12 school in Canada, there are many other things that need to be completed in timely fashion in a university faculty. These are things that are not considered part of the regular committee duties, but nonetheless, still need to be completed to keep programs running. For example, each year in our faculty, doctoral and master's applications arrive and need to be reviewed. SSHRC applications need to be reviewed. Ad hoc committees are struck and the individuals who join them have to meet and create propositions and prepare plans for oversight by faculty members. Some people create social activities for our staff to attend that will build culture and community—otherwise the staff may become disengaged and disconnected from each other. In the world of online teaching and learning, this reality is showing itself more and more as university teachers, particularly those teaching in graduate studies are teaching online and are mostly outside the faculty (i.e., working from their homes). Visiting scholars have spent time in our faculty and asked, "Where is everyone?" They soon learn that many faculty members do not spend much time on campus anymore due to their contemporary arrangements for teaching and research. It is important for people to socialize outside of committees

as it does contribute to faculty growth and health. However, new academics must be careful that they do not take too much of these types of commitments on early in their tenure trek.

3. Create a career path.
"If you don't have a purpose, you must give yourself one." Since 2001, when I began my graduate studies at the University of Lethbridge, I have harbored this wisdom close to my heart. I have always attributed the phrase to the poet Irving Layton, but I am not sure. What is relevant is that when I heard it, I wrote it down on a piece of paper, and have found inspiration in the phrase ever since. Whenever I have lost sight of my educational purpose or concept of my professional identity as I engaged new educational terrains, I have reflected on these words to help me take action again. Silly perhaps, but during my darkest moments in 2015–2016 when I lost track of my purpose during both assessment reviews (and new academics, you may lose yours during the course of your journey if my story holds up), I would think about the phrase, then reset myself through purposeful planning. These were moments when I would take stock by writing down my projects in a prioritized list in my field notebook. In this way, I could see my projects written out and then make further notes on them about how important they were, how much energy and time it might take me to complete them, and who I was completing them for as far as the audience or research grant was concerned. I would then check off projects as I completed them, or move some projects up or down the list depending on my energy levels or funding I had that supported the project at that time. I don't know if my colleagues do this or not; but I often wonder about how specifically detailed their plans for action are. But for me, to put things on paper and then to jot notes around my projects has been very helpful in getting the projects to completion or to further stages of completion.

I have found that projects—journal articles, book chapters and proposals, poster development and book reviews—take a lot of time. Often, the best articles that an emerging scholar (Anderson, 2010) writes and eventually publishes go through several revisions, reviews, rejection, and often further reviews before finally being accepted. This has been my experience over the last five years; I have had to learn to be patient as this all occurs long before publication—long after your final edits are completed, approved and the article is signed off on. Even then, it still might not get into a journal for some time. I came into this aspect of my job blindly other than what I had learned by listening to my professors in Alberta talk about their own writing and publishing. Admittedly, their stories made little sense to me at that time because I was simply writing papers as assignments and trying to grow as a thinker; not necessarily trying to get published. My papers were informing my work in my K–12 roles. I now follow, almost in a religious sense, the publish-or-perish mantra and on more than one occasion, when I have had papers sent back to me with all types of critique, I have become discouraged, darkened, and nearly disengaged from my work. That is when I have heeded the quotation at the beginning of this section along with other words of wisdom on my office walls. Without the guiding statements in these dark moments, my mind has invited me to abandon some projects and move onto another one. I haven't done this yet out of fear that it will produce a bad academic habit in me. I have learned that writing rejection and critique comes with the role.

As an example, it took me nearly two years to get an article published in an international journal (Hamm, 2017b). The call for papers came through an email about mentoring and coaching vice-principals. I jumped at this writing opportunity because I had been a vice-principal for six years in Alberta. I assumed that this would be a guaranteed publication opportunity, but I was wrong. I blindly believed my practical field knowledge and experience as an educational leader would be well received and widely acknowledged (another incorrect assumption). After I had submitted my final draft, I waited for the reviews to return and when they did, they were not favorable. In fact, there were four reviews in total, with three of the reviewers concluding that my article needed major revisions if it was even going to be considered for publication. The fourth reviewer stated flatly, "Do not accept this manuscript for publication!" And there I stood, mystified once again, looking at all four reviews and trying to understand them. I was confused because each review was quite different: what one reviewer took issue with, another appreciated. After several months of researching relevant articles on mentoring and coaching principles, in addition to reading about the multiple roles vice-principals perform in schools, I felt my work was being wasted. I had read several books, conducted a study, analyzed the data, and then finally wrote the paper through several drafts. The negative reviews made me want to give up on this project and send the paper to another journal for review. I emailed one of the editors thanking her for her leadership and indicated that I would not pursue publication with the journal. I was delighted when she wrote back immediately and encouraged me to address the reviews as best as I could and send in the next draft for further review. Her encouragement boosted my resilience in that moment and I once again focused on my purpose. It paid off in spades because I got published in the journal and was invited to be part of a project at an international conference.

4. Choose scholarly projects wisely.
Every time I design a project or begin the process of writing a conceptual or evidence-based paper, I convince myself it will be the best one I ever produce. Again, this thinking may seem silly to the reader, but for me, it goes with knowing one's purpose; I find it energy-inducing. Giving a project life, then visualizing where it might go and how I wish to represent the voices of the people who are part of my studies, generates energy in me that leads to additional energy, enthusiasm, and creativity.

It is this support for scholarly projects that lets them contribute to the creation of a career path. I have represented all the projects in this manner with visualization and conceptualization being scholarly nourishment. So, individual projects have contributed to a themed career path with qualitative and constructivist case study methodologies throughout my research work (Greenfield, 1973; Stake 2000; Starratt, 2005) from my dissertation thesis (Hamm, 2009) to this chapter. My work continues to be broadly about understanding immigration experiences and the effects of immigration in New Brunswick and Canada, demographic change in our communities, and how increasing cultural and linguistic diversity are impacting the lives of people who work and learn in our schools. For me, my projects are meaningful and interesting to pursue and that provides motivation to keep chipping away at them.

5. Get support from mentors and peers.
In my first chapter (Hamm, 2017a), I briefly discussed the leadership of one of my first mentors at UNB. At that time, I reflected on the importance of finding the right person who could help me quickly build my confidence and get established in the academy (Bell & Treleaven, 2011). At that time, it was important that I went looking for mentoring support because I had arrived on campus in the middle of

summer and few faculty members were on campus. I had two online courses to prepare, a dissertation to unpack and write about, and I really didn't know how to do either. I was encouraged in my early interactions with our graduate studies program leaders, but having been a mentee and mentor in previous educational positions, I knew the importance of working with someone directly who knew the academic game and would share their knowledge willingly.

I also knew at that time how critical it was for me to stay away from toxic individuals and, instead, to work with colleagues who loved their jobs, felt energized by their challenges, and were firmly embedded in a growth mindset. As Dweck (2006) states, "People in a growth mindset don't just seek challenge, they thrive on it. The bigger the challenge, the more they stretch" (p. 21). I needed to be around people who were like this. Becoming an academic and pursuing tenure was a big challenge requiring I stretch. I needed to know how people actually operationalized their roles on a day-to-day basis. I also needed to acquire the language and terminology of academia. For instance, I didn't know what "promotion through the ranks" meant, or what "faculty and inter-faculty assessment committees" were. Both proved to be important to know about. Further, I didn't want to have a mentor without giving back; I wanted to contribute in whatever way I could; ideally it would be a working relationship that was reciprocal and meaningful.

In recent years, I have adhered closely to Searby's (2014) protégé mentoring mindset framework. In her work, she argues there are multiple indicators of the presence of a mentoring mindset that can be observed in the protégé. Of significance, she writes about how important it is for a mentee to initiate contact with a mentor, accept their advice graciously, and become adept at building relationships with colleagues and other professionals, and articulate reflections out loud. In previous positions in public education, I had been mentored and served as a mentor. However, it was clear that in higher education it would be totally different. I was now part of a paradoxical game based on productivity and gentle competitiveness (at least in our faculty) among colleagues who also had to embrace and contribute simultaneously to a collaborative growth culture of teaching, learning, and research.

Of the many mentors I have had prior to arriving at UNB and then while on-campus striving to learn my job, two, Alan and John, stand out for me and they have both become my dear friends. I am not sure if either of them ever really pictured themselves as my mentor in a formal sense. However, without them, I know very well that I would not have made the progress I have over the last five years. Our relationships were formed through common teaching and research topics as well as shared personal interests, such as hockey. Our professional and personal relationships evolved organically, and I would agree with others (Bell & Treleaven, 2011) that this might be best for relational sustainability. We can discuss multiple topics, disagree with each other, and still be friends and trusting colleagues. I had been in previous educational environments among strong teachers and this was not always the case. Arguments often led to standoffs and then disengagement, which then contaminated the culture.

In their research on mentoring relationships in academia, Weijden, Belder, Arensbergen, and Besselaar (2015) argue "The benefits of mentorship in academia can be classified within three main categories: (increased) job satisfaction, network building, and (higher) performance. These are necessary conditions for academic career advancement" (p. 277). Among so many things, Alan shared pedagogical and content knowledge with me and provided connections to his research colleagues across Canada and in Europe. He invited me to be part of a SSHRC funded research project while I worked to get my own research program rolling. We later wrote together and Alan invited me to an international conference where his coaching and mentoring continued among many international scholars. He clearly took me into academic places that would have taken me several years to get to. Thank you Alan.

John provided me essential institutional roadmaps that I needed to navigate and calibrate myself for my new working conditions. John also connected me to people in the community as well as to community organizations where I could participate and contribute service. His efforts, guidance, and friendship diminished my loneliness and longing for western Canada while I became acclimatized to New Brunswick. Thank you John.

I feel it is important to also thank additional colleagues. Lauren, Al, Martin, Leah, Tim, Ann, Kirk, Sarah, Clive, Dave, Kathy, Carolyn, Carol Ann, Randy, Gardiner, Lisa, Wendy, Laura, Melody, Ken, Steve, Kevin, Ernie, Eileen, Dad and Mom. In one lived life, when a person is surrounded by solid individuals like yourselves, as I have been, their growth and success is expedited. And I am aware that I have not attained tenure as I am writing this, but it just doesn't matter anymore. I am forever grateful to the kindness you have all shown to me and Lauren. Thank you all.

6. Be organized for engaging teaching and learning . . . each class, each week, each term.
I work in a Faculty of Education where one of my roles is to contribute to teacher growth. Humbly, I am astonished that the pedagogical reach of the role is truly international as I teach so many students in our online courses who are not physically studying in Canada. In conversations with my wife and friends, I tell them I could never have imagined a professional life such as this one when I began teaching in Cessford, Alberta in 1991. I feel so fortunate because, as I plan and teach, I am perpetually learning. There is no border to cross anymore between teaching and learning because when I am working, I am always engaged in both. There is no distinction for me anymore.

It is incumbent upon academics in education to pay attention to the fact that they have the potential to reach thousands of children in classes all over the world through their service. Consider the math: one of the students you might be teaching may have 25 children in their class. Or, they might have 150 junior or senior secondary students. Or, they might be an administrator leading a school with over 100 teachers and 2,000 students. It requires being committed to teaching and planning your courses and lessons carefully and with intentionality. The impact necessitates engaging your students with passion.

7. Be accessible for your students and colleagues.
I remember a sticky situation I found myself in during work for my Master's degree. It was one of those common conundrums that many part-time graduate students get themselves in while they are studying and teaching full-time. I was enrolled in too many courses one academic term when I was teaching in junior high and my life went out of control. When I phoned my professor and explained my dilemma, she was more thoughtful than I was expecting. She listened very carefully, honed in on the things that I wasn't saying in my anxious tone, and she could clearly sense that I was headed for burnout. Through her care and consideration, I was able to calm down, get healthy and get back on track in my job, my studies and in my life. In the fury of my plea for help, she gently told me over and over, "Breathe, Lyle. Breathe."

I now find myself in the position of having to gently coach many of my students to slow down and breathe so they can catch themselves before they burnout. I have recommended to several of my students that they take off a term from their graduate studies, and collect themselves before returning. I remember thinking when I came to UNB, that I would have regular office hours where students would make appointments and then drop by to discuss their programs, their courses, or their assignments. This hasn't been my reality, due to the online delivery model used in our graduate program.

Often I am listening as carefully as I can to what students aren't writing in their emails. When I perceive they are in positions similar to where I was once, I try to be accessible. It can be very sticky, because I don't want to pry into the private lives of my students, and yet, when I see that they might be in a complex situation leading to personal and professional agony, I feel I have to learn more about their context to be able to guide them through their program in their darkest moments. Being accessible in person, online and on the telephone for students off campus is part of this job. It isn't something graduate school directly trains one for.

8. Write every day. Read every day.
I haven't been able to follow this suggestion as well as I would like to, but I do feel I have been productive writing, submitting, revising, and publishing during this five-year journey. When I am not actively sitting at my computer writing, I am often engaged in thinking about writing. It never ends. I have observed my key mentors at work on their computers in their offices and asked them questions about their own writing. I have been invited into projects and subsequently from the guidance I received, developed my own research and writing team—with members from our graduate and Bachelor of Education programs joining and exiting at various stages due to their life and work situations.

While sitting with a colleague at a conference, I asked her how she has been so productive in her academic writing and she kindly told me to "write what you care about" (C. M. Shields, Personal Communication, May 29, 2018). Other scholars have told me to write every day, even if it is just a paragraph or for 15 minutes. When I was struggling to get a project going in my third year, my mentor Alan said that his mentor told him that "writing doesn't get any easier tomorrow [so get on with it]." The advice I offer my graduate students who struggle with their writing is the same advice I gave junior high students years ago and comes from the movie Finding Forrester: "You write your first draft with your heart; you re-write with your head" (Connery & Mark, 2000). I agree with Gleich (2016) who tells new scholars that when you are firmly entrenched on a tenure trek, write first, and ask questions later. That is probably the best way forward, but try to have as much fun as you can doing it and don't let writing become a chore.

Conclusion

9. "Don't forget to live the life you are living, not the one you are searching for." (Prakash collection of James Wilson Morrice at the Beaverbrook Art Gallery)

Here I am once again . . . at my computer, at 4:00 a.m. I am either writing or teaching online by this time most mornings. For me it works because I love watching the sunrise as I sit by a warm fire (in the winter time) and wait for my wife to get up so we can enjoy a coffee and conversation before we leave for work. When I was a first year teacher in 1991, I could barely get out of bed by 8:00 a.m. and then I had to scramble to be in my first class by 9:00 a.m. I was lucky I lived in a district-provided teacherage that was located beside the rural school or I wouldn't have made that first year. Now, my educational experience has evolved in a way I could never have imagined. I work with graduate students from all over the world. I am paid to conduct research and write in my dream job. I am invited to present aspects of my work and sometimes even my opinions in our community and abroad. And yes, I still have to prepare my tenure application package, submit it for review, and wait several months for that final decision before I learn if I have "made it!" For the time being, I will continue to live this autoethnographic experience as fully as I can, exposing the "multiple layers of consciousness" (Ellis & Bochner, 2000, p. 739) that I continuously examine within my daily thinking.

One day earlier this spring, when my mind was at odds with itself once again over some work-related matter that I was stretching through, my wife and I spent an afternoon in our city's fine art gallery. Having grown up in a family of artists, I know how a human mind might get intentionally lost for a while and recover itself when there is, as Yeats suggested, "a fire was in my head." As I wandered my way through the many collections, stopping to wonder what this or that artist was thinking and perhaps what their lived experiences were like when they were in the moments of creating, I found myself staring at a quote from James Wilson Morrice, that was part of the A. K. Prakash collection that was given in trust to the National Gallery of Canada. It read, "live the life you are living, not the one you are searching for." Wow. That was it. I had coached myself to focus on one day and maybe the next, but truly, trying to get tenure has seemed at times like a constant battle of self-measuring, doubt, and frustration. This struggle has gone on for almost five years. Why should the process be like this? Just as Tilley-Lubbs (2014) was asking during her tenure torture and inquisition, I asked myself, "Will I ever be able to fully reclaim the Self that matters" (p. 53). The experience of working toward tenure has been wonderful, yet excruciating.

If I could provide myself encouraging advice when I entered the academy it would be this:

> Have fun and enjoy the ride, because one day it will all end! Certainly you may wonder, as I have along the way, how much is enough? How many articles, chapters, conference presentations, and funding applications should I produce? How many service committees should I be on? How many graduate students should I supervise? What matters most – quality or quantity? It all matters, and yet it doesn't. As you progress through the tenure-track let the concerns go and just live your life. Have fun and work as hard as you can while striving for balance. Because one day, it will end. Learn to control your mind and to free yourself of the anxieties, which will greet you in this position. You must borrow a line from Dylan Thomas and "rage and rage against the dying of the light," then rage intelligently with mentors, friends and family who are around you and will help you navigate your academic conundrums. Finally, give thanks and gratitude every day. In fact, "In everything, give thanks." (M. Chytracek, Personal Communication, November, 2015)

Keep in mind that academics are the lucky ones to be serving in higher education positions. Don't take anything for granted. All the best.

References

Anderson, K. (2010). *The leadership compendium: Emerging scholars in Canadian educational leadership.* Fredericton, NB: Atlantic Centre for Educational Administration and Leadership.

Bell, A., & Treleaven, L. (2011). Looking for professor right: Mentee selection of mentors in a formal mentoring program. *Higher Education, 61*, 545–561.

Coke, P., Bensen, S., & Hayes, M. (2015). Making Meaning Of Experience: Navigating The Transformation From Graduate Student To Tenure-Track Professor. *Journal of Transformative Education, 13*(2), 110–126. DOI: 10:1177/1541344614562216

Connery, S. & Mark, L. (Producers), & Van Sant, G. (Director). (2000). *Finding Forrester* [Motion picture]. United States: Columbia Pictures.

Dweck, C. (2006). *Mindset: The new psychology of success. How we can learn to fulfill our potential.* New York, NY: Ballantine Books.

Ellis, C., & Bochner, A. (2000). Autoethnography, personal narrative, reflexivity: researcher as subject. In N. Denzin & Y. Lincoln (Eds.), *Handbook of qualitative research* (2nd ed., pp. 733–768). Thousand Oaks, CA: Sage.

Gleich, J. (2016). Write first, ask questions later: Publishing and the race to tenure track. *Cinema Journal, 55*(4), 133–138.

Greenfield, T. B. (1973). Organizations as social inventions: Some considerations for those who would design schools to serve human ends. Toronto, ON: *Ontario Institute for Studies in Education.*

Hamm, L. (2009). 'I'm just glad I'm here:' Stakeholder perceptions from one school in a community undergoing demographic changes on the Alberta grasslands. Unpublished doctoral dissertation, University of Calgary, Calgary, Alberta.

Hamm, L. (2014). The culturally responsive classroom: A proactive approach to diversity in Canadian schools. *Education Canada, 54*(4), Web Exclusive. 5. https://www.edcan.ca/articles/the-culturally-responsive-classroom/

Hamm, L. (2016, December 9). Culturele diversiteit in het klaslokaal. *Nivoz*, Web publication, http://nivoz.nl/artikelen/culturele-diversiteit-in-het-klaslokaal/

Hamm, L., Doğurga, S., & Scott, A. (2016). Leading a diverse school during times of demographic change in rural Canada: Reflection, action and suggestions for practice. *International Journal of Citizenship, Teaching & Learning, 11*(2), 211–230. https://scholar.google.ca/scholar?hl=en&as_sdt=0%2C5&as_vis=1&q=Leading+a+diverse+school+during+times+of+change+in+rural+Canada+Hamm&btnG=

Hamm, L. (2017a). Just today and just tomorrow: Building capacity on the tenure track in New Brunswick. In T. Sibbald & V. Handford (Eds.), *The academic gateway: Understanding the journey to tenure* (pp. 249–264). Ottawa, ON: The University of Ottawa Press.

Hamm, L. (2017b). Becoming a transformative vice-principal in culturally and linguistically rich diverse schools: 'Pace yourself. It's a marathon, not a sprint.' *International Journal of Mentoring & Coaching in Education, 6*(2), 82–98. http://www.emeraldinsight.com/doi/pdfplus/10.1108/IJMCE-11-2016-0072

Searby, L. (2014). The protégé mentoring mindset: A framework for consideration. *International Journal of Mentoring and Coaching in Education, 3*(3), 255–276.

Stake, R. (2000). Case studies. In N. Denzin & Y. Lincoln (Eds.), *Handbook of qualitative research* (2nd ed., pp. 435–454). Thousand Oaks, CA: Sage.

Starratt, R. J. (2005). Responsible leadership. *The Educational Forum, 69*(2), 124–133.

Thomas, D. (n.d.). *Do not go gentle into that good night*. Retrieved from https://www.poets.org/poetsorg/poem/do-not-go-gentle-good-night

Tilley-Lubbs, G. (2014). The inquisition/torture of the tenure track. *Creative Approaches to Research, 7*(2), 51–70.

Weijden, I., Belder, R., van Arensbergen, P., & Besselaar, P. (2015). How do young tenured professors benefit from a mentor? Effects on management, motivation and performance. *Higher Education, 69,* 275–287. DOI: 10.1007/s10734-014-9774-5

Yeats, W. B. (n.d.). *The song of wandering Aengus*. Retrieved from https://www.poetryfoundation.org/poems/55687/the-song-of-wandering-aengus

CHAPTER 14

Relationships, Associations, and Authority

Lee Anne Block

Tenured

The role and meaning of context in developing curricula is central to my teaching. The intention is to authorize teacher candidates "both to teach within the context they are located and to question that context" (Block, 2017, p. 47). Bridging the contexts of the university and the practicum is an ongoing difficulty. My desire for teacher candidates to experience their agency within the structures of the education program adds another level of complexity: Has the change in my individual context, occasioned by receiving tenure, affected my ability to deal with these issues in my teaching? I do not experience any major differences in how I position myself or how I am positioned by others. This chapter examines questions of relationships and authority.

I received my official letter of tenure and promotion at CSSE in May 2016, indirectly as a result of the presentation with co-authors of *The Academic Gateway*. Prior to our presentation, my colleague from the University of Winnipeg (who was applying for tenure at the same time I was), explained he had received his official letter of tenure/promotion. Where was my letter? Had I checked my mailbox before leaving for the conference? With the help of another colleague, I reached the administrative assistant in Winnipeg and gave her permission to check my box and open my letter. She read it to me over the phone. It was now official, tenured and promoted. A flurry of text messages to my family, followed by an impromptu celebration with University of Winnipeg colleagues on the terrace at University of Calgary, marked the end of waiting for recognition of my place in the Academy.

My discussion of the tenure process in *The Academic Gateway* included my questioning of the success/failure binary: "If I get tenure, I succeed within an academic system I chose to compete within. If I do not get tenure, it is because I failed to meet the expectations of that system. And where is my agency in the tenure process? . . . If I ask my students to reject the limitations in the discourse of success and failure, can I reject it for myself?" (Block, 2017, p. 48).

On May 31, 2016, I received the official notice that I had succeeded in meeting the requirements for tenure and promotion to associate professor. At the University of Winnipeg, tenure and promotion are awarded simultaneously; an assistant professor is awarded both or neither. I was now established in my role at the university and I would not have to re-construct my work identity yet again. How would I position myself in the academy and would this public, professional recognition change the way I positioned myself? Would I keep categorizing my work as teaching, research or service, or could I integrate these compartments and emerge as a less-policed professor?

My recent research on teacher education has taken up the Foucauldian notion of self-surveillance or internalized regulation (Foucault, 1983) that I had examined as part of the tenure process in the *Academic Gateway*. I am concerned with how faculties of education and teacher educators are implicated in the production of teacher candidates as "docile bodies" (Betts & Block, 2018) whose self-surveillance maintains dominant social values. If the construction of the bourgeois subject (Davis, 1995; Foucault, 1965) depended on "self-surveillance," then does the construction of a teaching identity also depend on that concept?

Foucault's Panopticon can serve as a metaphor for teacher education theory when that theory is limited to a list of competencies to be achieved, and then assessed by expert teacher educators and finally reflected on by teacher candidates according to direction and surveillance by those experts. Teacher candidates internalize those competencies and participate in the self-surveillance, which will engender their "successful" completion of the education program.

Teacher candidates' experiences in faculties of education replicate the success-failure binary most of them experienced in their K-12 schooling (Alsup, 2006; Britzman, 1991; Sarason, 1996). In turn, the "successful" teacher candidates may model this binary as beginning teachers. As an "expert" teacher educator with the authority to pass or fail a teacher candidate, I replicate and legitimize this cycle of success and failure. As a tenured professor, might I address and authorize a shift away from these binaries?

If achieving tenure is, in part, taking up the role of professor as institutionally defined and socially positioned, will the process have reinforced my self-surveillance, my need for respectability, my docility in relation to authority? Or will the seal of approval free me to redefine authority in this changed context? A different understanding of authority may interrupt my policing of teacher candidates. If I interrupt that policing, will it assist teacher candidates to interrupt their self-surveillance? Can agentic co-participation in teacher education be a possibility? If so, what would that look like?

My association with the university has grown over time and strengthens my individual voice. That is, I now understand tenure as an indicator of my growth within the context of the academy, as well as a marker of professional achievement. The collaborations or associations with my colleagues (both within and external to the University of Winnipeg) support my understanding of the work I am engaged in and reinforce my ability to take action grounded on those understandings. These deeper connections or "relatedness' (Sibbald & Handford, 2017) support my participation in making agentic co-participation part of teacher education.

Agentic Co-Participation in Teacher Education

The starting place for transformation of relationships in teacher education is epistemology. If we begin with an understanding that knowledge is multiple, partial and emergent (Davis, Sumara & Luce-Kapler, 2008; Haraway, 1988), that knowing is contextual and that pedagogy is relational, the relationship between teacher educator and teacher candidate is changed. The context of that understanding removes the expert role of the professor, while allowing for expertise. Authority becomes the ability or power to author and co-author our learning experiences both agentically and collaboratively.

Rather than focusing on the learning of individuals, relational pedagogy involves learning with others by focusing on developing equitable, supportive, and resilient relationships. Collaborative pedagogies can integrate multiple viewpoints, synthesizing perspectives that could not have developed from individuals (Smith, Betts, & Block, 2017). Relational and collaborative pedagogies construct a milieu within which teacher candidates can develop the ability to respond critically to teaching and learning contexts. Requiring that teacher candidates engage in complex collaboration is evidence of my belief that learning is socially situated (Brydon & Coleman, 2008; Davis, Sumara, & Luce-Kapler, 2008). Collaboration is a strong tool for countering the neoliberal version of success. Teacher education is often focused through a psychological lens, rather than a sociological perspective (Haberman, 1996; Luke, 2009). My emphasis is on the sociological perspective. In teaching social studies methods from a social justice orientation, my focus is on how the discipline encompasses both the individual and the social. Integrating the socio-cultural perspective—that is, moving from a focus on the personal to a focus on shared social experiences within which inequities exist—can be difficult for teacher candidates.

Teacher candidates often face discomfort in dealing with the tensions inherent in negotiating difference (Boler & Zembylas, 2003; Kanu, 2016). Understanding cultural and individual differences involves questioning one's assumptions, investigating one's social position and examining one's privilege. Together with my students, we discuss how dominant popular culture resists the move from the personal to the social and how the Manitoba curriculum insists on it. Both a critique of dominant culture and strategies for developing community and collaborative learning are pursued, more or less effectively depending on the individuals' and the cohort's experiences, cultures and values (Richardson, 2003).

In my courses, I demonstrate the disparity between the enacted curriculum and formal curriculum documents and provide an orientation to what I term the interactive curriculum, a curriculum theory focused on the contextual relationship between teachers, students, and content. Curriculum development is understood to be both a collaborative process of knowledge production and a reflection of social values. Thus curriculum must be analyzed for what stories are not told, or are misrepresented.

Aboriginal (the existing Manitoba curriculum documents use the term Aboriginal while current discourse includes the term Indigenous) history and cultures have been missing or misrepresented in social studies and science curricula (Borden & Wiseman, 2016; Greenwood, 2009; Scully 2012). Like many other teacher educators (Tupper, 2011; Scully, 2012), I have been inspired by the Truth and Reconciliation Commission to rethink how I teach Aboriginal/Indigenous perspectives. I want to do better. In the course of my research, I initiated a community-based project, the Healing Forest Winnipeg. The Healing Forest is a response to the Calls to Action (Truth and Reconciliation Commission, 2015). The Healing Forest is a place for learning and healing in St. John's Park in the North End of Winnipeg. The Healing Forest is a living memorial to Indigenous children lost to or affected by the residential school system. The Healing Forest is also an outdoor learning space where place-based learning and intergenerational learning connect students to their histories and cultivate citizenship and sustainability.

The Healing Forest project opened up possibilities for further research into Indigenous perspectives and for action through community engagement. The community engagement through the Healing Forest connected me both to current activism and to tradition in parts of the Aboriginal community in Winnipeg. It bridged some of my concerns about the limitations of a non-Indigenous person as lead for such a project, about my position and relative privilege. Constructing the Healing Forest as a place for learning outdoors was a process that pulled together my past experiences as a youth worker and teacher in the inner city of Winnipeg and my present work with teacher candidates at the University of Winnipeg, where the Faculty of Education has a specific focus on inner-city education. My research and teaching are focused on locating and engaging with difference in educational settings and on cultural sustainability. I recognized that the differences I was taking up with my students needed greater attention to Aboriginal cultures.

Collaborative Relationships
Working with Indigenous/Aboriginal community activists, and studying Indigenous worldviews, foregrounded how relationships and relationship building are valuable for learning. This influenced how I worked with partners in the Healing Forest project. It led to reconsidering how I build relationships within my teacher education

practice. I realized that I have not always given much energy to relationship building with teacher candidates. I had to think about why that was.

Before the move to teacher education, I had been a classroom teacher for twenty years, teaching grades seven and eight for the last ten years. Prior to being certified as a teacher, I had been a youth worker in inner-city settings. As a beginning teacher, I had learned to balance my need to nurture with my role as a facilitator of learning. However, as a beginning professor, I felt less need to nurture my adult students and a greater need to affirm my authority in the new role and as part of the tenure process. I wanted to maintain professionalism and be respectful of teacher candidates' agency. At the same time, I missed the intimacy of being a classroom teacher and volunteered to supervise practicum in the After-Degree program, in order to stay in contact with classroom experience and with children. In addition, practicum supervision allowed me to observe and learn about teacher candidates' experiences in practicum.

As part of the teaching team in the After-Degree (AD) program, I am committed to linking course work and practicum experiences. The layered contexts of the AD Program were designed to deliberately and explicitly connect university course work and school practicum experience, commonly seen as distinct sites for theory and practice. Two structures are central to that connection. First is a required course in general theories of teaching and learning designed to articulate its content with practicum experiences, including a group school-based project and individual assignments based on the practicum experience. School-based Professional Learning Meetings (PLMs) are timetabled into that course and are integral. Second is the organization of the first practicum where teacher candidates are paired with one cooperating teacher and have faculty supervisors (including both course instructors and retired teachers) who work collaboratively to structure PLMs. These two structures are augmented by an orientation to situated knowledge and collaborative leaning (Block & Betts, 2016).

My relationships with students in the two year After-Degree Program tend to be stronger than with students in the five year Integrated Program because of my involvement in practicum supervision and PLMs with those after-degree students. In addition to practicum supervision, I requested to teach Social Studies methods to this same group in their final year of the AD Program. Working with the teacher candidates over two terms enabled deeper learning, a more deliberate working relationship, and sometimes deeper relationships.

The value of collaborative relationships with peers in the field is modeled for all teacher candidates. I require teacher candidates to develop strategies for collaborative learning and attempt to model such strategies. In initial classes, I discuss and demonstrate three teaching positions based on Freire's model (Giroux, Freire, & McLaren, 1988). These are transmission (banking model), transaction, and transformation. I explain that each position has its usefulness, but emphasize the value of the transaction position for learning in early years and in general. As I review my own teaching, what teaching positions do I occupy?

When I visualize myself teaching, I see my students looking at me from their table groups. Although I visit at those table groups during many classes, and most classes are structured for group work, my primary image is of the students looking at me or me looking out at them as I stand at the front of the classroom. These images suggest my favoured teaching position is transmission, a position I relegate to training pilots rather than educating future teachers. I perceive how that transmission position is mediated through a transactional style where informality, humour, anecdotes enact relatedness. It is also mediated by providing time for collaboration among students. But to what extent am I collaborating with students?

My teaching positions indicate that my sense of authority continues to be invested in the traditional role of a tenured professor. Although I do not portray myself as an authoritarian guardian of knowledge, I do feel responsible to author, construct or "curate" student experience based on my theory and practice of education, my scholarship. My sense of authority emerges from my own schooling and social positioning and perhaps self-surveillance. To what extent do I experience my authority as a keeper of knowledge? To what extent do I perform as an "owner" of knowledge, rather than as a collaborator in knowledge production, in knowing?

The neoliberal professor who sells shares or ownership of knowledge is a function of the structure of the Academy (Ragoonaden, 2015). The structure of the academy disciplines my students as well. Teacher candidates expect me to perform that traditional role and to showcase my expertise. When my performance includes self-critique, for example when I deconstruct my teaching at the end of a class or discuss my limitations, I feel vulnerable and have actually become vulnerable to a loss of status. For example, since introducing the inquiry process as a central strategy in middle years social studies courses, teacher candidates regularly give me bad reviews on university course evaluations and on anonymous surveys I ask them to complete. The first time I gave the survey, I noted that "confusion" was thematic in the teacher candidates' responses. My initial reaction to reading the responses was that I had taught badly and confused my students, which was a partial truth. Further analysis provided additional possibilities. For example, in a response to the survey question about what was difficult about doing inquiry a teacher candidate wrote: "I have never done it before, I had to research more about it to achieve what I wanted to." Reading this response reminded me that much of learning involves what one 'has not done before' and that the inquiry process includes researching to learn more. Thus, what was difficult for this particular teacher candidate also appears to have been valuable. Although doing inquiry was equated with "chaos" by many teacher candidates, I have persisted.

I believe in the value of inquiry-based teaching and learning. It is risky to persist in teaching from an unpopular framework, although risk-taking is less risky when one is tenured. I have always believed my teaching must demonstrate my values. I ask teacher candidates to question dominant cultural assumptions, and I must be prepared to demonstrate that questioning in my teaching. Teaching for change has been a credo. Can I change my teaching positions and give more time to relationships?

Transformative Teaching

> Education was considered important in inducing or otherwise facilitating harmony between a person and the world. The goal was to produce a person with a well-integrated relationship between thought and action. This idealized outcome was anticipated as following naturally from the "right education." The "right education" is, of course, a culturally defined construct, one of whose main criteria are socializing the individual to the collective culture of a group. However, this sort of socialization is only one dimension of education, a first step in a lifelong path of learning. In reality, "right" education causes change, which in

> time creates a profound transformation of self. This transformation is a dynamic creative process, which brings anything but peace of mind, tranquility and harmonious adaptation. (Cajete, 2010, p. 1129)

The transformative teaching position changes the relationship of teacher and learner. Transformative teaching and learning involves risk and vulnerability. There is the risk of blurring the boundaries between teacher and learner, resulting in less autonomy. Working collaboratively with students, rather than more simply constructing space for them to collaborate with each other, can be transformative. This collaboration requires relationship. The story of Tom (pseudonym), an AD teacher candidate I taught and supervised several years ago, is embedded not only in the teacher/student relationship between us, but also in the relationship with my colleagues in the AD program and the structures of the program we have developed.

I have discussed above how practicum supervision of AD students, to whom I also taught Curriculum, Instruction and Assessment courses, enabled deeper relationships. The excerpt below is part of an analysis of a first year AD student's practicum experience. My colleague and co-author, Paul Betts, had taught math methods to Tom and supervised his practicum in the fall term; I had taught Tom social studies methods and supervised his practicum in the winter term. The winter term practicum takes place in March and April. That spring, the river near Tom's practicum school was very high. Tom designed an inquiry-based unit for his grade 1/2 class, integrating science and social studies and focused on the potential for the Red River to flood the local community. Although Tom had not yet encountered place-based learning theory, as his supervisor I experienced his place-based teaching, both its ups and downs. Working with Tom as he planned and facilitated the inquiry was transformative; it was rooted in our shared actions over time, while building relationship in both university and field settings.

> This cyclical inquiry into his teaching took place across the sites of university courses and the school practicum. Having a faculty supervisor who was also his professor supported Tom's inquiry across sites, as did an orientation that included emergent knowledge. Tom's conflicts about addressing the curriculum

and also including the learner in his planning process did not need an immediate resolution. Tom worked at it through his teaching and his coursework. In the second practicum block, his planning and teaching evidenced a growing ability to plan differentiated learning activities and to develop curriculum in response to the teaching context. His teaching identity included the understanding that teachers (as agents) construct, as well as respond, to teaching contexts. (Block & Betts, 2016, p. 12)

The structure of the AD Program makes possible deep (Egan, 2010) and slow learning, (Shiva, V., personal communication, November, 2014), both of which I connect to relationship or relatedness. In the context of the AD Program, the transformative teaching position is enabled through structural change, that is, through the constructive association or collaboration of professors, faculty supervisors, cooperating teachers, the director of Student Teaching, and teacher candidates.The collaboration with others in the AD Program is important, as it supports my ability to take action at a systemic level. Structural changes in teacher education require such collaboration. I believe transformative teaching emerges from shared values and shared work. The associations developed within the academy animate deeper connections or relationships. In turn, that strengthens my participation in making agentic co-participation part of teacher education. An ongoing critique of our shared values and how they are enacted is part of a deliberate collaboration experienced and held onto over time and in place. The root word for tenure is *teneo*, Latin for "hold." My (untenured) authority was dedicated to developing teacher candidate agency. Over time (and with tenure) a different sense of authority may hold deeper relationships and further collaboration with students. Understanding tenure as growth within the context of the academy and experiencing how that growth engenders deepening relationships with colleagues and students is sustaining.

References

Alsup, J. (2005). *Teacher identity discourses: Negotiating personal and professional spaces*. New York, NY: Routledge, Taylor & Francis Group.

Block, L. A. (2017). Re-locating: Moving between the field and the university. In T. Sibbald & V. Handford (Eds.), *The academic gateway: Understanding the journey to tenure*. Ottawa, ON: University of Ottawa Press.

Block, L. A., & Betts, P. (2018). Interrupting the success-failure binary in teacher education: Our experience of Foucault's panopticon, In K. Nolan & J. Tupper, (Eds.). *Social theory for teacher education*. Unpublished chapter.

Block, L. A., & Betts, P. (2016). Cultivating agentic teacher identities in the field of a teacher education program. *Brock Education Journal, 25*(2).

Boler, M., & Zembylas, M. (2010). Discomforting truths: The emotional terrain of understanding difference. In P. P. Trifonas (Ed.), *Pedagogies of difference: Rethinking education for social change* (pp. 110–136). New York, NY: Routledge.

Borden, L. L., & Wiseman, D. (2016). Considerations from places where Indigenous and western ways of knowing, being, and doing circulate together: STEM as artifact of teaching and learning. *Canadian Journal of Science, Mathematics and Technology Education, 16*(2), 140–152.

Britzman, D. P. (1991). *Practice makes practice: A critical study of learning to teach*. Albany, NY: State University of New York Press.

Brydon, D., & Coleman, W. D. (2008). Globalization, autonomy, and community. In D. Brydon & W. D. Coleman (Eds.), *Renegotiating community: Interdisciplinary perspectives, global contexts* (pp. 1–28). Vancouver, BC: University of British Columbia Press.

Cajete, G. A., & Pueblo, S. C. (2010). Contemporary Indigenous education: A nature-centered American Indian philosophy for a 21st century world. *Futures, 42*(10), 1126–1132.

Davis, B., Sumara, D. J., & Luce-Kapler, R. (2008). *Engaging minds: Changing teaching in complex times*. New York, NY: Routledge.

Davis, L. J. (1995). *Enforcing normalcy: Disability, deafness, and the body*. Kbh.: Nota.

Egan, K. (2010). *Learning in depth: A simple innovation that can transform schooling*. Chicago, IL: University of Chicago Press.

Foucault, M. (1965). *Madness and civilization: A history of insanity in the Age of Reason* (R. J. Howard, Trans.). Pantheon.

Foucault, M. (1983). *Michel Foucault: Beyond structuralism and hermeneutics* (2nd ed.). New York, NY: Harvester Wheatsheaf.

Foucault, M. (2000). On the genealogy of ethics: An overview of work in progress. In P. Rabinow & H. Dreyfus (Eds.), *Ethics: Subjectivity and truth*. London, UK: Penguin Books.

Giroux, H. A., Freire, P., & McLaren, P. (1988). *Teachers as intellectuals: Toward a critical pedagogy of learning*. Westport, CT: Greenwood Publishing Group.

Greenwood, D. A. (2009). Place, survivance, and white remembrance: A decolonizing challenge to rural education in mobile modernity. *Journal of Research in Rural Education, 24*(10).

Haberman, M. (1996). Selecting and preparing culturally competent teachers for urban schools. In J. P. Sikula (Ed.), *Handbook of research in teacher education* (2nd ed., pp. 747–760). New York, NY: Routledge.

Haraway, D. (1988). Situated knowledges: The science question in feminism and the privilege of partial perspective. *Feminist Studies, 14*(3), 575.

Kanu, Y. (2016). Integrating Aboriginal perspectives for educational wellbeing: Minimizing teacher candidate resistance. In F. Deer & T. Falkenberg (Eds.), *Indigenous perspectives on education for well-being in Canada* (pp. 139–156). Winnipeg, MB: Education for Sustainable Well-Being Press.

Luke, A. (2009). Race and language as capital in school: A sociological template for language education reform. In R. Kubota & A. Lin (Eds.), *Race, culture, and identities in second language education: Exploring critically engaged practice* (pp. 286–308). New York, NY: Routledge.

Ragoonaden, K. (2015). Setting the path towards emancipatory practices. In K. Ragoonaden (Ed.), *Contested sites in education: The quest for the public intellectual, identity, and service* (pp. 9–20). New York, NY: Peter Lang.

Richardson, V. (2004). Preservice teachers' beliefs. In A. R. McAninch & J. Raths (Eds.), *Teacher beliefs and classroom performance: The impact of teacher education* (pp. 1–22). Greenwich, Conn, CT: Information Age Pub.

Sarason, S. B. (1996). *Revisiting 'The culture of the school and the problem of change.'* New York, NY: Teachers College Press.

Scully, A. (2012). Decolonization, reinhabitation and reconciliation: Aboriginal and place-based education. *Canadian Journal of Environmental Education, 17,* 148–158.

Sibbald, T. & Handford, V. (2017). Is there a metric to evaluate tenure? *Academic Matters,* (Winter), 9–13.

Smith, C., Betts, P., & Block, L. (2017). Openings for social change through critical relational collaborative pedagogies. In M. Hirschkorn (Ed.), *What should Canada's teachers know? Teacher capacities: Knowledge, beliefs and skills* (pp. 15–31). Canadian Association for Teacher Education (CATE).

Truth and Reconciliation Commission of Canada. (2015). Calls to action. Retrieved 2019, from http://www.trc.ca/websites/trcinstitution/index.php?p=3

Tupper, J. (2011). Disrupting ignorance and settler identities: The challenges of preparing beginning teachers for treaty education. *In Education, 17*(3), 38–55.

CHAPTER 15

It's Not Me, It's the Process

Kathy Snow

As I write this chapter I am in the final stages of the preparation of my application for tenure. This process sometimes feels like a make-work project, alternatively like an egomaniacal field trip down memory lane, and occasionally like a five monkeys science experiment[1] (which never happened but gained viral attention in social media). Tierney and Bensimon (1996) describe the advice given to tenure candidates as an "odd potpourri of folk wisdom and half-truths" (45) and at the risk of presenting the same, this chapter outlines my reflections on the tenure process from the standpoint of fostering learning organizations and organizational management. Admittedly, this process is still very close to home for me, and the frustration of accepting the way it works around here in parallel with the social pressure from the system to fit in has left me feeling a little weary. I find it disconcerting that in institutions of higher learning, where we work to promote critical thinking, dialogue, and personal growth in our students, the institutionalised approach to tenure appears to result in a different, almost opposite, assessment experience for faculty members. After four years and my own monkey experiences I have reached the point that I'm no longer confused about the way it works around here, and I feel ready to support new academics in their indoctrination to organizational culture. However, I cannot do it through the institutional ethos that appears to be the norm of the tenure and review committees I have observed both in my institution and others.

I am sure somewhere in the history of the development of the tenure process there was wisdom in the development of a peer-reviewed accountability system. To increase fairness and rigour through evidence and quantifiable measures of success is a good idea; who is better positioned to evaluate academic success than someone in your own field and department? I agree, a person's achievement of tenure should not be based solely on opinion and peer impressions; it requires a rigorous process that is evidenced through clear stages with feedback to allow for improvement along the way. However, the process does not always reflect this objective approach. Achieving tenure has been described as "fraught with contradictory criteria and unwritten rules" (Rice, Sorcinelli & Austin, 2000, 9) and a "mysterious, politicized and stressful crapshoot" (Chait, 1997, p. B4). Few have the luxury of a job that offers so much freedom, flexibility, and security as a tenured professor; the privilege is earned through tenure. But like all assessment, the way the tenure process appears in collective agreement documents and what pre-tenure faculty experience is variable.

The results of the tenure review assessment process have been linked to creating collegial tensions, undesirable organizational outcomes, diminished citizenship behaviour, productivity, and job satisfaction, even for those who have achieved it (Cameron & Hyer, 2010; Hearn & Anderson, 2002; Lawrence, Celis & Ott, 2016). It is no wonder faculty frequently report increased levels of stress (Jakob & Teichler, 2011; Winefield & Jarrett, 2001), isolation (Shaw, 2014), and challenges related to being valued contributors to the organization (Kinman & Wray, 2015) pre-tenure. The aforementioned experiences are in direct conflict with the desired culture of learning organizations. In my experience, the road to tenure is not only the institution developing trust in you, but you building trust in the institution. At this point I am confident the institution now trusts me, but I am still not sure I trust it, regardless of or perhaps because of the layers of process that are involved in the tenure decision.

Trust Building and Learning Organizations

The organizational leadership theory of Senge (1990) when applied to schools, can be summarized as being purposeful about the group learning process with a critical emphasis on social processes for acquiring and sharing knowledge that improves learning and development for all (Leithwood, Steinback & Jantzi, 2002; Manjounes, 2016). DuFour (2004) posits that organization learning, through collaboration, is necessary and generally understood by all school members as desirable, but can be undermined in organizations through oppressive accountability measures. While Zucker (1986) states that accountability in an organizational setting is not in itself problematic, however without trust (a frequently overlooked aspect of organizational cohesion), accountability does not lead to school or individual improvement. Further, low trust environments are costly to institutions (Handford & Leithwood, 2013) because they lead to a withdrawl of organizational citizenship behaviours, burnout, departure, and the inevitable re-training of new employees (Friedman, Lipshitz, & Overmeer, 2001).

In the past five years I have watched with trepidation as the cycle of desire to improve learning, being stymied by organizational processes and its subsequent demotivating effects—has repeated itself in my institution. This is not unique to my institution, nor is it unique to educational institutions. As friends and colleagues, both in my institution and others, have reached out to each other to talk through the review process, whether year one probation, year-three review, tenure, or promotion to associate or full professor, the personal experiences are all parallel. Few have come out the other side without feeling anxiety about how the process will function. Even colleagues I would consider high performers in their field have shared concerns and hurts with me, and some have even quit. As an educator, the process challenges everything I have learned about assessment for learning, leadership, and learning organizations.

To reiterate, I position myself and my goals for assessment and organizations from within the construct of learning organizations; it is through that lens that I see the tenure process. Learning organizations are defined by Senge (1990) as groups work towards creating a shared vision of the organization for the future. This vision goes beyond individual motivations. It involves building shared mental models, developing personal and collective mastery, and collaborations where everyone benefits. In the context of graduate teaching, my colleagues and I teach these concepts, but then step out of the instructor role to face a different reality in the same institution. I claim to be working in an organization of higher learning, but it is not always a learning organization. It is not the institution's fault, nor departmental nor individual resistance, but rather that "monkey experiment" type thinking, an indoctrination into a specific organizational behaviour and culture, that is dictated by external regulatory bodies and fears of disrupting collective agreements, procedures, and policies, that both offer security and hand-cuffs when trying to think differently.

I present here the impressions from countless conversations with colleagues, and the literature supporting organizational learning, personal insights about how to address this critical yet highly convoluted path to success or failure in academia. This chapter is intended to be helpful for those facing tenure and promotion committees. My approach is not the only one or necessarily the best way, nor is it a critique of colleagues who are all facing the same challenge from the system. Rather, through this chapter, and this book, my hope is that extended discussions arise which transform the process itself. This chapter summarizes four critical aspects of my own actions that developed as I wound my way through a process I came to trust less and less as an accurate assessment, the longer I was engaged.

Humility and Grace

The tenure process, by nature, is a socialization system that initiates new faculty into the cultural norms of the institution (Tierney & Bensimon, 1996). Part of that initiation is about finding your position and role in the university. As you enter the tenure process, regardless of age or achievements outside of the institution, you are re-starting. For those in education particularly I think this is a difficult shift as joining Higher Education usually means leaving a full career of teaching in the K-12 system behind you. This is not the same for all Faculties so you can find yourself junior to those with less teaching/professional experience across the university. I found this was a challenging mental shift as I went from school leader in the K-12 system to an absolute beginner in Higher Education. I was not the director anymore. I was not in charge of my classroom or departmental procedures, and had little to no influence in the operations of the university as a whole. I have watched colleagues (including myself) rail against this shift, through comments like "at my last organization we . . .", only to be quickly shut down with statements like, "But you are not there now." The reality where previously I would be listened to now required re-establishing respect in the new system. In the past when I had changed jobs, it usually came with a promotion, my status moved with me through the title of the new position even though I may have changed school districts or governance levels. It is not the same with the change to Higher Education. Within the university tenure process, you engage in a five- and seven-year probationary period where you develop autonomy and trust through each stage of the process (Lawrence et al., 2016). You re-start at the bottom. Respect must be earned through your contributions, not your past experience. You have to put in your time, teaching the courses no one else wants to teach, saying yes to some task, when you are mentally screaming "no!" But, there is a need to balance and be strategic in saying yes and no because working conditions early in this process can impact your ability to put together experiences that will build a strong dossier (Cawyer, Simmonds & Davis, 2002; Kaminski & Geisler, 2012). Asking myself why I wanted to say yes or no was a significant part of the learning. Do I want to say no because I feel the task is unjust, for example taking all the high enrolment courses at unpopular teaching times, or am I saying no because I just cannot do the job in the way it is proposed in a way that benefits all? Am I saying yes to support others as part of building our team, or for self-serving purposes? Or worse, am I seeking out high profile tasks, to gain visibility and feed my own ego and insecurities?

Additionally, in the face of job insecurity, it is tempting to remind others of significant achievements in your former career or, alternatively, reminding others of your academic lineage (for example, I studied under X, at amazing university Y). As I sought to find my place, I saw in myself a return to an academic version of teenage angst around branding, and cliques that I didn't like. According to Inger Mewburn, who has been publishing a popular blog for new academics called *The Thesis Whisperer*, many academics resort to academic bullying, which she calls "cleverness," as a form of currency in academia. In her descriptions, cleverness involves, among other things, belittling behaviours through academic snobbery and narcissistic self-promotion. This set of behaviours can be a powerful social control and can be highly contagious as group members seek to join the insider circle either consciously or unconsciously. Somewhere around year two I became aware of the cleverness around me as well as the cleverness I was propagating, in my own insecure attempts at self-promotion and expectations of privilege based on former career achievements, and I did not like who I was becoming. Why was I embroiled in this hyper-critique of others? Why this need to prove myself and rise to the top of the clique? I needed to stop, take a step back, and re-establish not only my own humility but also my care for others. I needed a healthier mental space. In a recent conversation with a colleague, who asked me for advice when she reached a similar point in her own tenure development she reminded me of the simple advice I had given her several years ago: "don't worry about others, keep your head down, do good work, and let your work stand for itself, not the politics around it, and you will be fine." It was not particularly wise or complex, but according to her, it was the best advice she had received. The message was, don't worry about what people think or say, just do good work that fulfills you, with humility and grace, and it was that teaching, which I adopted after my three-year review. I began to become a better academic and person. However, I still need constant reminders of my own advice, particularly on challenging days.

Compassion
Extending the notions of humility and grace is compassion for self and others. I have faced more rejection and negativity in my academic role than I have in any other role during my career. In the last five years I have submitted many funding applications of varying sizes. I have submitted applications on my own as well as working on small and large team project proposals. I have experienced a reasonably high acceptance rate—but there is always the presence of rejection. Rejection is not, in itself, the problem; the problem is academics never talk about it. There was a lot of work invested in all the applications, including those that were rejected. Writing them, learning to write them better, reviewing them, having them reviewed and editing them, represents a significant investment of time, but also of self. Silva-Ford (no date), in describing academic job rejections stated "job rejections felt personal" and indeed critique, be it not receiving a job offer, a funding award or during your three-year tenure review, can hurt. In the case of article reviews for publication, I have personally found that reviewer responses frequently seem to be geared to adding insult to injury. On one unsuccessful funding proposal that was co-authored with an established colleague who is an expert in the field in question, the reviewer wrote "It appears your team has limited knowledge of the instructional discipline and should seek out someone with more experience before attempting to re-submit this proposal." Though the example cited here does not

deal specifically with tenure process feedback, it is representative of the peer-review responses that academics regularly experience during that process. As I described my response to my three year review to a colleague, her response was, "Oh yes, it was just like that for me too, you shouldn't expect anything different, in fact mine was worse because . . ." Another colleague who successfully mitigated an appeal within the tenure and promotion process stated, "I was successful, but I got bruised." Why are we doing this to each other? Again, I liken this to the Monkey Experiment, with the mentality appearing to be, because my process was one of high critique, or of duration X, etc., then yours must be the same as mine. I cannot imagine the same tone and language would be used grading student assignments if you want your students to feel motivated to progress.

A parallel experience of misguided assessment practice occurs when publishing research. I have received a considerable amount of feedback that I do not consider constructive or timely. Two things the literature on learning organizations and positive development for students tells us we must do: provide developmental feedback, in a timely manner. I publish several articles a year, but most of them have been in some stage of review or editing for more than a year before they are published. I have heard stories from colleagues who claim to have had publications intentionally slowed down to allow one of the reviewers to publish a parallel article ahead of the one under review. Over the past five years I have drifted into that margins of paranoid thinking, but it did not last long because I honestly (naively?) did not believe that colleagues would do that to one another. However, faced with non-constructive comments from reviewers being almost normal, I can drift into a defensive space. The culture of marking rather than supporting learning through assessment for time-pressured faculty seems to permeate much of the feedback mechanism in academia.

It is not surprising the tenure review process is the same. During my three-year review I felt graded rather than nurtured. Rebounding took some time and was only accomplished by accepting that it's the process, not me. Evaluation felt more a reflection of the review teams' collective experience with tenure than the actual merit of my dossier. The act of peer-review has, to some degree, established a negative normalizing effect within the university construct. In discussions with colleagues I found some are afraid of appearing too eager, shining too brightly, for fear of jealousies arising during peer-review, while others both under review and some of those conducting reviews try to measure themselves against each other and conflicts arise, with comments like "X has not published in five years; who is he to judge me?" Or "Y might have won two awards for teaching, but has he really been supporting teaching here?" Insecurity on the side of the reviewers and reviewees leads to a tightening of ranks, and less than constructive treatment of one another. It's not as much a part of human nature to celebrate others successes with them as I would like to think. As long as the peer-review system exists, there will be a constant comparison of each other to each other and we are hard on one another. When I stepped back, and viewed the process through the lens of compassion why it is the way it is became clearer and I could objectively evaluate my own review process. But it involved developing compassion for myself and others. Neff (2003) outlines the concept of self-compassion as a means to improve job satisfaction. Self-compassion involves being discerning and gentle towards self in the face of hardships or perceived inadequacies. Self-compassion has also been paralleled with mindfulness, or the ability to be thoughtful about the actual phenomenon one is experiencing rather than reactionary (Hollis-Walker & Colosimo, 2011). I've adopted this for my own peace of mind, but compassion should extend beyond the self towards shifting workplace culture.

Mutual Respect
Inherent in compassion is respect for self and others. If the peer-review process causes academics to feel insecure I posit this is because academics tend to be overachievers, and we need to recognize this in ourselves and others. If, for example, you want a coveted tri-council grant or publications in top-tier journals, then the competition is tough, because everyone is trying to gain these prizes. Learning to write in the academic genre that is expected is essential. I was self-diagnosing what was wrong with my work from the rejections, sometimes taking things personally and sometimes feeling disrespected or disrespecting those who critiqued me. In a small university like mine, in the face of the national budget cuts that all universities in Canada have felt, there are few people around with spare minutes to mentor a beginner in the process. Isolation in the tenure process has been cited frequently in evaluations of faculty experience as detrimental (Frazier, 2011; Johnsrun & Des Jarlais, 1994;

Lawrence et al., 2016). I've needed to be proactive about re-learning what I thought I knew from my rejections, but to do that I needed to trust my colleagues enough to share my challenges. Carmeli and Gittel (2009), claim that mutual respect among colleagues is critical to learning from failures, and developing high quality working relationships, which the peer-review process needs to thrive. Furthermore in highly diverse but interdependent collections of colleagues, as are found commonly in universities, mutual respect for different disciplines and areas of expertise is foundational for psychological safety. Although Carmeli and Gittel (2009) cite examples of medical teams, with anesthesiologists, nurses, and surgeons working together, the concept is the same throughout tenure where faculty from diverse disciplines set out to evaluate what is excellent, satisfactory, or unsatisfactory in an area that may be very far from their own expertise. I observed a colleague challenge his tenure evaluation when the review committee deemed the academic publications were not representative of a sufficient level of research and rigour based on the criteria of the reviewer's disciplines; this, too, leads to hurt and demotivation. In the face of this and a dearth of mentorship from my own tiny department, I turned to faculty from other disciplines and institutions for mentorship. Another colleague told me she regularly attends a particular conference because that is where the reviewers of tri-council grants tend to go. Her thoughts are that it is good to be seen so that her ideas stay fresh in the minds of reviewers as they set out to blind review papers. Being visible and personable is her approach to developing respect and trust needed for successful reviews of any type.

As previously mentioned, my thoughts have always been that good work will be rewarded, not that I needed to network on behalf of my research to have it gain traction or acknowledgement. Yet self-promotion seems to be an important part of academia, in developing a reputation that encourages respectful interactions, and as I sit in an untenured space that possibility is scary. I have observed and benefited from academic gardening, where highly respected researchers have brought me forward on grants, which has increased my likelihood of success in future grants based on their reputations. I appreciated the help, but I don't like working in a system where that seems to be needed, rather than a default position of respect. In saying that, I appear to be contradicting my earlier statements, in which respect must be earned; however I don't think the two, earning respect and evaluating one another respectfully, are mutually exclusive. To me, the golden rule, which we all should have learned in Kindergarten, always applies—treat others as you wish to be treated, and insecurities about trust, failure, success, and evaluation begin to soften through an ethic of reciprocity.

Balanced Perspective

At the risk of citing a cliché, Sayre's (1973) quote in *The Wall Street Journal*, which has become known as Sayre's Law, states: "Academic politics is the most vicious and bitter form of politics because the stakes are so low." I've quoted that to myself many times as I have sat listening to or engaging in extended debates on issues or semantics that will have little meaningful consequence. Ren and Caudle (2016) outline that faculty adopted a range of techniques to balance work and life, which fall into three categories of coping strategies: behavioural, interpersonal, and intrapersonal. Behavioural strategies included practical adaptations such as setting boundaries around when and how work was to be conducted. Interpersonal includes how you draw upon social connections for support, and intrapersonal describes the psychological approaches adopted, which are used to shape perceptions. All of these became visible at the time of my three-year review when, unrelated to the review, I obtained a small flock of chickens, which allowed me to observe "the pecking order" from a healthy distance. As I watched all five chickens run and fight for a single strawberry top, while a pile of other tops lay unwanted in the corner of their enclosure, I gained some perspective. On another occasion, I watched two of the larger birds try to leave the coop at the same time only to get stuck in the door. Neither bird would give way to the other, so they remained stuck. No other bird could leave the coop until a small bird jumped over their backs and got ahead of them to the corn. I don't know which bird yielded to the other, but their jealousy of the little bird caused them to work together to get out of their predicament and chase the little one away. When I observed the behaviour, I laughed out loud because I saw examples of academic behaviours in their actions. There is also nothing like a proud rooster, with a look in his eye only a rooster can have, marching around his domain and, in our case a rooster half the size of the hens, to help gain perspective about the organizational structures one is immersed in. Realistically, the chickens experience negotiations of life in the coop that are not very different from my own in achieving tenure, and the consequences are about as significant. Knowing that, laughing through observations of the chickens and myself, brought a very needed balance to the problem of tenure for me.

Conclusions

Hooper, Wright, and Burnham (2012) refer to the tenure process as having an impact on an individual's family, professional, and individual life. From personal experience I would agree: The tenure process represented a significant disruption in my ability to just get on with things, as long as I worried about it, or attempted to join in the process in the way I felt was expected from observations. As I look back at this chapter, which attempted to discuss the assessment system of tenure, but essentially only discussed what I needed to change in me to negotiate the system, I see the process is not about the tools of assessment, but the relationships built with peers during the process. Pavel, Legier, and Ruiz (2010) refer to the process as a challenging time of critical examination, often resulting in a negative emotional experience. I would argue that it is an important time of critical reflection as you develop into the academic you want to be, and it can be negative if you let the challenging aspects of the process infect your own thinking. It is not the same for everyone, as I have presented here, arguably based on the degree of adoption of learning organization principles that support peer cohesion and trust. I believe the tenure process does not have to be negative for anyone if we as a collective academy decide to break the cycle of enculturation through our response to the evaluation and support processes involved in tenure. We can build a more trusting and learning-centric place involving humility, compassion, respect, and balance.

Endnotes

1   The Five Monkeys experiment, originally published in a 2011 *Psychology Today* blog post by Micheal Michalco under the title "What monkeys can teach us about human behavior," told the story of the successive training of five monkeys to avoid a banana based on the initial monkey's negative experiences reaching for the banana. Even though no physical

threat existed for new monkeys they were said to avoid the banana and teach others to avoid the banana based on pressure from the previous monkey.

References

Cameron, T., & Hyer, P. (2010). *An examination of departure trends and tenure rates among pre-tenure faculty: A ten year cohort study (1996–2005)*. Retrieved from https://vtechworks.lib.vt.edu/handle/10919/72140

Carmeli, A., & Gittel, J. H. (2009). High-quality relationships, psychological safety and learning from failures in work organizations. *Journal of Organizational Behaviour 30*, 709–729.

Cawyer, C. S., Simonds, C., & Davis, S. (2002). Mentoring to facilitate socialization: The case of the new faculty member. *International Journal of Qualitative Studies in Education, 15*(2), 225–242. https://doi.org/10.1080/09518390110111938

Chait, R. (February 7, 1997). Why academe needs more employment options. *The Chronicle of Higher Education*, B4. Retrieved from: https://www.chronicle.com/article/Why-Academe-Needs-More/77478

DuFour, R. (2004). What is a 'Professional learning community'? *Educational Leadership 61*(8), 6–11.

Frazier, K. N. (2011). Academic Bullying: A barrier to tenure and promotion for African-American faculty. *Florida Journal of Educational Administration and Policy, 5*(1), 1–13.

Friedman, V., Lipshitz, R., & Overmeer, W. (2001). Creating conditions for organizational learning. In M. Dierkes, A. Berthoin-Antal, J. Child, & I. Nonaka (Eds.), *Handbook of organizational learning* (pp. 757–774). Oxford, UK: Oxford University Press.

Handford, V., & Leithwood, K. (2013). Why teachers trust school leaders. *Journal of Educational Administration, 51*(2), 194–212.

Hearn, J. C. & Anderson, M. S. (2002). Conflict in academic departments: An analysis of disputes over faculty promotion and tenure. *Research in Higher Education, 43*(5), 503–529. https://doi.org/10.1023/A:1020197630478

Hollis-Walker, L., & Colosimo, K. (2011). Mindfulness, self-compassion, and happiness in non-mediators: A theoretical and empirical examination. *Personality and Individual Differences, 50*(2), 222–227.

Hooper, L. M., Wright, V. H., & Burnham, J. J. (2012). Acculturating to the role of tenure-track assistant professor: A family systems approach to joining the academy. *Contemporary Family Therapy 34*(1). https://doi.10.1007/s10591-011-9171-5

Jakob, A. K., & Teichler, U. (2011). *Der Wandel des Hochschulleherberufs im internationalen Verglieich: Ergebnisse einer Befragung in ben Jahren 2007/08*.

Berlin: Bundesministerium fuer Bildung im Forschung. Retrieved from: https://www.uni-kassel.de/einrichtungen/fileadmin/datas/einrichtungen/incher/T_12__BMBF_Hochschullehrerstudie_2011.pdf

Johnsrun, L. K., & Des Jarlais, C. D. (1994). Barriers to tenure for women and minorities. *The Review of Higher Education, 17*(4), 335–353.

Kaminski, D., & Geisler, C. (2012). Survival analysis of faculty retention in science and engineering by gender. *Science, 335*, 864–866.

Kinman, G., & Wray, S. (2015). *Taking its toll: Rising stress levels in further education UCU Stress Survey 2014*. Retrieved from: https://doi.org/ 10.13140/ RG.2.2.31578.64967

Lawrence, J. H., Celis, S., & Ott, M. (2016). Is the tenure process fair?: What faculty think. *The Journal of Higher Education, 85*(2), 155–192.

Leithwood, K., Steinbach, R., & Jantzi, D. (2002). School leadership and teachers' motivation to implement accountability policies. *Educational Administration Quarterly, 38,* 94–119.

Manjounes, C. K. (2016). How tenure in higher education related to faculty productivity and retention. *Walden Dissertations and Doctoral Studies collection*. Retrieved from: https://pdfs.semanticscholar.org/6ca1/8593d068c5604ef68a495491f283099128b3.pdf?_ga=2.66580909.2056677699.1566049633-386168268.1566049633

Neff, K. (2003). Self-compassion: An alternative conceptualization of a healthy attitude toward oneself. *Self and Identity, 2*(2003), 85–101.

Pavel, S. R., Legier, J. T., & Ruiz, J. R. (2010). Promotion and tenure perceptions of University Aviation Association (UAA) collegiate aviation administrators and faculty. *Quality Progress, 43*(1), 16–47.

Ren, X., & Caudle, D. (2016). Walking the tightrope between work and nonwork life: Strategies employed by British and Chinese academics and their implications. *Studies in Higher Education 41*(4), 599–618.

Rice, E., Sorcinelli, M. D., & Austin, A. E. (2000). *Heeding new voices: Academic careers for a new generation*. (New Pathways Working Paper Series, Inquiry No. 7). Washington, DC: American Association for Higher Education.

Sayre, W. S. (1973, December, 20). In Politics and people, Otten, A.L. *The Wall Street Journal*. p. 14

Senge, P. (1990) *The fifth discipline: The art and practice of the learning organization*. New York, NY: Doubleday.

Shaw, C. (May 8, 2014). *Overworked and isolated-work pressure fuels mental illness in academia*. Retrieved from: https://www.theguardian.com/higher-education-network/blog/2014/may/08/work-pressure-fuels-academic-mental-illness-guardian-study-health

Silva-Ford, L. (n.d.) in Schuman, R. (June 2, 2014). *Why is academic rejection so very crushing?* retrieved from: https://www.chronicle.com/article/Why-Is-Academic-Rejection-So/146883

Tierney, W. G., & Bensimon, E. (1996). *Promotion and tenure: Community and socialization in academe*. Albany, NY: SUNY Press.

Winefield, A. H., & Jarret, R. (2001). Occupational stress in university staff. *International Journal of Stress Management, 8*(4), 285–298.

Zucker, L. G. (1986). The production of trust institutional sources of economic structure, 1840–1920. *Research in Organizational Behavior, 8*, 53–111.

CHAPTER 16

Jill Revisited—Still Struggling With Mental Illness Within Academia Post-Tenure

Joan M. Chambers

I first began working on a chapter contribution for this book over nine months ago! During the past months, I have continually struggled with writing, this piece in particular; the progress has been haltingly and painfully slow (for me and the poor editors). The reasons for my struggles are complex with both constant and changing elements. Let me explain, beginning with who I am.

I am a female academic and an associate (tenured) professor at a small university in Northern Ontario, Canada. I am a teacher. I am a researcher. I provide service to the university—the three pillars of an academic's role (Greenbank, 2006). In order to receive recognition and to experience career growth and autonomy—perceived as a desirable outcome and need (Deci & Ryan, 2000; Broeck, Ferris, Chang, & Rosen, 2016) within academia—it is expected that I carry out all of the duties framed within an academic's role equally well, but with emphasis on research followed by teaching. However, the reality . . . my reality . . . is that I cannot easily do so because I am an academic with mental illness. My mental illness significantly affected my personal journey to tenure as explained in The *Academic Gateway* (Chambers, 2017). I won't go into the details of my tenure journey—suffice it to say that though the journey was extremely challenging personally, I was able to achieve tenure in spite of mental health issues. Yet one might comment, "you were given tenure, it couldn't be all that bad for you"; or "now that you are a tenured professor, life is more relaxed and easy-going, right?" Wrong. Achieving tenure does not ease the pressure and job expectations for academics. In some ways it actually increases tensions, because the supports often put in place to help new academics are no longer there.

Since I began my career as an academic in 2009 I have learned to hide my illness (as best I can) and soldier on because, for the most part, the academy does not want to know about or have to deal with the "impairment effects" (Williams & Mavin, 2015) of mental illness. Further support for the necessity (perceived or otherwise) of keeping my illness out of the eyes and ears of my employers is provided by Dalke and Mullaney (2014) as they draw upon the work of Margaret Price (2011):

> Margaret Price has conducted an extensive analysis of the ways in which the academy's structuring of itself around schedules—placing importance on appointments, deadlines, the completion of timed tasks—excludes and discriminates against those with mental disabilities; she shows how the demands of academia can exacerbate symptoms which may be manageable in a less stressful environment. It is relatively easy for a college to imagine accommodating physical disabilities, Price argues, but much harder for a place that prides itself on mental accomplishment to envision accommodating mental diversity and difference—to adjust, in particular, to the altered *pacing* that differently minded minds might require. (para. 51)

Whether successfully hidden or not, the effects of my illness are very real, are not accommodated by the institution, and are the primary reasons for my struggles in writing this piece.

When I began trying to write this post-tenure chapter many months ago, I was in a deep depressive phase. In the beginning I wrote:

> I have mental illness. My illness shifts like the waves in an ocean, sometimes rough and high, threatening to pull me under. Sometimes the waves are small ripples, rolling through my life, troublesome perhaps but mostly manageable. Sometimes the ocean is calm, easily navigable. Like the waves in an ocean, my illness is unpredictable, sometimes leaving me unable to rise from my bed and face the day. Sometimes I am able to cope, but

> it's not easy. Sometimes I am . . . "normal" or as I prefer, neurotypical. My cognitive abilities have changed since becoming ill; I do not know when or even if my abilities will ever return to what I once knew.

This is, perhaps, somewhat melodramatic, but it rings true for me, especially at the time of writing. Now, at this moment, I am not in a severe depressive phase and, consequently, am not as disabled by my illness, but my illness continues affecting me in unanticipated ways. After my first bout of major depression,[1] I believed that, once better, I would be able to work as before and perform as expected by the academy. I was wrong. The cognitive changes are a reality I try to deal with on a daily basis—the ability to focus, sustain mental thought processes, articulate my thinking, hold thoughts or ideas in my head long enough to express them or write them down, maintain mental (and physical) energy, and short-term memory—abilities I possessed before but now struggle with. Some days are better than others, some worse, but what is particularly challenging is not knowing, or being able to schedule, when a difficult day will arise.

All it takes is for some small thing to go awry and it can trip me up and send me down the hill—the unexpectedness of which makes it difficult to complete work as planned. Consequently, I feel as though I am always behind, continually playing catch-up, and failing at my job as an academic. Some of these feelings may be exaggerated in my mind, but they further act to sabotage my productivity and work. And because I never want to let others down, my teaching and students are my priority, followed by my service duties to the faculty and the university. My own research and writing falls to the bottom of the to-do list, a list I never quite seem able to complete; there is never enough time, thus, my inability to complete a chapter for this book by the required deadline. Not that I place any blame with the editors—they have their own deadlines to work within—no, I believe the problem lies within academe where time is measured and appropriated by the system; time is a demanding, non-negotiable requirement of the job.

Through my struggles I have found that there are advantages to challenging the thinking about dis-abilities. Consider, some telling thoughts:

> Many disability studies scholars include time in their systematic "cripping" of normative assumptions about human

experience.... The concept of "crip time" could also conceivably be used in a third sense, to identify the possibility—the profound *need*—for some time that (as the anonymous reviewer of this essay observed) is "just plain wasted ... sometime we are just 'doing time'—in depression, in illness, in times when there is nothing really beyond surviving to do." Although the field of disability studies has evoked, and advocated for, the variability of "crip time," it has not wrestled directly (so far as we know) with this notion of wasting time.... the disability movement seems particularly, and somewhat paradoxically, invested in a narrative of "overcoming" particular impairments, in order to be taken seriously in the academy. The field hasn't yet offered us, we think, the tools we need to interrupt the narrative of academic achievement, to find a space where nothing happens, to discover gaps in which normative time is ruptured, suspended.

And so we gesture, here, toward some of those possibilities that lie in empty and "unproductive" time.

... do the gossamer clocks meld or resist?
protest
or conform? ...

"Does the demonstration of coherence indicate a stronger mind?"
—Margaret Price, Mad at School

Does getting your work in on time indicate a stronger mind? (Or: why is punctuality so important?) (Dalke & Mullaney, 2014, para. 49–50)

For me, there are two faces to the issue of mental illness. First, the ongoing personal struggle that can be difficult for others to understand, react to, and accept. Mental illness is an unpredictable, invisible, and stigmatized dis-ability with challenges that are often misunderstood—perhaps even more so within academia. Second are the challenges posed by normative processes that impose a rigidity and characteristics that lack responsiveness—a responsiveness and "altered pacing" (Price, 2011) that is necessary from time to time for those academics with mental illness, like me.

Endnote

1   I first became ill in autumn 2009, following the first term of my academic appointment. I was formally diagnosed with major reoccurring depressive disorder and complex PTSD in late fall 2010.

References

Broeck, A., Ferris, D. L., Chang, C. H., & Rosen, C. C. (2016). A review of self-determination theory's basic psychological needs at work. *Journal of Management, 42*(5), 1195–1229. doi:10.1177/0149206316632058

Chambers, J. M. (2017). Meet Jill–She fell down the hill but came back up again: Struggling with mental illness while on the path to tenure. In T. M. Sibbald & V. Handford (Eds.), *The academic gateway: Understanding the journey to tenure* (pp. 29–39). Ottawa, ON: University of Ottawa Press.

Dalke, A., & Mullaney, C. (2014). On being transminded: Disabling achievement, enabling exchange. *Disability Studies Quarterly, 34*(2). doi:10.18061/dsq.v34i2.4247

Deci, E. L., & Ryan, R. M. (2000). The "what" and "why" of goal pursuits: Human needs and the self-determination of behavior. *Psychological Inquiry, 11*(4), 227–268.

Greenbank, P. (2006). The academic's role: The need for a re-evaluation? *Teaching in Higher Education, 11*(1), 107–112. doi:10.1080/13562510500400248

Price, M. (2011). *Mad at school: Rhetorics of mental disability and academic life*. Ann Arbor, MI: University of Michigan Press.

Williams, J., & Mavin, S. (2015). Impairment effects as a career boundary: A case study of disabled academics. *Studies in Higher Education, 40*(1), 123–141. doi:10.1080/03075079.2013.818637

CHAPTER 17

In the Trenches

Greg Rickwood

The academic marathon known as track to tenure ended for me in 2016 after learning I had attained tenure and promotion. The on-going stress of proving my worth to institutional administration had temporarily been relieved as I finished my last lap of the tenure-track. As at most finish lines, athletes collapse from physical, mental and emotional exhaustion. Similarly, my body and mind were spent; refueling came by way of quality family time and temporary escape from deadlines, student demands and committee obligations. Days of nothingness followed this achievement; it was as if I had subconsciously activated my biological and psychological reset buttons. I had to redefine my mental space from job insecurity and watching over my shoulder to absorbing the newfound realization of a second career.

Validation and acceptance described my preliminary feelings as I read the letter outlining I had achieved tenure. I reflected back on the years of graduate school; the autonomous journey and the imposing fear of failure. According to Ivengar and Lepper, (2002), the autonomous element of self-determination theory drives tenure-track faculty to justify their presence due to minimal feedback from their tenured peers. As such, tenure-track faculty attempt to establish an academic niche they believe is useful to the institution and to their tenure application. Thus, the tenure-track path is the one least travelled, one of great resistance and difficult to define pre-tenure.

The internship of tenure-track involved academic supervisors who guided me forwards, sideways and backwards trying to open a path to a tenured faculty position. However, the more I listened and acted upon the advice from others, the less confident I felt about my progress. What may have worked for my mentors was not resonating with me—their feedback was foreign and advice was foggy. I had to connect the dots and make it about me. This was a difficult concept to embrace as an experienced secondary school teacher who always placed student priorities before my own.

A strong sense of relief came across my immediate family support network that had battled through the tenure circumstances with me. Endless sacrifices by my partner and two children were now perceived as purposeful and character building. Ostensibly, my children could transfer their lived experiences of hardship associated with their father pursuing his goals and apply it to their own life-long pursuits. Living years absent and distant (500 kilometres from campus) from our extended family made us closer and bumped us out of our comfort circles.

This chapter contains short vignettes that highlight significant stories in my pursuit of tenure. These stories are chronologically assembled and detail the personal interactions, experiences, relationships and outcomes associated with my track to tenure. Although these stories are unique to my journey, I learn regularly from other tenured faculty across academic disciplines and geographical borders who recall similar stories within their own contexts. I believe these vignettes speak beyond me personally and may reflect the experiences of many academics.

Vignette #1: First Week on the Job

My research agenda examines the various cultural components of elementary and secondary schools. School cultures can be segregated into three main categories: first, beliefs and values of cultural members; second, policies and practices that reinforce core values; and, third, artifacts (see, hear, touch, feel, taste) that outwardly represent institutional beliefs (Schein 1985; 1999). Therefore, starting a new position at a post-secondary institution was a time in which I could begin to examine its culture relative to secondary school where I lived and worked for many years. I was granted my wish on the Friday of my first week of tenure-track during a scheduled meeting with an administrator to clarify my new role. I had not met the administrator in the interview process so I was eager to understand more about her expectations of me, and how I fit into the fabric of the institution. Talking with my colleagues in advance of this meeting, they described this introductory meeting to be informal with a meet-and-greet atmosphere. On the contrary, as soon as I sat down in front of her, it quickly became apparent I was in for a lecture, not a conversation. Absent from any small talk, she told me I was only as useful as my last publication, I was to dedicate my waking hours to meeting the requirements of tenure, and my current portfolio lacked depth and direction. The conversation involved what I could do for the institution, not what the institution could do for me. The meeting ended after 30 minutes of one-way communication and degradation directed toward me. Rather than being embraced into the culture by one of the institution's most influential leaders, I was perceived a burden and sub-par to the other individuals walking the halls. Overall, I left feeling concerned if our academic leader acted in this manner, how would the faculty structure unfold in departmental sub-cultures.

It was clear I was back at the bottom of the institutional hierarchy. After 13 years in teaching, leading departments, designing curriculum and mentoring teacher candidates, and in spite of being successful in the eyes of the hiring committee, I was now construed as one who had to prove my worth to the institution. This first meeting felt as if they (the university) were doing me a favour by bequeathing me this tenure-track opportunity; I was to be subservient to their wishes and enhance their reputation within the postsecondary community. My needs, requests and aspirations as a new employee were of no significance at this juncture. The message was to discard other interests beyond gaining tenure.

Vignette #2: Motor Home Mentality

At the conclusion of my second year of tenure-track an administrator asked if I would be interested in covering a sabbatical at one of the satellite campuses. The satellite campus was located four hours from the main campus but the teaching timetable was a good fit for my background. That summer, however, my family had decided to move closer to the main campus so this offer came at a precarious time. During the discussion with the administrator, I asked her if there was potential for me to remain at the satellite campus beyond the sabbatical replacement timeframe because the campus was located in my hometown, with many of my extended family still residing in this region. She indicated there was the opportunity for me to remain long-term at this satellite campus due to retirements. Hearing this generated feelings of relief knowing that my four-hour weekly commute, extended time away from family, and the costs associated with a second dwelling could be in the past. I stated I would be willing to move my young family to the area of the satellite campus based upon a long-term commitment and confirmed again with administration that this would be permanent. In the administrator's words, "We are 99 percent confident that you will continue teaching at the satellite campus and encourage you to move closer. It will be beneficial having one of our full-time faculty members actually living in the same community." All things considered, and being tenure-track, I wanted to demonstrate flexibility and a willingness to expand my academic comfort zones, so my wife and I decided to move 10 minutes from the satellite campus. We decided it was a much better lifestyle option than our existing work-family dynamic.

Within two months of moving my family to the satellite campus community, I was informed by university administration that my role would be relocated back to the main campus at the end of the academic year. All of the university's satellite campuses were being sold and closed and faculty moved to the main campus. A new university president believed in a centralization model of running school business; all business would be conducted out of one campus.

After receiving this information, I quickly reflected on the significant life changes my family recently made (i.e., my daughters were in a new school, we had purchased new home, there were changes associated with the move to the new city such as a new doctor, etc.). All of this was done to support my career choices. My daughters were in grades 4 and 5 at the time of this move and were devastated to be uprooted from a school and a friendship network they thoroughly enjoyed being a part of, and one they had just settled into. Shortly after making the adjustment to their new school, I had to tell them even though we moved to this area to spend more time together, Dad was only going to be home three days a week because he was going back to North Bay. Additionally, my wife received the news with great angst because she deeply valued our home and life in the city we resided in for many years before the change of address. She had established productive business connections and friendships that were hard to leave behind. From a personal perspective, I was disappointed with the false information I received from the administration about the security of my satellite campus role and the promise of remaining in this new community until the end of my career. Ultimately, I concluded that I was asked to fill in for a sabbatical leave because I was the cheapest and most convenient fit for the University. Administration told me what I wanted to hear to satisfy their objectives of sealing a temporary hole in the faculty complement.

Completing the academic year at the satellite campus, knowing what I now knew, was a challenge. Maintaining professional relationships and investing wholly into a campus and program I was leaving in a few short months seemed futile. Two months after the announcement was made to the close the campus, the university president spoke to faculty about the major changes ahead for faculty and the university. The message was clear—the satellite campus would survive with minimal resources until closure and faculty had two years to find new employment or move to the main campus. In response, faculty and campus administration were ready with feasible alternatives to campus closure but these solutions garnered no attention and were quickly dismissed. Thus, my family's response to this future reality was the next hurdle to overcome.

Encapsulated in the tenure-track bubble after two years devoted to the profession, was I going to move the family again or remain steadfast in the satellite campus community? The fear of the main campus closure was in the back of our minds. If satellite campuses were being closed, was closure of the main university next? At this point, moving closer to the main campus offered no guarantees and would further disrupt our children's education. The decision was made to stay in the community and resume the four-hour commute, extended periods of time away from family, and once again absorb the added cost of a second residence. This was our family reality in the tenure-track years, and it has remained our reality into tenure.

Vignette #3: Camaraderie

The biggest adjustment for me during tenure-track was the marginalization of colleague interaction. The tenure-track learning culture was lonely and very unlike the high school staff room table. Sharing like-experiences with secondary school teachers finding their way when I was early in my teaching career was soothing. It reaffirmed what I was doing in my classroom and daily evidence of student engagement (verbal and written) offered constant feedback for me about whether my teaching methods were relevant. This was not true in the university environment. Contact with students was not as personal or regular contact with colleagues was almost non-existent. There was no shared staff room table where informal conversation was instructive. There was no shared anything.

During tenure-track, there were days when I emotionally craved and actually seized the camaraderie of a school family unit including teachers, administrators, parents and students. I wanted to walk through the school doors and be acknowledged by the institutional community and asked about how my daughters and wife were doing. In tenure-track, you are your own entity. Meaningful relationships with students could mean getting to know their names by the end of the four-month term. Furthermore, socialization with colleagues can be limited and informal. This may stem from the rarity of faculty in each area of specialization leading to the lack of commonality that enhanced collegiality in the secondary school context. In turn, many faculty members are not residents of the community in which they work making it a challenge to engage socially outside of the workplace. Distinct from the colleagues on the floor in your building, the university spirit can be disjointed and endemic to departments.

Conversely, since achieving tenure, colleagues are reaching out to partner with me in research endeavours, stopping by my office to share stories of course and service experiences, and inquiring about my family life with sincerity. It now feels that I have earned their respect and overcome the barriers they once faced in tenure-track. It may be the belief of tenured professors that tenure-track employees are disposable until they have achieved tenure. However, looking back, it could have been my body language or my lack of interest in my colleagues' research agendas and personal lives that led to isolation. I was in survival mode for the years leading to tenure and possibly now, I have become more approachable and open to workplace relationships. The insecurities that accompany tenure-track may have leaked into my outward expressions or the lack of mentorship and inclusion may have provoked my isolation.

Overall, these personal experiences have led to me taking on a mentorship role with the new tenure-track employees in my department. I make an effort every day to check in with their progress, offer any assistance that I can, and be someone they feel comfortable asking the tough questions to. As I step into the early years of tenure, I find that the cliché holds true: If you do not like something, take the steps to change it or learn to live with it. In the small institution I work in, it is imperative that cultural membership matures together; our collective actions directly influence the expansion and reputation of the institution.

Vignette #4: Cultural Shift—Part A

In line with the scarcity of colleague companionship during my tenure-track years, I witnessed the loss of 32 limited term instructors because of institutional re-organization. Many of these instructors helped introduce me to the university culture, had offices near mine and understood the risk I was taking. It was easy to communicate with these individuals and appreciate the challenges they faced towards gaining full-time status. Several had resigned from their school board teaching careers to extend their contracts with the university. Upon the discontinuation of their contracts, these instructors had very little if anything to fall back on. Most of them were middle-aged with children, living in a small northern Ontario community—employment opportunities are limited. I put myself in their shoes—if I did not achieve tenure by the end of my contract, I would be in a similar position. This brought fear regarding the risks associated with my decision to enter academia. Questions cascaded daily in my head: What have I done? Am I next to be pushed aside? How will my family recover?

The physical loss of one third of our limited term teaching faculty changed the internal culture instantly. Anger and disbelief spread across the university. The emotions took a variety of forms. Some lashed out in local news outlets and social media, others protested at Senate and Board meetings. It was a tumultuous time to be a university faculty member. The visceral mentality of each person for themselves grabbed hold of those who remained. Instead of a culture of collegiality, which I was searching for, the change moved faculty into self-preservation mode.

With all this in mind, the tenure-track position was beneficial from a lifestyle perspective. Instead of my day being defined through the secondary school system's timetable, my time outside my teaching responsibilities became my own. I was used to coaching high school sport teams early in the morning and late into the evening each day of the week. I never had time for a formal lunch break and my preparation time (75 minutes) was often consumed with on-call duties for other teachers. I recall specifically during my first year of tenure-track asking my director for permission to be off-campus on a Friday to coach a minor sport team in a tournament. He laughed and replied. "As long as you are doing what you need to be doing, you can work from where you want to."

Vignette #5: Cultural Shift—Part B

My sophomore year of tenure-track included a faculty strike that absorbed two months of the academic year. Walking the picket line on both the main and satellite campuses introduced me to some of the internal issues that had been weighing on faculty for some time. I have never been an employee who helps drive the union or interrogates the collective agreement for inequalities, but this experience made me appreciate the people who do. Ironically, these weeks afforded me the opportunity to meet colleagues I may never have encountered in the university. I began to feel a part of something bigger and learned about my place in this conflict. The unity and strength shown by the university and local community throughout these difficult weeks produced closer bonds between colleagues, departments and administration.

Participating in the strike movement as a tenure-track employee triggered a paradigm shift in my drive to tenure. The university had yet to make a formal, long-term commitment to my services but walking and talking with colleagues at the same career stage as me brought reassurance and motivation to continue forward. So much of the tenure-track experience is spent alone, in wonder of what could have been, or doubting decisions to enter academia. Through the walk and talk, I learned there were others grappling to find their place and position within their own academic departments. For me, finding a home within the sub-culture of tenure-track fueled my fire to achieve tenure. Thus, meeting and greeting with tenure-track colleagues on a consistent basis early in one's academic career may enhance one's ability to attain tenure and promotion. Additionally, being able to compare and contrast tenure portfolios leading up to tenure application may also increase the tenure success rate. Rather than operating in silos, tenure-track colleagues are encouraged to collaborate around their experiences moving towards tenure.

Table 17.1

Tenure-Track survival kit

Requirements	Strategy
Directional focus	Begin with the end in mind and never lose track of the end goal. Achieving tenure might be thought of as setting tenure as "due north." Everything needs to be oriented towards that goal of tenure. Schedule personal time into your calendar so that what really matters beyond work continues to know it really is important to you.
Resilience	Rejection is an inevitable part of success. There will be multiple publication and grant rejections. Some students may not appreciate you. Some peer evaluations may not be completely glowing. Learn what you can and keep moving forward.
Relationships	Keep the value of relationships beyond the university in clear focus. These are the people who make life meaningful. Do find a trusted colleague or two at work. There will be guidance needed to navigate the tenure-track.
Office supplies	Caffeine may be important. It will help with some long and dark days on the tenure-track. Make your office welcoming. If others can drop by and enjoy a relaxed and comfortable space, maybe they will do just that. Keep your expense forms at the ready—be prepared that many expenses are not covered. So, be careful about what you choose to spend your limited dollars on.

Survival of the Fittest

Drawing upon the aforementioned vignettes, I have compiled a list of items that could be included in a tenure-track survival kit (Table 17.1). The kit contents may be fluid relative to individual contexts but the core components should resonate with new academics.

Discussion

The vignettes speak to the gritty moments of my move into the academy. They are not representative of the glorified success stories that many gravitate towards. I could speak to some of those moments but instead I have chosen to speak about the grievous challenges I experienced along the way. In spite of being successful achieving tenure, the vignettes illustrate the complexity of multifarious circumstances involving grief and cultural loss.

The Kubler-Ross model of grief (Kubler-Ross & Kessler, 2005) and Levy-Warren's (1987) cultural loss construct effectively structure my track to tenure. In these constructs, feelings of denial, anger, bargaining, depression and acceptance associated with grief and loss are examined and expanded upon. Relative to my personal tenure-track experiences, anger arose closer to the tenure decision because I realized how those around me could have guided my progress. I was asked to teach courses outside of my area of specialty, take on time-consuming service roles and establish a research agenda while fumbling my way through the early years of tenure-track. I have heard across my years in academia from peers my senior that they had to do it on their own, so it is expected others follow the same traditions—a hazing of sorts. These traditions may be rooted deep in the autonomous nature of the tenure-track role (Ivengar & Lepper, 2002). Fortunately, a mentorship program was established in my department a year after I achieved tenure. To witness how new tenure-track faculty are led around the academic potholes that I succumbed to generates feelings of anger, knowing that I could be further ahead.

Highlighted throughout the vignettes are undertones of cultural loss moving from a secondary school environment to a post-secondary context (Levy-Warren, 1987). Also, being transferred to a satellite campus two years into tenure-track, and then told unexpectedly to return to the main campus within 12 months of the transition bred cultural confusion. Overall, my first three years of tenure-track were spread between two campuses (500 kilometres apart) and three academic departments. My adjustment to the post-secondary culture (beliefs/values, policies/practices/artifacts)(Schein, 1985) had not been established before I was introduced to another post-secondary cultural system. Compounded among these cultural changes, I was attempting to develop a strong portfolio for tenure application. Upon reflection, I was unable to initially grieve the loss of my long-time secondary school environment (people, places), adapt to my new post-secondary culture and function efficiently as an academic. Furthermore, the autonomy of the tenure-track role (Ivengar & Lepper, 2002), together with exposure to multiple work environments in a short time span, pushed me further into isolation – survival mode. I lost interest in socializing with colleagues, learning more about the inner-workings of post-secondary institutions and making contributions to the academic culture outside of my classroom and research. In turn, these series of events also provoked feelings of anger towards university administration and my decision to enter academia, and triggered depressive tendencies that ultimately seeped into my private life. In general, perceiving I had not achieved acceptance in the post-secondary culture (tenure-track) while ineffectively grieving the loss of my secondary school culture made me, in a sense, homeless. It was not until I achieved tenure that I began cultural recovery and acceptance at the university. Those around me became more welcoming and the university became a place I wanted to be.

Although I achieved tenure, I am reluctant to refer to my tenured status as a success. I was successful in meeting the predetermined criteria for academic tenure but I believe the failures outweighed the gains. My tenure-track years consisted of countless sacrifices, isolation, financial and familial strain, and wonderment whether daily decisions would help or hinder my tenure application. In my opinion, tenure-track is a state of mind that demands one's psyche to become one with the process. It is a multi-year emotional addiction and character-building cycle that requires a supportive network of human resources; it is the Olympics of education and as in sport, getting there is difficult, but winning gold is the ultimate test of mental and physical endurance.

My tenure-track journey left me with unresolved emotional issues that have plagued my progress beyond tenure. Certain sacrifices were too great and the consequences of poor choices are now coming to fruition. Achieving tenure requires the efforts of many people but only one person receives the reward. It is a bittersweet feeling when tenure knocks on your door knowing that those closest to you have given so much to the fight but come away with very little. There is no doubt that tenure-track takes its toll. Rather than thinking tenure is the end, it can, conversely, be the beginning of repairing strained relationships, seeking out post-secondary cultural integration opportunities, and understanding the benefits and drawbacks of the tenure-track years. Tenure permits those granted to actively explore the profession and enjoy the moments with students and colleagues that once drove our passion to secure a permanent place in post-secondary education folklore.

References

Ivengar, S. S. & Lepper, M. R. (2002). Choice and its consequences: On the costs and benefits of self-determination. In A. Tesser, D. A. Stapel, & J. V. Wood (Eds.). *Self and motivation: Emerging psychological perspectives*. Washington, DC: Amercian Psychological Association.

Kubler-Ross, E. & Kessler, D. (2005). *On grief and grieving: Finding the meaning of grief through the fives stages of loss.* New York, NY: Scribner.

Levy-Warren, M. H. (1987). Moving to a new culture; Cultural identity, loss and mourning. In J. Bloom-Feshbach & S. Bloom-Feshbach (Eds.). *The psychology of separation and loss.* San Francisco, CA: Jossey-Bass Inc.

Schein, E. H. (1999). *The corporate culture survival guide: Sense and nonsense about culture change.* San Francisco, CA: Jossey-Bass Publishers.

Schein, E. H. (1985). *Organizational culture and leadership.* San Francisco, CA: Jossey-Bass.

CHAPTER 18

Who Am I? Professional Identity on the Path to Tenure

Cam Cobb

When joining a university, an assistant professor is expected to take on a certain role. In terms of research, the beginning scholar is likely expected to continue exploring certain interests applying familiar research skills, or methods. It is also likely that that assistant professor is expected to teach courses that are linked – in one way or another, or to one degree or another – to those research interests and skills. To fill certain needs in a faculty, a new scholar is hired to contribute through research, teaching, and service. Although that person may be starting a career in the academy, he or she already has already developed a research portfolio and professional identity. Beginning scholars join faculties with a variety of experiences already behind them. Moreover, they have already been on a path, or trajectory, for years. Yet none of this is static. According to Clarke, Hyde, and Drennan (2013), "Professional identity is not a stable entity; it is complex, personal, and shaped by contextual factors" (p. 8).

In this chapter, I reflect on some of my experiences as I figured out my role as an assistant professor. While preparing for tenure, I took on different sorts of responsibilities within the realms of research, teaching, and service. During that time, I have shaped and reshaped my professional identity. Pursuing a range of interconnected research interests and learning how to carry out new (at least new for me) research strategies has kept me energized. Admittedly, it has been frustrating at times. Yet pursuing these different avenues has always been engaging.

When an assistant professor arrives on campus to begin work, things are already different. It is already a different place than it was when that person was interviewed weeks or months earlier. The faces in the faculty, even the hiring committee, may have changed, with staff and faculty movements and retirements. Along with the start of a new school year, the context at the university has shifted. There is a new group of students entering the academy for the first time, while a departing group is not returning for the first time. For new professors teaching concurrent education courses, some of these first-year students may be in classes or advisory groups. Amidst all these changes, a new assistant professor is starting out. As you read about some of my experiences in those early years, think about your own path as a budding scholar.

Travelling from Toronto to Windsor takes about four hours by train. There are eight stops between the metropolis and the line's terminus. Glancing out the window, you can watch the flat countryside and various small towns of Southern Ontario as you speed forward. The largest city you pass through is London, which rather symmetrically, falls at the midpoint of the journey. First time, or infrequent travellers sometimes strike up conversations, while regular commuters often keep their noses in their computers, books, binders, phones, or some other object or task that occupies their attention.

Late one August afternoon, I took this trip on my way to a job interview. It was nearly two months since I had graduated with my PhD. I had taken the day off from my summer job with a language program that operated at Trinity College at the University of Toronto. Working at Trinity was a routine for me during my summertime breaks. For years, I had enjoyed working with an ever-changing cadre of international students on a campus that is perhaps best described as Toronto's architectural answer to Oxbridge. Of course, that was my summer routine. By that point, I had been teaching with the Toronto District School Board (TDSB) for over a decade—and before that, in what seemed like another lifetime, I had lived, studied, and taught in South Korea.

As the train sped forward that afternoon, I looked over my notes. Over the past couple of weeks, I had put together two sample course syllabi—one undergraduate and one graduate. I had also designed handouts for exemplar classroom activities. Preparing for the interview and presentation, I had printed copies for the hiring committee, so there was no way I could tinker with what I had already written. Yet I could review things, and reflect on my words and ideas, anticipating different sorts of clarification or critical questions I might encounter. I had studied the short profiles of each professor on the Faculty of Education website. There were about 25 in all, and my acting experiences came in handy for the task of memorizing names, faces, and lists of research interests. Shuffling through my papers, I pulled out the short piece of writing I had submitted with my application back in late June. It outlined some details regarding my aims and experiences in teaching and research. Nervously perusing all these documents as the train dashed forward, I tried to calm myself.

"Try not to worry," I thought silently. Gazing out the window, I forced myself not to shuffle though my notes. "The folks on the committee just want to know about you," I reflected. "They will ask who you are, and what you know, and what you have done. They want to know about what you can do and your plans at the university. It's as simple as that." I knew they would ask me about the intersection between special education and social justice because it was my primary area of research. Particularly, I expected they would ask me about the body of literature on different issues in special education, as well as qualitative research on the subject. After all, those were things I had worked on, read about, and (at least in theory) was supposed to know inside and out.

If you become immersed in something, the journey from Toronto to Windsor is not just fast, it flies-by—and that is what happened to me on that afternoon in August 2010. A month later, I started working at the University of Windsor. Accepting a position, I capriciously resigned from the TDSB; no longer a school teacher, I had become an assistant professor on tenure-track.

Arriving in Windsor I began to learn about my new role. No longer would I take part in parent-teacher interviews, parent council meetings, community barbecues, and other such events. No longer would I write Individual Education Plans (IEPs) or report cards. No longer would I conduct running records to assess reading levels and then use levelled readers with different groups of learners. Although I was continuing to work in education, the nature of that work was changing. In many ways, my upcoming role was going to be shaped by the new environment I was immersed in, namely the university and faculty. Yet this shift was not simply a passive experience as I was also shaping my professional repertoire.

As a new faculty member, I was expected to have a certain level of knowledge and skills in relation to the courses I taught—which, largely dealt with special education, social justice, and curriculum theory. I was also expected to carry out research and then communicate those findings in various ways, including faculty sharing sessions, conference presentations, and peer-reviewed scholarly journals. According to Austin, Sorcinelli, and McDaniels (2007), new faculty are expected to thoroughly know their discipline and discipline-based research. Expanding on this point, they note "New faculty need to have some significant sense of their professional identity as scholars" (p. 53).

It was a time of change, also a time of uncertainty. My understanding of my newfound role was incomplete. As such, I was unsure of what my professional identity would or could become. In short order, I sat on faculty committees, joined a research team, and started taking part in thesis committees and defences. Taking on different responsibilities for the first time and learning about the habits and routines of the faculty, I gradually came to understand various expectations that were placed upon me as an assistant professor. During those early weeks and months, as I struggled to better understand my new role, I gazed into my past.

Throughout my experiences in graduate school, I had worked for (or with) numerous professors. While most were seasoned, some were new to the academy. Through those varied experiences—working on studies, presenting at conferences and in classes, writing and publishing, copyediting, and so on—I developed certain notions of what I thought a professor's work entailed. Of course, I carried those notions with me as I started working at the University of Windsor.

Perhaps most clearly, I understood that professors took on a teaching load yet I did not fully grasp what that entailed. I knew the total number of hours of teaching time per week was significantly less than that of a school teacher's; beyond that I was at a loss. I knew professors kept office hours, but I was not sure as to what that involved in terms of weekly work. On another front, I understood professors were expected to conduct research and then present and publish their findings, yet I did not have a clear idea about what those research-driven expectations entailed. Naïvely, I did not really understand what teaching and research meant for new professors.

I certainly did not know what was at stake in terms of the tenure application procedure.

While I knew professors taught graduate and undergraduate courses, supervised graduate students, sat on thesis committees, worked on faculty and university committees, and reviewed for journals, I did not have a clear picture as to how much time, or exactly what *sort* of work those responsibilities involved. So, when I started out as an assistant professor, I brought with me a partial understanding of a professor's role and identity. As time passed, I came to realize there were many gaps in that initial understanding.

Though I did not realize it at the time, my experience was consistent with the body of literature on new faculty. Over the years, researchers have noticed that new professors tend to form their image of a professor's role during their graduate studies—a time of intense, early socialization into the academy (Austin et al., 2007). Yet, as the literature indicates, budding academics do not often form an accurate picture of what that role entails (Austin et al., 2007). In their early years, assistant professors tend to perceive "a lack of clarity about their new role . . . [with] disparities [existing] between their expectations and reality" (McDermid, Peters, Daly, & Jackson, 2015, p. 52). While the image I had developed of a professor's role was incomplete, it *was* a picture nevertheless—and it was something to hold onto, and work with as my first semesters at Windsor unfolded.

During my first semester as an assistant professor, I came to learn more about my new role in both formal and informal ways. On a formal level, I was acquainted with various benchmarks set out in my employment contract and faculty documents, which included brief descriptions of tenure expectations. On occasion, an administrator would sit down with me (during performance evaluations, for example) to review my progress in the areas of teaching, research, and service. We would go over the wording of various parameters for a tenure application in relation to my own performance and timeline. My experience in this regard was by no means unique. Considering the post-secondary education context, Clarke et al. (2013) noted that faculty take on "roles, which are strongly determined by the communities and institutions of which they are members" (p. 9). In my case, expectations often linked to my role as a researcher and educator, and my perceived expertise stemmed from my ongoing research in special education.

Yet the process was reciprocal. Not only did the faculty and university shape my role, but my own field of research also shaped how I came to understand (and take on) my role and identity as an assistant professor. "Discipline-based cultures," Clarke et al. (2013) observed, "are the primary source of faculty members' identity and expertise and include assumptions about what is to be known and how tasks [are] to be performed, standards for effective performance patterns of publication, professional interaction, and social and political status" (p. 7). From that perspective, I saw myself as someone who focused primarily on special education, someone who carried out qualitative research, and someone whose teaching and research involved digging into social justice issues.

In retrospect, having a list of tenure-based expectations gave me a sense of relief, as evaluation became an ongoing endeavour of carrying out tasks, demonstrating skills, and monitoring progress—rather than engaging in some sort of political campaign of wooing. As I prepared my dossier during those first few years, tenure always seemed to be an elusive destination, something that lurked in the back of my mind, something always beyond the horizon. While it was nice to have formal goals, having those goals also formed a source of—it was not exactly stress but it was a pestering doubt. Highlighting the demands of the tenure preparation and application process, Clarke et al. (2013) flatly state "faculty face extraordinary challenges to gain membership into the profession" (p. 11).

Throughout my first year, I learned about my new role, that of an academic, in other ways. On a less formal level, I became aware of various expectations through my day-to-day interactions with students, staff, colleagues, administrators, and so on. When I collaborated with others on committees, I honed my understanding of what sort of work we were expected to do to support the faculty and university. When graduate and undergraduate students asked me questions, and when they asked for help, I came to better understand what students expected of me as a teacher and scholar.

Yet there was another dimension to all of this. I felt a certain sense of obligation. The university had hired me, invested in me. It had selected me over others. And to prove they made the right decision, I had to produce according to their expectations—I had to produce as a researcher and an educator, and I had to meaningfully contribute to the faculty and to the university itself. This was not something that was pressed upon me in any way. It was something that lurked in my mind, something I felt internally.

As a budding scholar, my research primarily delved into social justice issues involving Culturally and Linguistically Diverse (CLD) families navigating the special education landscape. To explore the phenomena of CLD student and parent voice in special education decision-making, I conducted qualitative research applying a blend of narrative inquiry and case study analysis. During my first year at the university I felt I needed to explore different research approaches and topics. New faculty need to engage in all parts of the research process, Austin et al. noted (2007). Getting into more specifics, Mabrouk (2006) observed that new faculty need to navigate the terrain and persist in their pursuit of research projects, external grants, conference presentations, and peer-reviewed publication.

Slowly but surely, I honed my ability to write different sorts of journal articles—ones written in the third person, first person journal articles, articles with a shifting voice, qualitative research reports, Systematic Literature Review (SLRs), action research papers, policy analyses, and so on. Over time, I also developed new skills in selecting journals, addressing and responding to constructive feedback in the peer review process, and better understanding how to communicate with journal editors and assistant editors along the way. These skills are nearly as important as being able to carry out research projects and write about meaningful findings. Yet my learning in these areas continues today. Developing teaching and research skills, after all, is a process that never ends.

Balancing time between teaching and service work, I carved out hours here and there to conduct research, write new pieces, and then carefully rewrite and resubmit articles in the peer-review process. Time management was crucial. As Mabrouk (2006) astutely noted, learning how to strategically manage time is fundamental to new professors (p. 1030). That said, a new professor's writing schedule can become rather haphazard, which was certainly the case for me.

Although I was setting out regular times for research and writing, I often worked intensively on a project—toiling days and nights for weeks on end—followed by a cooling off period of relative inactivity. Perhaps it was a bad habit I had formed decades earlier. Teaching writing courses to faculty and students led Belcher (2009) to observe that "Most academic writers learned as undergraduates to write to deadline and developed procrastination/binge habits" (p. 191). Yet I am not convinced that this is always (or even often the case). Sketching, drafting, and revising a piece of writing demands close attention and intensive thinking. It requires persistence and after the process is finished, having a cooling off period (what Belcher labels "procrastination") seems only natural. Of course, it could be a bit of both. Perhaps my binge writing *is* a bad habit, one that is perhaps also a natural outcome of my writing process.

Either way, I was well aware that as I approached tenure evaluation, I had to produce peer-reviewed publications to complement my teaching and service portfolio. Thinking back, I recall feelings of frustration when journals took months (or, in one case, over a year) to send feedback. Yet I was not alone. As Austin et al. (2007) observed, journal backlogs mark a tangible source of stress for assistant professors amidst a climate that demands greater and greater productivity in research. In spite of these challenges, I was published in a variety of local, national, and international journals.

With each new school year, I navigated tasks and routines that were becoming more and more familiar. Over time, I learned how to chair defences, chair committee meetings, put motions forward at Faculty Council, order textbooks for courses, create course websites, provide detailed rubrics as well as exemplar assignments, and so on. In terms of research, the matter of sending out articles for peer review and then responding to reviewers' feedback became more of a natural routine.

As I think back, the whole process of becoming familiar with my role and responsibilities seems natural. However, I realize that, as a whole, it was something that required ongoing concentration and patience. It was a lot of work.

Throughout those early years, I reflected on the different tasks I was carrying out as I worked my way through them, and all the while I was adjusting my approach. As Creed and Zutshi (2012) observed, "Learning is a move from one state of understanding to another" (p. 3). Elaborating on this point, they added, "The cycle of feedback suggests a need to adapt to feedback from learning experiences. Learning, as a change from one state to another, is therefore a response to feedback" (p. 3). Shifting from implicit to explicit knowledge, our growth moves in a spiral rather than a straight line (Nonaka, 1994; also see Creed & Zutshi, 2012). And just as our students learn though contemplation and both peer- and self-evaluation, so do we (Dunham-Taylor, Lynn, Moore, McDaniel, & Walker, 2008). Receiving feedback from journal reviewers certainly marked *one* way that I was adapting to feedback. Repetition of the process facilitated changes along the way that slowly spiralled in the sense that

I became more proficient. Dialoguing with colleagues, friends, and family, I continually reflected on what I was doing and learning. With tenure, this process does not stop, of course. It was and still is a natural cycle. Ultimately, as Creed and Zutshi (2012) observed, "As a process involving reflection and action upon feedback, there is a spiral of learning implied in reflective evaluation" (p. 3).

As the school years passed (with intersession and summer session courses sometimes binding one year to another) I began to feel more confident with my tenure portfolio. My understanding of the scholarly role was solidifying. While I did not yet have tenure, I knew that I was on the right path. By my fourth year, I was starting up a new qualitative study on beginning principals and venturing further into what were newer areas of research and writing for me, namely the SLR and policy analysis.

Then, something unexpected happened. Just as I was settling-in to my role as a special education researcher I felt compelled to pursue a variety of interconnected avenues. It was not that I wanted to leave special education research behind; far from it. But there were other things I felt I had to pursue, to research—and, in a sense, there was something else I wanted to become. As a result, I started exploring new terrain. While continuing to work in the qualitative domain, I have delved into the interconnected areas of the arts, arts education, and adult learning. All the while I have been learning new things about research and writing—and about myself. Of this turn of events—which is not uncommon among new faculty—Cake, Solomon, McLay, O'Sullivan, and Schumacher (2015) note "Reflexivity is not just about probing practice; it is a means of taking control of one's own practice" (p. 473). Pursuing different avenues has led my professional identity to transform. This often makes for interesting conversations when someone asks, "So, what exactly do you do as a professor?" I'm not always sure how to answer that question. In May 2018, I had this sort of experience after giving a radio interview.

In the late spring of 2018, I gave my first CBC radio interview. It was not about special education. It was not about adult learning or policy or arts education either. Booked a few days earlier, I was scheduled to meet with radio host Tony Doucette to chat about my new book on his program, *Windsor Morning*.

Over the last year-and-a-half I had put together a book about an almost tragic San Francisco rock band from the heady days in and around the Summer of Love. Drawing from a punchline that was behind that band's name, I entitled the book, *What's Big and Purple and Lives in the Ocean? The Moby Grape Story*. Applying research approaches and writing styles I had learned about over the years, the book combined first-person narrative with dream sequences, speculative fiction, oral history, third-person basic history, and impressionistic music analysis.

The interview flew by in what seemed like seconds. Tony was cheerful and warm and genuinely curious about this band that featured a Windsor-born songwriter. Afterwards, I had one of those conversations where explaining my work at the university resembled a detective novel, or comedy sketch. After leaving the broadcast booth, one of the co-ordinators handed me a complimentary CBC coffee mug. Cheerfully, she asked me about my work at the university. Unsure of how to respond, I rapidly blurted out a few things about two policy analysis projects I was working on in the areas of school leadership and special education. What follows is a short dramatization of that conversation:

> "Oh," she replied, a bit surprised. "I didn't realize you're an education professor." Pausing for a moment, she added, "Perhaps we could call you in to speak about news items in education from time to time."
>
> "Of course," I replied. "I'd be happy to."
>
> In the uncomfortable silence that followed I could tell that she wanted to ask me something else. "So," she interjected, "was this music book a one-off thing, or are you working on another music book now?"
>
> "Well," I replied hesitantly, "I'm working on some articles for a few UK and US music magazines this month. They'll help promote the book hopefully. I've been writing them to go beyond what's already in the book, so I've done some new interviews for them."
>
> "And when you're finished those articles, it's back to those policy studies you were telling me about?"
>
> "Not exactly," I replied.
>
> "Ah," she exclaimed knowingly. "You *are* writing another music book."

"No. Maybe. Hopefully in the future. I'd love to write another music book someday. But I'm co-editing a different sort of book right now. It's about teaching Ernest Hemingway in post-secondary classrooms."

"How did that come about?"

"A few months ago, a friend and I put together a book proposal and we sent it to Kent State University Press (KSUP). They specialize in Hemingway scholarship. After some emails back and forth, they told us to move forward with the project. The book is going to be a teaching resource of sorts. It's going to be a part of the *Teaching Hemingway* series—it'll be called, *Teaching Hemingway and Film*. It'll look at things like close reading, film theory, and critical pedagogy when using Hemingway texts in the classroom."

"So, you mainly write about education and literature, but sometimes you write about music?" she asked.

That was a very good question, I thought to myself. Perhaps it would have been simpler if I had just focused on talking about music and education at the start of our conversation.

It is now a few months later. The summer is winding down. In a matter of days, I will begin my ninth year at the University of Windsor. It is three years since I completed the tenure process. In that time I have continued to research and write in special education. Yet I have also pursued projects in film, literature, music, and adult education. Collaborating with people in different fields, I have gotten to know scholars in a variety of countries and contexts. While some of these collaborations have been unexpected each has been rewarding. Austin et al. (2007) noted that a professor's first few years "is a period of intense socialization and satisfaction" (p. 54). From my experience, the statement is true. Similarly, Clarke et al. (2013) have drawn from social network theory and narrative inquiry to look at the relationship between agency, dialogue, and identity construction among new faculty.

While certain stresses arise when joining the academy, the intrinsic rewards (given the amount of agency assistant professors often have) are tremendous (Austin et al., 2007; Stupnisky, Pekrun, & Lichtenfeld, 2016). Before and after I completed the tenure review process, I pursued a variety of research and writing interests. Perhaps unsurprisingly, this multi-front research approach has led me to quickly learn that imposter syndrome can be a very real part of a new professor's life (Hutchins, 2015). It continues today. Whenever I interact with those who purely research in the arts, or those who purely focus on adult education, I realize that I am not a typical member of these communities—and when I am with other researchers in special education I realize that I do not singularly devote myself to that field as so many others do.

During my preparation for tenure, I came to realize my role as an assistant professor went beyond being a researcher and educator in special education. Pursuing multiple research paths has brought on a number of challenges and, sometimes, frustrations. Yet it has also been fulfilling. Whatever path you are on, as you pursue tenure, be aware that you have a range of possibilities that lay before you, as you continue to shape your own professional identity.

References

Austin, A. E., Sorcinelli, M. D., & McDaniels, M. (2007). Understanding new faculty: Background, aspirations, challenges, and growth. In R. P. Perry & J. C. Smart (Eds.), *The scholarship of teaching and learning in higher education: An evidence-based perspective* (pp. 39–89). Dordrecht, Netherlands: Springer.

Belcher, W. L. (2009). Writing for publication to graduate students and junior faculty. *Journal of Scholarly Publishing, 40*(2), 184–200.

Cake, S. A., Solomon, L., McLay, G., O'Sullivan, K., & Schumacher, C. R. (2015). Narrative as tool for critical reflective practice in the creative industries. *Reflective Practice, 16*(4), 472–486.

Clarke, M., Hyde, A., & Drennan, J. (2013). Professional identity in higher education. In B. M. Kehm & U. Teichler (Eds.), *The academic profession in Europe: New tasks and new challenges (The changing academy – The changing academic profession in international comparative perspective, volume 5)* (pp. 7–21) Dordrecht, Netherlands: Springer.

Creed, A, & Zutshi, A. (2012). The spiral of learning: 4 R's of education. *TMC Academic Journal, 6*(2), 1–16.

Dunham-Taylor, J., Lynn, C. W., Moore, P., McDaniel, S., Walker, J. K. (2008). What goes around comes around: Improving faculty retention through more effective mentoring. *Journal of Professional Nursing, 24*(6), 337–346.

Hutchins, H. M. (2015). Outing the imposter: A study exploring imposter phenomenon among higher education faculty. *New Horizons in Adult Education & Human Resources Development, 27*(2), 3–12.

Mabrouk, P. A. (2006). Advice to a new faculty member. *Analytical Bioanalytical Chemistry, 384*(5), 1029–1033.

McDermid, F., Peters, K., Daly, J., & Jackson, D. (2015). 'I thought I was just going to teach': Stories of new nurse academics on transitioning from sessional teaching to continuing academic positions. *Contemporary Nurse, 45*(1), 46–55.

Nonaka, I. (1994). A dynamic theory of organisational knowledge creation. *Organization Science, 5*(1), 14–37.

Stupnisky, R. H., Pekrun, R., Lichtenfeld, S. (2016). New faculty members' emotions: A mixed method study. *Studies in Higher Education, 41*(7), 1167–1188.

Conclusion

Taken as a whole, the chapters in *Beyond the Academic Gateway* provide demonstrative evidence that the journey to tenure and earning of tenure is not a simple process. The chapters of this book show myriads of experiences, none of which say it is a walk in the park. This is not to suggest graduate schools are not preparing students with relevant skills—they are—yet in spite of years of preparation, this collection says the experience remains arduous.

To help gain an overall understanding of the collection the editors first speak to the larger context of developing the book. While this has implications for the interpretation of the chapters, we chose to discuss it here rather than in the introduction because we did not want our explanation of the process to influence the reader before they read the chapters. However, we do feel that the process needs to be disclosed so that its influence on the book can be considered.

The contextual considerations are followed by considerations of what the chapters mean for the period around the decision on each author's tenure. The third, and final, area of interpretation is the assessment of the theoretical model we had provided to the authors for consideration during their preparation for writing their chapters.

Crafting the Book

We noted changes in how the authors have written their chapters, in comparison with their chapters in *The Academic Gateway*. The authors expressed themselves with a greater degree of precision and greater conformity with standard requirements of academic publishing. The use of references was better and the academic support for particular positions generally seemed stronger. The greater coherence and focus within the writing was reflected in our comments and recommended considerations when working with the authors. Overall, we interacted about 75 percent less with the authors in this book. In summary, the quality and clarity of writing has improved and less editing was requested or required. While we have grown as editors, we do not believe our style of editing has changed significantly nor that it is the reason for the level of change in writing for each individual author. In line with Occam's razor, we see personal growth by the authors as the primary reason for improvements in the quality of writing.

Another clear change was the pace of chapter completion. With this book, managing the deadline was more complex because we wanted each chapter written within six months of the writer's tenure and promotion decision. As well, the writing process was more difficult for some authors to schedule because of conflicts with teaching and other roles, including, for some, a much more demanding research and publishing schedule. We surmised that virtually all of the authors were (and are) busier. For *The Academic Gateway* it was relatively straightforward—there was a deadline and the authors adhered to it almost without exception. Capturing the moment of tenure was more complicated.

Learning From *Beyond the Academic Gateway*

The focus period for this book was the tenure decision, which often coincides with promotion. The distinction is that tenure is interpreted as providing permanence, while promotion has a financial impact and involves achievement of slightly more arduous benchmarks. In the call for chapters, we emphasized tenure as the milestone of importance because it is decisive and divisive—failure to achieve it generally leads to leaving the institution or being in contract positions without a research mandate.

We did indicate to authors that we were interested in the period around the tenure decision and asked them to speak about it. We did not mention promotion because it is a separate process nor did we advise against mentioning it, yet in this book for every six mentions of tenure there is a mention of promotion (a 6:1 ratio). The ratio suggests that promotion to associate professorship is seen as significant, and perhaps we should have inquired about this aspect of the process. Perhaps the writers mentioned it because there are good reasons for seeking both at the same time, including that it requires the preparation of a single dossier.

Notably, several authors made remarks indicating they thought there would be positive changes after receiving tenure and that this was not the case (also noted by Nelson, 2018). Romero, for example, rapidly moved into a position running her own laboratory as a full professor and realized a new collection of challenges and stresses. Badenhorst, along with Penney et al., found many beneficial changes but also stress associated with the potential implications of collective bargaining and power dynamics within the university. Handford remarks about the difficulties of negotiating the service aspect of the role: How does one say no when there seem to be genuine needs? This is consistent with Rosborough remarking, post-tenure, that she still struggles with keeping up with the workload, which we understand to be a matter of balance between work and life outside of work.

Once again, we received remarks from authors indicating that preparing their chapter had been "cathartic." There were positive remarks about the experience, and there was evidence of a few authors having considerable animosity about their treatment; some had difficulty writing about their experiences. In one instance, after drafting a chapter, the author started again and even had trouble with the second effort. It was evident from editing conversations that authors were circumspect about avoiding the potential for negative repercussions from their institution or colleagues. We did not, and ethically could not, pry beyond asking clarifying questions based on what they submitted. One remark that speaks to this pertained to difficulties sustaining the writing effort because thinking about the tenure process made the author angry about their treatment. Rangoonaden (2015) expressed the feeling of completing the tenuring process: "I felt exhausted, disconnected, and alienated from my personal and scholarly contexts" (p. 81).

The introduction identified two key dimensions that are quite pronounced. The first ranged from choices about how much personal narrative was provided and the extent to which they placed themselves in the institutional context. An example of the personal/institutional continuum, Greg Ogilvie speaks of academics as pawns in the context of this much larger political environment of the institution. At the other end of this continuum, Cam Cobb articulates how academic freedom allows choice in spite of political circumstances.

The second dimension has to do with change. At one end of this spectrum are individual changes and at the other end, systemic changes. However, individual changes are dichotomous. One can change for private reasons or because of normative demands. Similarly, systemic changes can work toward improvements in one's individual institution or improvements by altering the normative situation of the academy. Badenhorst exemplifies individual changes when she speaks of rhythms. One can envision day to day changes being a back and forth of choices and responses to the needs of others. Deer, along with McIvor and Rosborough, speaks to the systemic need for the academy to genuinely be inclusive of Indigenous scholars. All the authors seem to be placed differently with respect to these two dimensions, a reflection of their different perceptions about their place in the institution and also their desire or willingness to call for change.

Did the Framework Hold Up?

As described in the introduction, we developed a theory using *The Academic Gateway* that relies on the Kubler-Ross model of grief to address cultural loss and rebirth for those people who make significant moves associated with joining the academy. It is interesting that for mid-career academics, Peter Milley suggests grief may apply separately to cultural loss and rebirth of the workplace transition separately from the graduate student to faculty member transition. In our theory, we tied the grief component to self-determination theory to address intrinsic motivation and autonomy as two key elements that seem to be promoted within graduate programs and that are fundamental to engagement as a researcher in the academy.

While this theory seems to work well for some chapters, it does not fit universally. Some authors seemed to have difficulty identifying with the abstract components of self-determination theory. In some circumstances, however, the proposed theory misses the mark. When we examined how our proposed theory may not be applicable, we realized that not all aspects of self-determination theory are completely relevant. Rather, it is the high functioning aspects, where competence has been established. Success in graduate programs and careers, as well as through the vetting processes for being hired into an academic tenure-track role means this is a very high-functioning group.

Were the limitations of the theory due to authors having moved beyond the early stages of the tenure-track? Perhaps the proposed theory is best suited to the first two years of the process? Are gaps in applicability emerging as even greater competence (and confidence) is achieved?

We also considered whether there are missing components or considerations in the theory. We suspect it is a combination of authors having grown beyond the applicability and through discussions about the chapters in this book we have come to recognize missing components.

Our theory is a combination of grief and self-determination theories, one that is fundamentally based on individual experience and personal interpretations of the experiences. We anticipated that following tenure the writers would experience increased acceptance by peers within the institution and that collective efforts would become more important. This focus on collective effort and sociological elements was missing from the originally proposed theory. While the chapters in *The Academic Gateway* focused on the individual experience, the autoethnographic writing of the authors indicates a slow transition of integration into the collective effort of the institution. Our sense is that collective efforts will become increasingly common as these authors gain experience beyond the tenure decision.

Within this, we find interplay between the needs of the individual (reflected in self-efficacy) and the institution (reflected in collective efficacy). The individual does seem to be well-represented through aspects of grief and self-determination theory. However, we did not anticipate that the needs of the institution would emerge as clearly as they do during the tenure-track period. This is now evident and we are not going to resolve this theoretical issue because of a larger implication it has that extend beyond our sampling.

The implication is that by the time faculty members reach their tenure decision they are at the confluence of various personal considerations reflected through self-efficacy. We claim these are strongly associated with self-determination and point to intrinsic motivation and autonomy as two key attributes of the theory. However, there is also a confluence of community considerations—those of peer groups, academic groups, and the institution. The community considerations are reflected through collective efficacy. However, there are two problematic features to address if this is to be reconciled with the existing theory. First, there are organizational models, but are any analogous to self-determination when applied to an institution? Secondly, there is a further complication of universities being a mixing of different interconnected networks—peers within the institution, peers beyond the institution, the institution itself, and so on—it does not suffice to model a singular institution. Perhaps it is more appropriate to consider academics to be interconnected through various networks with the university being only one network (albeit an important one). If this is the case it calls for a sociological theory of the collective efforts that swirl around the academic.

It is clear such a theory requires reconciliation with a multitude of existing efforts to address specific issues within the academy. The possibility that we might arrive at an overarching theory for the experiences of academics and be able to bring that to bear on individual issues within the academy is looming. An overarching approach would not dismiss work on specific issues; rather, it would meet those issues in a coherent and constructive manner. Understanding gaps between our theory and theories related to specific issues will require significant effort. However, the present work is moving toward a significant broad theory of experience within the academy, which will provide a framework that must be connected to specific issues (and where it does not connect well, it may reveal deep structural issues).

Limitations

While this book examines academics with a tenured trajectory we would be remiss not to acknowledge that institutionally they represent a smaller proportion of academic faculty than in previous years (Flaherty, 2018). The use of faculty who are "off the tenure-track" should be a concern when one considers the overwhelming evidence of talent and capacity represented in this book. The concern is that 69 percent of doctoral students in education aspire to be professors but only 15 percent actually achieve that outcome in the first three years after graduation (Etmanski, Walters, & Zarifa, 2017). The very limited market may explain a former faculty association president communicating that success with tenure is very high because of the quality of the candidate pool. However, as we saw in *The Academic*

Gateway and this book, that outcome is clearly not evident to those in the tenure-track. Furthermore, we do not address the challenges of the employment situation undermining doctoral programs. We know that doctoral students, in large numbers, find employment outside the academy. They are valuable resources in the many environments where they work, as they have profound knowledge and skills that are useful in a myriad of contexts.

The individual authors are academics in education. We believe the results are generalizable to other disciplines, but limit that suggestion by pointing to the need for care in doing so. Our model of tenure-track seems to be consistent with the view of generalizability as well but, as noted, it is a model that has some imperfections.

Last Thoughts About Achieving Tenure

Given how much achieving tenure and promotion to associate professorship mattered to our authors it is interesting that, with the exception of Margarida Romero, none speculated about whether they might now want to achieve full professor. It seems likely that they have chosen to pause and enjoy where they are before trying to scale the mountain further. Some individuals have speculated privately with us about moving to other universities or considering opportunities to take on administrative roles.

Finally, we are aware of at least one dean who has supplied copies of *The Academic Gateway* to new tenure-track faculty. Clearly, some deans are willing to consider the need for support for this faculty group. To that end, as editors we have had numerous conversations with each other about the efforts institutions could make to address the needs of new faculty members. We believe that opportunities with minimal fiscal impact exist and so would encourage academics and administrators to discuss how to implement improvements.

We will close by suggesting one potential change—the sharing of relevant parts of institutional reviews. One author in this book, who has received tenure, recounted how the reporting on an Institutional Quality Assurance Process (IQAP) process could have been used to inform new faculty. The report, which was in excess of 2,000 pages, was shared with faculty. That is far too much information for new faculty members to be provided, let alone absorb. However, a dean could extract 25 pages from the IQAP report that would detail the structure of programs, the publication record of faculty over the last few years, and the outcomes emphasized by each course. This would provide new faculty members with a sense of how their courses fit in the larger program context and insight into publication norms. This would not replace the role of peer review, but would give individuals a better sense of institutional norms than hearsay in hallways.

Until We Meet Again. . .

Our final thought is one of thankfulness. Each of these authors has become a friend, with one or both of us. Friendships have developed between authors as well. We have journeyed as a group, sharing successes and failures in emails, at conferences, on Twitter feeds and on the telephone. We are a community.

Each author revisits a portion of their story from *The Academic Gateway* in *Beyond the Gateway*. Yet, if you take their chapter in the first book and read it with the chapter in this book, you will find that they tell their story differently. Many of those original anxious moments have faded. No longer are the moments a paragraph, they are now a short sentence if included at all. The past is not gone, but is understood as part of the journey. We circle back, retell, and move on. If we are fortunate enough to maintain our relationships with these authors, and each can find time to write a chapter in another few years—we think the story will change again. Yet, within its core will be the people doing their best to help colleagues who are starting on the tenure-track and continuing through the gateway to see themselves in aspects of the experiences and ideas recounted in these books.

References

Etmanski, B., Walters, D., & Zarifa, D. (2017). Not what I expected: Early career prospects of doctoral graduates in academia. *Canadian Journal of Higher Education, 47*(3), 152–169.

Flaherty, C. (Oct. 12, 2018). About three-quarters of all faculty positions are off the tenure track, according to a new AAUP analysis. *Inside Higher Education*. Retrieved from www.insidehighered.com/news/2018/10/12/about-three-quarters-all-faculty-positions-are-tenure-track-according-new-aaup?utm_source=Inside+Higher+Ed&utm_campaign=d2917333f7-WNU_COPY_01&utm_medium=email&utm_term=0_1fcbc04421-d2917333f7-198897417&mc_cid=d2917333f7&mc_eid=c6d8c7b783

Nelson, M. (Apr. 11, 2018). The benefits of post-tenure reviews (opinion). *Inside Higher Education.* Retrieved from www.insidehighered.com/print/advice/2018/04/11/benefits-posttenure-reviews-opinion?width=775&height=500&iframe=true

Ragoonaden, K. (2015). Self-study of teacher education practices and critical pedagogy: The fifth moment in a teacher educator's journey. *Studying Teacher Education, 11*(1) 81–95. http://dx.doi.org/10.1080/17425964.2015.1018886

Contributors

This section lists the authors of chapters in alphabetical order.

Cecile Badenhorst MA (UBC), PhD (Queen's) is Associate Professor in the Adult Education/Post-Secondary program, Faculty of Education, at Memorial University, Newfoundland, Canada. She has conducted research and published in the areas of doctoral education, doctoral writing, graduate writing, thesis/publication writing pedagogies, academic literacies and faculty writing. She engages in qualitative, arts-based and post-structural research methodologies. She has written three books in the area of graduate student writing: *Research Writing* (2007), *Dissertation Writing* (2008) and *Productive Writing* (2010). She is a co-editor of *Research Literacies and Writing Pedagogies for Masters and Doctoral Writers* (Brill, 2016).

Lee Anne Block is Associate Professor in the Faculty of Education, University of Winnipeg. Her research and teaching are focused on how we name and engage with difference in educational locations. Of particular interest are cultural sustainability, reconciliation through healing and place-based learning. For twenty years, she was a classroom teacher in Winnipeg.

Joan M. Chambers is Associate Professor in the Faculty of Education at Lakehead University, Ontario, Canada. She teaches elementary science and environmental education to teacher candidates in the BEd program. Dr. Chambers also teaches in the graduate program—introductory and qualitative research methods courses, and Science, Technology, Society and Environment (STSE). Her research interests include primary science education, environmental education and [eco]literacy for young children, climate change education, and teacher resiliency. Though she completed her BEd in 1985, she chose to stay home with her children, entering graduate school 15 years later. Moving from her life-long home in Alberta to Northern Ontario, Dr. Chambers began her academic career at Lakehead University in January 2009.

Cam Cobb is Associate Professor at the University of Windsor. His research interests include social-justice, special education, co-teaching, and the arts. His writing has been published in such journals as *Per la Filosofia, Cinema: Philosophy and the Moving Image, British Journal of Special Education, Journal on Excellence in College Teaching,* and *Journal of the Scholarship of Teaching and Learning*. Books featuring his work include *Hemingway and Italy: Twenty-First-Century Perspectives* and *Critical Essays on Twin Peaks: The Return*. His most recent book published by Jawbone Press in 2018 is *What's Big and Purple and Lives in the Ocean? The Moby Grape Story*.

Frank Deer is Associate Professor and Canada Research Chair of Indigenous Education in the Faculty of Education, University of Manitoba. Frank is Kanienkeha'ka from Kahnawake, a community that lies just south of Tiotia'ke in the eastern region of the Rotinonshonni Confederacy. Frank holds an earned PhD in Educational Administration from the University of Saskatchewan and is published in the area of Indigenous education. Frank conducts research on Indigenous language education and Indigenous religious and spiritual orientations. Frank has previously served as a classroom teacher in Northern Manitoba and in the inner city of Winnipeg.

Lyle Hamm is Associate Professor of Educational Administration and Leadership in the Faculty of Education at the University of New Brunswick (UNB) in Fredericton. His teaching and research, broadly speaking, focuses on provincial and national immigration, demographically changing rural schools and communities, intercultural education and peace-building, and social justice and transformative leadership. Steamer served as a K–12 educator and administrator in Alberta for 22 years prior to joining UNB in 2013.

Victoria Handford is Associate Professor in the Faculty of Education and Social Work (Leadership) at Thompson Rivers University. Tory is also the Coordinator of Graduate Programs, a role of service that consumes considerable time. Tory held multiple roles in education prior to moving to her university position, including teacher, vice-principal, principal, education officer (Leadership) for the Ontario Ministry of Education, and program officer (Standards of Practice and Accreditation) for the Ontario College of Teachers. Her research interests include school and school district leadership, and trust. Her husband and now-grown children continue to be central figures in her life.

Lloyd Kornelsen has worked in the field of education for the past 32 years, primarily as a high school social studies teacher. In addition to teaching, he has developed curricula, facilitated international practica and, as an adult educator, acted as a conflict mediator and trainer for both local and national organizations. His recently published book, *Stories of Transformation: Memories of a Global Citizenship Practicum*, is based on research for which he was awarded the Manitoba Education Research Network award for outstanding achievement in education research. For the past six years, Lloyd has been a member of the Faculty of Education at the University of Winnipeg (UW). In July 2018, Lloyd was appointed Director of the Human Rights program at Global College (UW). http://www.uwinnipeg.ca/global-college/who-we-are/lloyd-kornelsen.html.

Heather McLeod, PhD, is Associate Professor (arts education), in the Faculty of Education, at Memorial University. She is Editor-in-Chief of the *Canadian Review of Art Education*. Heather has received national, university, and faculty awards for excellence in curriculum development and teaching. She served as Associate Dean (Undergraduate Programs). Her current funded research initiatives include a community Open Studio/Art Hive project, and a poetic inquiry project. Previously she taught in the public school system in British Columbia and Nunavut. As well she worked in communications and policy development for a provincial teachers' organization and for government.

Onowa McIvor is maskékow-ininiw (Swampy Cree) from Treaty 5 territory in Northern Manitoba but grew up in Treaty 6 territory. Onowa is Associate Professor and was the former Director of Indigenous Education in the Faculty of Education at the University of Victoria from 2008–2017. Onowa is a lifelong adult learner of her mother tongue nehinaw/nehiyaw/nehithaw, and her research focuses on Indigenous language revitalization, various aspects of additional language learning and language education; language learning assessment and links between language use, health and well-being. However, her most important job is raising two daughters with the help of her extended family.

Peter Milley is Associate Professor in the Faculty of Education and Senior Associate of the Centre for Research on Educational and Community Services at the University of Ottawa. Peter teaches and conducts research on topics related to educational administration, policy and evaluation. His recent focus has been on administrative ethics via collected edition book co-edited with Eugenie A. Samier entitled *International Perspectives on Maladministration in Education* (published by Routledge). He is also conducting research on the leadership of social innovation initiatives in universities.

Sylvia Moore, PhD, is Assistant Professor at the Faculty of Education of Memorial University. She is the lead in program development for the Inuit Bachelor of Education (IBED) and the Labrador MEd cohort. She is also the Labrador lead researcher for the National Centre for Collaboration in Indigenous Education. Her research focuses on Indigenous pedagogies, land-based learning, and Indigenous language rejuvenation. Sylvia's community-based work is with Indigenous knowledge holders and educators to develop culturally relevant teacher education and K-12 education in the circumpolar.

Greg Ogilvie is Assistant Professor in the Faculty of Education at the University of Lethbridge. He is a passionate educator who has worked as a language teacher and teacher educator in Canada, Ethiopia, and Ukraine. His scholarly interests include task-based language teaching, critical interculturality, restorative justice pedagogy, culturally and linguistically responsive teaching, and supervision practices to foster professional growth.

Sharon Penney, PhD, is Associate Professor in the Faculty of Education at Memorial University, and Certified Teacher and Registered Psychologist with the Newfoundland and Labrador Psychology Board. She has worked in both clinical and school settings for over 20 years and has held a variety of positions including serving as a behaviour therapist, guidance counsellor, children's mental health therapist, and school psychologist. Her research is focused on special education, autism spectrum disorders, home and school partnerships, as well as positive mental health. She works primarily with qualitative methodologies and mixed methods research.

Sarah Pickett is Assistant Professor in the Faculty of Education, at Memorial University, Registered Psychologist and the faculty founder/advisor to the Gender and Sexuality Alliance (GSA) in Education at Memorial. Her research has focused on affirmative sexuality and gender practice and pedagogy in education and healthcare. Dr. Pickett is interested in narrative and autoethnographic methodologies; how researchers may use these methods to engage in evocative conversations about educational contexts; and she actively publishes in this area from the position of parent, lesbian/queer, psychologist, educator of educators, counsellor educator and academic.

Greg Rickwood is Associate Professor within the Physical and Health Education and the Schulich School of Education at Nipissing University in North Bay, Ontario. He is a certified physical education specialist with teaching experience in Kenya, Amazon, and the West Indies. Dr. Rickwood's research encompasses teacher-coach mentorship, physically active schools, and minor hockey player/coach attrition rates. Recently, Dr. Rickwood contributed to the book *Ingenious* authored by Canada's 28th Governor General designed to nurture innovation in schools. In 2018, Dr. Rickwood coached an elite group of U18 female hockey players to a Silver medal at the World Selects Invitational tournament in Czechoslovakia.

Of Kickapoo ancestry and Mexican heritage, **Carmen Rodriguez de France** has been a grateful visitor on the land of the Coast Salish people for 22 years. Born and raised in beautiful Monterrey, México, her career spans thirty-four years with participation in a broad range of educational, community service, and research activities. Carmen teaches courses on Indigenous education, pedagogy and epistemology in the Faculty of Education, and contributes in the Social Justice Program and the Latin American Studies Program at the University of Victoria. Her most recent research involves partnerships with community organizations to support the enactment of the Calls to Action from the Truth and Reconciliation Commission Report (TRC).

Margarida Romero is Research Director of the Laboratoire d'Innovation et Numérique pour l'Éducation (LINE), a research lab in the field of Technology Enhanced Learning (TEL). She is Professor at Université Côte d'Azur (France) and Associate Professor at Université Laval (Canada). Her research is oriented towards the inclusive, humanistic and creative uses of technologies (co-design, game design and robotics) for the development of creativity, problem solving, collaboration and computational thinking.

Trish Rosborough is from the Kwakiutl Nation on Vancouver Island. Prior to her appointment to the role of Associate Professor of Indigenous Education at the University of Victoria, Trish was Director of Aboriginal Education for the British Columbia Ministry of Education. She completed her doctoral studies in 2012 at the University of British Columbia. Trish's research area and life passion is Indigenous language revitalization. She is an adult learner and speaker of her mother's first language, Kwak'wala. Trish is a mother of five and grandmother of ten. It is with deep sadness we share of Dr. Rosborough's passing in August 2019, following a brief illness, prior to the book's publication.

Manu Sharma is Assistant Professor at the Thompson Rivers University in the Faculty of Education, where she teaches foundational courses in the Masters of Education. Dr. Sharma has previously taught a variety of undergraduate and graduate courses and supported field placements at University of Wisconsin–River Falls, Brock University, University of Toronto, and University of Windsor; in addition, she has also worked for the Toronto District School Board and in international settings as a public educator. Her research interests and publications in the field of teacher education are based on equity initiatives, teacher development, social justice pedagogy, deficit thinking, and international teaching experiences.

Timothy M. Sibbald is Associate Professor in the Schulich School of Education at Nipissing University. His primary focus pertains to mathematics education. Among other topics, he has investigated reflective practices with a lens of teacher development. On moving into academia, it seemed natural to extend that research to include the experience of teachers who move into the academy. He is, currently, the editor of *The Gazette*, a double blind peer reviewed math education publication for teachers produced by the Ontario Association of Mathematics Educators.

Kathy Snow, who was at Cape Breton University at the time of writing her chapter, moved during the preparation of this book. She is the new Coordinator of the Certificate in Educational Leadership (CELN), within the Faculty of Education at the University of Prince Edward Island. Kathy's research interests revolve around supporting student success and resilience for non-traditional learners at all levels.

Gabrielle Young, PhD, is Associate Professor in the Faculty of Education at Memorial University, where she teaches undergraduate and graduate courses surrounding understanding and supporting students with specific learning disorders, as well as the practicum in special education. Gabrielle's research interests surround the use of assistive and instructional technology in inclusive classrooms, applying the principles of universal design for learning and differentiated instruction to support students with exceptionalities in general education classrooms, and pre-service teachers' efficacy to support students in inclusive classrooms and facilitate positive mental health.

Index

A
ability, 16, 35, 46, 55, 115, 160, 178, 217, 251, 258, 265, 277, 299
accomplishments, 39, 109, 164, 166, 186–189
accountability, 34, 206–210, 220–221, 263
adaptation, 31, 62, 69–76, 270
administration, 14, 17, 58, 75, 92, 152, 175, 205, 281–286, 297, 313
   dean, 16, 33, 37, 39, 51, 128, 158, 174, 313
   president, 35, 40, 128, 148, 284
advocate, 40, 70, 149

C
capacity, 63, 97, 145, 236
commitment
   personal, 34, 49, 225, 227
   professional, 145, 158, 288
   service, 24, 69, 75, 93, 146, 194, 235
   teaching, 215, 232
   time, 91
competence, 4, 64, 73, 103, 114, 126, 160, 197, 311
complexity, 13, 28, 35, 40, 55, 87, 150, 218, 228, 249, 289
confidence, 52, 73, 98, 110, 125, 141, 161, 190, 198, 231, 239, 301
contract, 70, 104, 159, 200, 214, 232, 287, 297
costs, 71, 101, 196, 214, 284
creative, 22, 54, 90, 93, 108, 110, 149, 208, 239
criteria, 24, 55, 80, 127, 141, 148, 189, 212, 269, 291

D
dialogue, 139, 219, 261, 301
dissertation, 19, 53, 139, 203, 239
diversity, 27, 54, 180, 239

E
efficiency, 67, 206, 208, 221
email, 59, 72, 90, 104, 188, 194, 198–200, 243
energy, 87, 109, 114, 188, 220, 227, 237, 254
expectations, 24, 37, 58, 66, 92, 139, 141, 190, 197, 250, 265, 276, 296

F
family, 3, 48, 78, 95, 111, 114, 150, 189, 201, 229, 250, 282, 284
First Nations. *See indigenous*
Foucault, 87, 226, 250
freedom (Academic), 21, 54, 98, 132, 171, 220, 262, 310

G

gender (gender equity), 20, 26, 191
graduate studies, 4, 47, 92, 157, 215, 237, 297
guidelines, 39, 41, 192
guilt, 101, 113, 132

H

home, 36, 96, 113, 165, 179, 236, 261, 284

I

identity, 26, 37, 73, 80, 97, 101, 112, 174, 178, 204, 233, 250, 293
immigrant, 37, 47, 239
Indigenous
  community, 142
  dual tradition scholar, 41
international, 37, 53, 131, 170, 214, 241, 294
interview, 47, 62, 139, 167, 174, 283, 295, 301
institutional logics, 57, 66–80
isolation, 24, 81, 199, 262, 268, 286, 290
introjected regulation, 103

K

Kubler-Ross, 3, 34, 163, 290, 310

L

lifelong, 127, 146, 282
lifestyle, 166, 284
lived experience, 60, 87

M

maladaptive traps, 61–63, 69
management (see administration), 21, 98, 175, 204, 261, 284
mental health, 24, 58, 65, 103, 114, 266, 275, 281
merit, 128, 207–211, 267

N

narrative inquiry, 139, 299
negotiate, 170, 225
neoliberalism, 204–205
normal (normative), 74, 96, 155

O

office, 36, 59, 72, 143, 188, 198, 233, 243, 286
online, 59, 68, 89, 236

optimism, 36, 58, 65, 115, 188, 201
organization (institution), 55, 68, 76, 103, 162, 254, 261–264

R

ranking, 19, 109, 207
reciprocity, 66, 71, 140, 149, 211, 270
recovery, 61, 193, 291
rejection, 160, 198, 237, 266, 289
resilience, 58, 239, 289
respect, 36, 40, 126, 138, 183, 264, 268, 286
rhythms, 87

S

sabbatical, 115, 171, 195, 283
security (job), 15, 21, 60, 146, 281
social justice, 138, 217, 252, 298
SSHRC, 94, 128, 200, 236, 241
storytelling, 139
stress, 3, 16, 49, 64, 68, 98, 232, 281
strike, 166, 288
student evaluations, 36, 58, 71, 165, 190, 216, 256
supervisor, 20, 71, 200, 212, 257, 282
supports, 56, 64, 115, 150, 258, 276

T

tensions, 49–50, 74, 92, 138, 193, 204, 211, 219
traditional, 25, 41, 52, 127, 143, 255, 290
travel, 162, 194, 210, 294

U

uncertain, 15, 24, 109, 125, 133, 227, 296

V

validation, 20, 188, 281
Vibot, 49–50
vulnerable, 182, 256

W

weekend, 59, 90, 193, 198
work-life balance, 56, 101, 113, 155, 168, 210
workload, 53, 59, 68, 102, 109, 114, 145, 166, 195, 220, 309
workshops, 38, 53, 92, 132, 159, 186, 233
writing group, 32, 101

Education

Series Editors: Nicholas Ng-A-Fook and Carole Fleuret

Our *Education* series seeks to advance thought-provoking research within the broader field of education. Scholarly works in this series examine educational research from a multidisciplinary perspective and address a variety of issues in the field, including curriculum studies, arts-based education, educational philosophy, life writing, foundations in education, teacher education, evaluation, and counselling.

Recent titles in this series

Anne M. Phelan, William F. Pinar, Nicholas Ng-A-Fook, and Ruth Kane (Eds.), *Reconceptualizing Teacher Education: A Canadian Contribution to a Global Challenge*, 2020.

Michelle Forrest and Linda Wheeldon, *Scripting Feminist Ethics in Teacher Education*, 2019.

William F. Pinar, *Moving Images of Eternity: George Grant's Critique of Time, Teaching, and Technology*, 2019.

Pierre Jean, *Planification de formations en santé : guide des bonnes pratiques*, 2019.

Thomas R. Klassen and John A. Dwyer, *Décrocher son diplôme (et l'emploi de ses rêves !) : comment maîtriser les compétences essentielles menant au succès à l'école, au travail et dans la vie*, 2018.

Timothy M. Sibbald and Victoria Handford (Eds.), *The Academic Gateway: Understanding the Journey to Tenure*, 2017.

Lise Gremion, Serge Ramel, Valérie Angelucci, and Jean-Claude Kalubi (Eds.), *Vers une école inclusive : regards croisés sur les défis actuels*, 2017.

For a complete list of our titles, see:
press.uottawa.ca

www.ingramcontent.com/pod-product-compliance
Lightning Source LLC
Chambersburg PA
CBHW070746020526
44116CB00032B/1984